Corruption, Character, and Conduct

Essays on Canadian government ethics

d by John W. Langford
Allan Tupper

Toronto Oxford New York
OXFORD UNIVERSITY PRESS
1993

Oxford University Press
70 Wynford Drive, Don Mills, Ontario M3C 1J9

Toronto Oxford New York
Delhi Bombay Calcutta Madras Karachi
Kuala Lumpur Singapore Hong Kong Tokyo
Nairobi Dar es Salaam Cape Town
Melbourne Auckland Madrid

and associated companies in
Berlin Ibadan

Oxford is a trade mark of Oxford University Press

Canadian Cataloguing in Publication Data

Main entry under title:

Corruption, character, and conduct:
essays on Canadian government ethics

Includes bibliographical references.
ISBN 0–19–540930–2

1. Political ethics – Canada.   I. Langford, John W.
II. Tupper, Allan, 1950–

JA79.C67 1993   172'.0971   C93–095327–4

Design: Jeffrey Tabberner

1 2 3 4 — 97 96 95 94

This book is printed on permanent (acid-free) paper ⊗.

Printed in Canada

Contents

Preface   v

List of Contributors   vi

1 The good, the bad, and the ugly:
Thinking about the conduct of public officials
John W. Langford and Allan Tupper   1

2 Quasi-crimes and eager beavers:
Public sector ethics in British Columbia
John W. Langford   20

3 Aboriginal political ethics
Tom Pocklington and Sarah Pocklington   42

4 Public sector ethics in Quebec:
The contrasting society
Jacques Bourgault and Stéphane Dion   67

5 Despoiling the public sector?
The case of Nova Scotia
Ian Stewart   90

6 The Canadian Federal Government:
Patronage, unity, security, and purity
Sharon Sutherland   113

7 Alberta: The search for an ethical balance
Allan Tupper   151

8 Rules are not enough:
Ethics, politics, and public service in Ontario
Kenneth Kernaghan   174

9 Cities:
'The dilemmas on our doorsteps'
James Lightbody   197

10 Small-town Canada
David Siegel   217

Preface

This book reflects the editors' concern that the debate about government ethics in Canada is becoming too narrow and fragmented. In the early 1990s, governments' efforts to regulate the behaviour of public officials, particularly politicians, have received extraordinary attention. But a fixation on this topic shifts attention from other salient issues including the values which underpin the behaviour of public officials and the impact of government ethics on the overall health and legitimacy of government. Our book tries to balance the debate somewhat by examining the rules by which public officials play and the impact of their behaviour, and attempts to regulate it, on the quality of Canadian democracy.

We are concerned by the degree to which discussions of public sector ethics in Canada tend to focus on events in a particular jurisdiction. But how do government ethics in Toronto or Ottawa compare with those in Quebec City, Halifax, or Victoria? Inquiring students and critical citizens have few opportunities to place events in their communities in a broader context. To this end, we commissioned essays on the federal and provincial experience. We also probe the distinctive world of aboriginal government and the ethical environments in small and large municipalities. Our introduction avoids a detailed review of the contents of the individual chapters. Instead, it provides an overview of lessons from recent Canadian experience about several complex, perennial issues of public sector ethics. Our concerns include the meaning of public sector ethics, the reasons for our contemporary concern with ethical government, and an assessment of several reform proposals.

Each chapter was written specifically for this book. Our first debt of gratitude is to our collaborators, all of whom energetically studied government ethics in the jurisdiction they examined. Several contributors also read and commented upon their colleagues' drafts. Sharon Sutherland deserves special thanks for providing provocative commentary on almost the entire text. Our publisher at Oxford University Press, Brian Henderson, enthusiastically supported the project from the outset. It was a pleasure to work with him and his colleagues. We owe special thanks to Terry Brown, Kim Nicholson, and Pam Ouimet in the Department of Political Science at the University of Alberta. Their word processing skills moved the manuscript to completion. Families always get the last notice when their names should be up in lights. Special thanks are extended to Kate and Peggy for their understanding as the project wore on and, in particular, for remaining stoically silent when the monthly telephone bills arrived. Whatever else the co-editors have wrought, in the course of producing this book we have moved from being professional colleagues to being close friends—an extra dividend at the end of a highly charged intellectual endeavour.

John W. Langford and Allan Tupper

Victoria, British Columbia and Edmonton, Alberta
May 1993

Contributors

Jacques Bourgault is a member of the Department of Political Science at the University of Quebec at Montreal.

Stéphane Dion is a member of the Department of Political Science at the University of Montreal.

Kenneth Kernaghan is a member of the Department of Politics at Brock University.

John W. Langford is a member of the School of Public Administration at the University of Victoria.

James Lightbody is a member of the Department of Political Science at the University of Alberta

Sarah Pocklington is a recent MA graduate (Native Studies) from Trent University.

Tom Pocklington is a member of the Department of Political Science at the University of Alberta.

David Siegel is a member of the Department of Politics at Brock University.

Ian Stewart is a member of the Department of Political Science at Acadia University.

Sharon Sutherland is a member of the Department of Political Science at Carleton University.

Allan Tupper is a member of the Department of Political Science at the University of Alberta.

The good, the bad, and the ugly

Thinking about the conduct of public officials

In the 1990s, Canadian politics are obsessed with the ethical conduct of their practitioners. The manifestations of this fixation are everywhere. Governments are constructing new regimes for regulating the conduct of public officials in response to assertions about their declining integrity. Patronage and party financing, topics that have intermittently evoked controversy in the past, are subjects of continuing debate. The private conduct of politicians as a determinant of their public personae, a seldom discussed topic until recently, is now a central feature of Canada's ethics agenda. The character of our leaders is now among our preoccupations. For example, an important biography of Brian Mulroney, *Brian Mulroney: the Politics of Ambition*, by John Sawatsky, ends in September 1984, as Mulroney assumes power.[1] Mulroney's performance as prime minister is not assessed—our judgements about that matter may apparently be shaped as we now understand his character through examination of his childhood, his friendships, and his marriage.

Our book examines the roots, contemporary manifestations, and future course of Canada's now-crowded ethics agenda. We approach our topic with a balance of scepticism and humility. We are sceptical because democracies are only intermittently interested in government ethics. For little-understood reasons, the conduct of public officials becomes highly controversial at particular periods before the public agenda changes and moves on. Is Canada in the 1990s merely at a high point in an ethics cycle, or are Canadians witnessing a redefinition of their standards of political morality and public conduct—a real break with past practices? Our humility flows from two sources. First, we are dealing with issues that have preoccupied thoughtful people for centuries. Government ethics are an area where difficult questions come easier than convincing answers. And without becoming too earnest, the study of government ethics demands humility on the part of its practitioners. In pursuing our task, we must avoid facile generalizations and after-the-fact condemnations of others' behaviour and decisions. The study of ethics carries its own ethical burdens.[2]

Each chapter explores government ethics in a Canadian jurisdiction or governmental milieu. Instead of reviewing our findings, our introduction tackles the overarching issues. We first consider the boundaries of our topic. What is the scope of public sector ethics? We then ask why the integrity of officials excites so much interest in the 1990s. What forces create this preoccupation with ethics? Is our societal concern with government ethics justified? Are contemporary officials bad? How does unethical conduct shape the long-term health and character of Canadian politics? We argue that the way we do our public business does matter, and then we discuss our capacity to improve the conduct of our officials. Can some combination of education and closer regulation of official conduct improve government ethics? Finally, we speculate on possible future directions for public sector ethics in Canada.

What do we mean by public sector ethics?

For many observers, public sector ethics are defined by the idea of conflict of interest. This narrow focus is not surprising. We are swept up in an orgy of concern about the intersection between the private interests of public office holders and the performance of their public duties. This intersection is now very crowded. The boundaries of private interests have been stretched to include the financial status of public officials and their spouses, children, friends, business associates, and even constituents. The public office holder is now a complex corporate entity who, like the ghost of Christmas past, shuffles about the public arena encumbered by the weight of private interests that he or she may be tempted improperly to service.[3] The notion of a private interest now transcends narrow financial interests to embrace aspects of the personal lives of public officials (for example, ideological or religious bias, strong ties to a single interest, substance abuse, sexual predilections) that might tempt them away from the exercise of undistorted judgement. In late 1992, a judge in British Columbia was reported as seeing considerable merit in the complaint that a devout Roman Catholic Crown counsel might be in a conflict of interest as public prosecutor in a case in which a Catholic bishop was to be tried for sexual assault of native women.[4] Finally, the definition of a conflict, and when it occurs, has changed. In many eyes, the idea of conflict of interest cannot be limited to the definition of situations where officials take an action in their private interests. In many jurisdictions, even the appearance of acting or an opportunity to act in less than an impartial manner is to succumb to conflict of interest.

If public sector ethics are no more than conflict of interest, then, at the very least, conflict of interest is now a substantial territory. This expanded terrain is more demanding than it was for the person who entered public life even twenty years ago, when ethics were defined almost exclusively by the anti-corruption provisions of the Criminal Code. Public sector ethics were then about fraud, bribery, influence-peddling, and breach of trust. These concerns are now the first crude landmarks on an increasingly complex ethical landscape.

The field of government ethics cannot be limited to corruption and conflicts of interest. It must also encompass relationships between citizens and their governors. Government ethics must embrace the dilemmas raised by governments' control of information. If information is an important determinant of power, then rules about how information is shared among politicians, civil servants, and the public are crucial questions for public sector ethics. Debates about secrecy reveal a range of ethical controversies. The capacity of citizens and corporations to keep information to themselves and the reciprocal duty of the state to keep information gathered about them confidential are central issues. Freedom of information laws deal with some of these important matters, but are silent about such ethically charged issues as whistle-blowing and the dissemination of propaganda and misinformation by governments.

Public sector ethics are also about coercion. Traditionally, the key issue has been the responsibility of politicians and administrators for the misuse of the state's capacity for violence. But coercion can also take subtle forms. It often coexists with other forms of ethical transgression. Fairness, another important public sector virtue, is tested during incidents of conflict of interest and during routine interactions between public officials and citizens. Public sector ethics are also about loyalty and accountability—especially the tug of war that sometimes pulls public servants between their political masters, the interest groups, and citizens.

The addition of questions about information, fairness, loyalty, and accountability to perennial concerns about corruption and conflict of interest helps to establish boundaries for the field of public sector ethics.[5] Seen together, these topics present a focus on *procedural* ethics—how business is done in government and politics, the means used to achieve ends, and the rules that guide the relationships between the governors and the governed. A focus on procedural ethics permeates this book. But some authors go beyond this view and examine the moral visions that underpin political communities. In their chapter on aboriginal political ethics, Tom Pocklington and Sarah Pocklington probe the obligations of citizens as well as those of office holders.

We recognize that public sector ethics cannot be entirely defined by procedural or power relationships involving public office holders and citizens. Public sector ethics must also embrace the 'business that we do'—the moral quality of public policies and the ends pursued by governments. Here, attention is focused on the ethical reasoning relevant to policy issues, such as whether to allow euthanasia, to use the death penalty, or to limit access to health care. In government, procedural and substantive public sector ethics cannot be easily separated. Some observers argue that the best way to discover a good public policy is to establish procedures that allow affected interests to participate in its development. When decisions are made, those interests that are negatively affected can be compensated. Controversy about patronage also highlights the links between procedural and substantive ethics in government. In some jurisdictions, patronage is a procedural issue of how we do business, a signal of the degree of adherence by those in power to the values of fairness and impartiality. But in other jurisdictions, it is a substantive policy issue, and it is attacked as an unfair distribution of government resources in favour of supporters of the governing party.

Why is there such a fuss?

What explains the contemporary interest in government ethics? First, it is possible that ours is an age of demonstrable moral degeneracy. Government officials may now reflect a particularly unhealthy combination of political ruthlessness in their pursuit of public goals and a craven disregard of the obligations of public office in their pursuit of personal enrichment.[6] A concern with government ethics is thus well placed because of the erosion of standards of government conduct. The assertion that morality is declining is important enough to merit detailed attention later in this chapter. Suffice it to say that we find claims of moral degeneracy hard to demonstrate. A better explanation lies in changing standards of conduct and the emergence of new definitions of morality. In any case, what accounts for either changing standards or a degeneration of conduct?

Any explanation of the contemporary fascination with government ethics must be multifaceted. A starting point is the Canadian party system. Here we observe assertions that a party system, whose parties exhibit few real ideological differences, is prone to a 'politics of ethics'.[7] The opposition can always differentiate itself from the government through a claim of ethical superiority and an offer of cleaner government to the electorate. At its worst, politics can degenerate into scandal-mongering, the circulation of lies about opponents, and character assassination. Such conduct brings politics into disrepute, creating the conditions in which ideology and ethics can join hands. The Reform Party, which sees itself as ideologically pure and which rejects the brokerage roles of the established parties, also contrasts itself with the other parties on the basis of a self-assessed ethical superiority. Its vision of New Canada rejects the politics of patronage and compromise. It claims to offer morally superior candidates who would transform our politics. In pursuit of these ends, Reform screens potential candidates to understand their lifestyles, their financial status, and their values, and hence their fitness for public office. Ideological politics is not necessarily an escape from a politics of ethics.

The interest in ethics is linked with what governments do and, increasingly in the modern era, what they fail to do. In an time of global economic change and competition, democratic governments have redefined their roles. The links between these changes and the ethics agenda are complex and straightforward at the same time. In an obvious way, economic restructuring enhances the political power of business. It is not surprising that, in the face of more obvious business dominance, the view exists that politics is unfair and that 'undue influence' is exercised. At the same time, citizens face a declining welfare state, increasing taxes, and promises from all parties that they can manage the economy better. The promises prove unfounded, cynicism abounds, and politics seems dishonest. Citizens lash out at politicians and officials who seem responsible for the malaise but ineffective in its resolution. Ironically, a Tory disdain for 'professional politicians' and their crass behaviour finds resonance in the electorate. Debate degenerates into complaints about the salaries and benefits of office holders, their personal conduct, and the way they conduct their business. It is 'them' (a self-indulgent political and administrative class) versus 'us' (an over-taxed and ignored majority).

The mass media have a major interest in political conduct. Political reportage is about personality and style, not policy or deeper political forces. Carl Bernstein, the American journalist who reported the Watergate scandal, argues that even the best American journalism now resembles a tabloid, with its emphasis on personality, the private lives of prominent people, and scandal.[8] Our contributors often note the media's role in shaping Canadians' perceptions of government conduct. Moreover, the contemporary interest in government morality is certainly reinforced, if not shaped, by modern electronic media with intense institutional and commercial interests in the issue.

What else underpins the modern concern with ethics? Modern feminism and the politics of women's movements are important influences. Feminists see the male-dominated state as responsible for a too-rigid separation of public and private spheres, which must be redefined. In their view, such private matters as sexual relations, family finances, and child-rearing practices involve the exercise of power, and hence are political. As far as ethics are concerned, this view injects into politics the interesting idea that the public-private distinction is too narrow, and thereby raises concerns about the private lives of public officials to greater prominence. As well, feminism is deeply concerned with such ethically charged policy issues as family violence and sexual harassment, which have long been ignored or defined away as private matters. An emphasis on these issues adds new elements to the list of conduct that must be avoided by public officials, and spurs debate about proper behaviour. These points help us understand such contemporary concerns as the marital fidelity of politicians, their sexual conduct, their views on harassment, and the abuse of public office for sexual gratification. In the same vein, affirmative action, sexual harassment, and family violence all raise a classic ethical issue—the cover-up and conscious neglect by powerful people of serious wrongdoing and injustice.

The Canadian Charter of Rights and Freedoms is also a factor. It has created an aggressive generation of rights-bearers and equality-seekers.[9] Moreover, the Charter's codification of rights is moving our politics from its traditional focus on region and territory towards a politics of rights, wherein fairness of treatment and equality are dominant values. These two powerful effects of the Charter—the generation of a less deferential citizenry and the creation of a consciousness of rights—intermingle with the ethics agenda in complex ways. A more demanding citizenry is more probing of its leaders' behaviour and more aggressive in seeking accountability. The politics of rights shapes and sustains a citizen interest in fairness that is at the heart of many concerns about unethical government practices.

Is the fuss justified?

In the early 1990s, government ethics are controversial and widely discussed. But has official conduct deteriorated significantly in the last decade? Are public officials now acting particularly badly? How do we know? Are we yearning for a golden age? Complex methodological and ethical issues plague the study of government morals. For one thing, measures of governments' ethical health are difficult to establish. In this vein, Gary Sturgess has constructed a peeping-Tom analogy that reveals several problems in the study of government ethics.

> We find ourselves, if you like, standing in the front garden of a house, trying to guess the intimate personal relationships of the family inside. Very occasionally . . . we are privileged to peek through a window and glimpse one or two scenes. Sometimes, a family argument spills out on to the front porch. But, most of the time, even with the powers of a royal commission, we are left standing out on the footpath trying to reconstruct the scenes inside according to our respective theories of corruption and the vignettes we have been lucky enough to glimpse.[10]

Sturgess's argument raises important points. First, data are not easily gathered. We have at our disposal publicly revealed episodes of public sector misconduct. But to go beyond these and to establish the ethical health of a jurisdiction, we would need to establish the range of officials' ethical values, attitudes, and behaviours. Not unexpectedly, officials are often uninterested in responding to questionnaires or scenarios designed to examine their integrity. When they do participate, they often see questionable behaviour all around them, but never in their own dealings. The lack of published studies in this genre and the reservations expressed about their methodologies attest to the difficulty.[11] Case studies of misconduct provided by oversight committees and the legion of auditors general, ombudsmen, and commissioners for information and conflict of interest often provide insights. But such cases provide only a partial view. They are those instances of misconduct, which for a variety of reasons, are intermittently politicized, debated, and reported in particular jurisdictions. Do they reveal patterns of misconduct or are they unrelated episodes from which it is difficult to make generalizations? Such problems cast doubt on sweeping assertions about the demonstrable deterioration of public conduct in the 1980s and 1990s.

We must also avoid the temptation of twisting facts to suit our potentially narrow views about how public officials *should* act. Sharon Sutherland captures this problem in her chapter, when she argues: 'We rarely come to grips with the way our most basic convictions shape and colour the stories we live and tell each other'. Universal standards must be embraced with care and an understanding that public sector ethics is an evolving discipline related to, but not necessarily defined by, the slow evolution of community ethical standards. Test your own ethical neutrality and sense of context by pondering that in the 1950s some federal cabinet ministers saw nothing wrong with adjusting their stock portfolios each morning before starting work.

We must also temper our conclusions about the state of public sector ethics with the understanding that many citizens either expect that public officials will act badly or advocate that they do so. This strain of thought is conventionally identified with Machiavelli's famous book *The Prince*. But hints of the argument are found in Book 1 of Plato's *Republic*.

The argument commonly takes two forms. As a law of public life, 'dirty hands' are seen as inevitable companions of power. Lord Acton's dictum that 'power corrupts and absolute power corrupts absolutely' is for many a self-evident truth. Some political philosophers, Plato and Aristotle, for example, argue that the strength of the axiom can be offset by institutional arrangements, a constitutional separation of governmental powers and ethical rules, for example. Even if one is persuaded by these claims, the apparent historical and psychological fact remains that humans are base and will use power selfishly and abusively. Contemporary perceptions of public officials as corrupt individuals prepared to use unethical means to retain and increase their power, enhance their perks, and divert state resources to themselves reveal the continuing appeal of Acton's assertion.[12]

The second form of the 'dirty hands' argument asserts that public life often requires officials to act in ways that would be unethical in everyday life. This is the territory explored by Machiavelli and many other philosophers.[13] The key part of this argument is its connection between effectiveness in public office and morality. A leader, bound by everyday moral rules, is not likely to do a good job. As Michael Walzer puts it: 'It is easy to get one's hands dirty in politics and it is often right to do so'.[14] Good behaviour then becomes, at least partially, a function of role. Coercion, violence, secrecy, deceit, and manipulation are all potentially good behaviours where one's role as a representative demands that one weigh the consequences of official action (or inaction) on the welfare of many citizens. As Dennis Thompson argues: 'As agents for citizens, officials are judged by different principles, or principles differently interpreted, than those applied to persons who act for themselves and for less inclusive groups'.[15]

A variation on the 'dirty hands' theme is found in chapters in this book that ask questions about the costs and benefits of patronage or kinship-driven allocations of government resources. It may surprise readers that some observers propose that corruption may make a positive contribution to some political systems. Patronage and pork-barrelling, for example, may be glues which integrate polities in the face of enduring divisions.[16] (Pork-barrelling is the allocation of public expenditures to advance a party's fortune in a geographic area.) Some self-serving actions by state officials are judged as essential to the functioning of 'developing' countries in their transition from political cultures in which obligatory gift-giving is a feature of public life. Some authors assert that limited amounts of bribery and theft of state resources may have positive economic effects.[17] But other studies argue that the alleged benefits of patronage are overstated.[18] Apologists for corruption, self-styled realists, are on the run, but they are certainly not routed.[19]

These arguments and questions raise complex problems for students of government ethics. First, poor data and problems of bias make it difficult even to describe the range of unethical behaviour in the Canadian public sector. It is difficult to compare contemporary ethical behaviour with past behaviour. Similarly, the ethical health of different jurisdictions is difficult to divine precisely. Second, everyday moral rules are probably not very useful as criteria for evaluating government actions. If Acton is right, then it is silly to expect that public officials can subscribe to the same standards of behaviour as the rest of us. Third, that expectation may even be dangerous to the survival of the state and the liberty of its citizens. The first and last points are joined by the concept of context. To understand, and possibly judge, unethical government behaviour, we must see it in its historical, social, and cultural settings.

How important is the ethical conduct of politicians for the health and quality of democracies? Can there be too much concern with ethics? We are reminded that until about two centuries ago, great civilizations were thought to fall because of corruption and the moral decline of their leaders and citizens; the Roman Empire is often given as an example of this. Economic and military weaknesses were seen as symptoms, not causes, of national and imperial decline.[20]

We know that abuse of public office for private gain is reprehensible, possibly costly, and often damaging to the integrity of government. We also know that politicians are role models whose behaviour, not merely the quality of their decisions, is an important determinant of our views about government. But beyond these assertions questions arise when we review the contemporary Canadian condition. Canadians have not witnessed a single cataclysmic scandal like Watergate, which might reveal our deeper thoughts about democratic values and arguably might constitute a watershed in the development of our political morality. We have had few opportunities to test whether major scandals cleanse politics and move public morality to a higher plane. On the contrary, our essays reveal jurisdictions where episodes of unethical conduct are hotly but episodically, and often inconclusively, debated. Few obvious lessons emerge about the longer term democratic consequences of incidents of misconduct.

Somewhat ironically, it is easier to sustain the case that we can worry too much about ethics. It may be that our concern with ethics is merely symptomatic of a deeper, albeit variously defined, malaise. As Sharon Sutherland argues in her chapter, scandals will at most reinforce deeper political contradictions; they are never regime-shattering by themselves. Finally, an obsessive concern with ethics is undesirable if it causes citizens to confuse minor wrongs with major transgressions or if it impedes debate about policy issues.

An interesting characteristic of our ethically aware age is its preoccupation with *government* ethics. To be sure, environmentalists bestow some of their outrage on business. There is also anxiety about the abuse of power by physicians, priests, and teachers, especially for sexual gratification. But society's indignation and moral anxiety is primarily about politics. For example, the National Hockey League's (NHL) weak response to alcohol and drug abuse among its players and management is not widely seen as morally outrageous, even after the death of John Kordic, a player for several NHL teams. Yet this matter reveals an indifference to bad procedures and cover-ups of athletes' wrongdoings and problems by the the media, the sports establishment, and the police. The exposure of such conduct in a government agency would cause genuine outrage. Yet the NHL, an important institution, faces little censure. Similarly, much misconduct that we label governmental or political involves many people who are not public officials but who misbehave with, tempt, and influence government officials. We seldom acknowledge this, nor do we often think about the motivations and roles of the private corrupters. If a society's capacity for moral outrage is a finite commodity, perhaps we should devote more of this scarce resource to private immorality and less to public sector misconduct.

To whose drummer should public officials march?

Canadian government ethics are assumed to differ widely across the country and to reflect the characteristics of the governments and societies that give rise to them. This state of affairs is seen as natural and to be expected in a physically large and diverse federal state. In Canada, talk of a universal political morality would strike most observers as strange and impractical.

Governments' capacity to regulate official conduct in Canada is allocated as one would expect in a federal state. The senior governments—federal and provincial—establish codes of conduct and other forms of regulation that follow their sense of the needs of their jurisdictions. They have no formal obligation to consult with, let alone emulate, each other. Canadian municipal governments are formally the dependents of the provincial governments. Cities and small towns, when approaching questions of public conduct, are subject to provincial government influence and legal authority. The situation of aboriginal governments is in flux. As the Pocklingtons argue in their essay, the Indian Act now gives the minister of Indian Affairs wide discretion to shape standards of political conduct on reserves. One assumes that the term 'aboriginal self-government' implies a capacity, equal to that of the senior governments, to regulate official conduct in Native communities.

In the face of such diversity, the provisions of the Criminal Code, as they relate to bribery and other forms of public misconduct, establish minimal national standards to which all public office holders must submit. The Criminal Code's provisions thus acknowledge the principle of a universal code for public officials —certain actions are criminal and unacceptable everywhere in Canada.

In Canada today, the provinces and the federal government employ different approaches to the regulation of conflict of interest. Governments employ different definitions of misconduct, use contrasting administrative machinery, and impose different sanctions on offenders.

Such intergovernmental diversity generates surprisingly little controversy. The Pocklingtons' essay decries the Indian Act's paternalistic approach to official misconduct on reserves. And provincial governments are occasionally lambasted for requiring or suggesting that municipal officials submit to controls that are more stringent than those applying to provincial officials. But the philosophical and political justifications for this diversity are seldom probed. For example, some provinces now regulate the post-political careers of ministers. After leaving public office, they cannot engage in certain activities that will bring them into direct contact with the public agencies they recently directed and the officials who were recently their colleagues. A revolving door between the public and private sectors is seen as an insult to democratic principles and a threat to the impartiality of government. Is it justified that a practice defined as an affront to democracy in one province is ignored in its immediate neighbours or in Ottawa? Will aboriginal peoples be expected to adhere to codes of conduct like those prevailing for other Canadians? Whose rules will operate when aboriginal governments interact with other governments?

Canada's deviations from a universal political morality are implicitly justified as reflections of enduring political and cultural differences. Nova Scotia's ethical agenda is assumed to differ from Ontario's, for example, because of long-standing differences in political culture, economic structure, and partisanship. But how convincing are assertions of cultural distinctiveness in modern Canada? In an era of homogenizing communications technologies, a mobile population, and the influence of the Charter of Rights and Freedoms, can we easily speak of distinctive regional, provincial, and local cultures? Or are differences really those of degree? Such questions are not academic. Questionable governmental practices can be justified by their perpetrators as reflections, indeed celebrations, of local distinctiveness. Those who criticize misconduct can be portrayed as spokespersons for the irrelevant standards of outsiders. Jacques Bourgault and Stéphane Dion's chapter on Quebec reveals how arguments of cultural distinctiveness were employed by conservative Quebec politicians to justify abuses of public office.

The advent of aboriginal government will cause us to think carefully about how to evaluate political morality in genuinely different cultures. How, for example, should we look upon aboriginal peoples' deep sense of obligation to members of their families? As the Pocklingtons argue in their chapter, two convenient approaches must be avoided. On one hand, it is wrong to say that obligations to kin should overcome impersonal considerations simply because the pull of kinship is traditional and indigenous, while an appeal to impartial policy making is a non-aboriginal notion and hence wrong by definition. On the other hand, obligations of kinship should not be dismissed as mere reflections, by non-aboriginal standards, of an underdeveloped political morality.

In their account of Quebec, Bourgault and Dion note how the private conduct of Quebec government officials is not a subject of public interest, unlike the practice in other Canadian jurisdictions. And Ian Stewart's assessment of Nova Scotia notes how a member of the legislature, found guilty of corruption, was removed from office by a special statute, subsequently reelected in a by-election, and then defeated in a general election. These events raise interesting ethical issues. And following our theme, both cases can be explained in cultural terms. For example, an interest in the sexual conduct of public officials is characteristic of the Anglo-Saxon democracies. It is a subject of relative public indifference in Quebec and in continental Europe. But while official misconduct and its definition may be explained in cultural terms, can they be so justified? Is morality properly judged by anthropological standards? Does the fact that some voters tolerate public officials who abuse their spouses mean that the conduct is correct?

Deviations from a universal public morality are also explained by a focus on the functions performed by different political communities or by their size. James Q. Wilson argues that broad changes in American political and economic life resulted in the situation where state governments were particularly fertile grounds for corruption.[21] Under these circumstances, a citizen could rationally maintain that special attention and especially strict controls should be visited upon the state governments. No such sweeping arguments emerge from our studies, but James Lightbody's chapter on large cities highlights the considerable political influence of realtors, land developers, and construction firms. The urban ethical agenda is dominated by interplay between the municipalities' authority in development matters and industry's awareness of the importance of political power. David Siegel's assessment of small towns argues that provincially imposed conflict-of-interest codes, which may be suitable for cities, are alien to small towns, where politics is still a part-time undertaking. How far should senior governments extend their rules to their subordinate jurisdictions? Should local school board trustees, who are normally part-timers but who make important decisions, be subject to provincial guidelines, local ones, some of their own devising, or none at all?

Another deviation from a universal code of conduct rests on the assumed need to treat different types of officials differently. That is, we suppose that what officials do and whether they are elected or appointed should determine the controls under which they labour and the ethical standards they must meet. In Canada, the activities of cabinet ministers, who wield great power in policy making and administration, are more rigorously regulated than those of ordinary members of legislatures. Other powerful political actors, notably senior civil servants and judges, work under different guidelines presumably because they are appointed, hence removed from politics, and because of their duties. One wonders, however, whether these different controls are as readily justified as we assume. Perhaps judges, as custodians of substantial policy making power through judicial review and sentencing, should be subject to standards of conduct like those of senior civil servants. Perhaps senior civil servants who influence policy development should be regulated by the same codes and moral precepts that govern ministers.

Should we fix public morality? Can we?

Our essays reveal anxiety about the ethical health of Canadian government. But how can we achieve better government? Three answers present themselves, answers that reveal differing diagnoses, and that have been advanced at other times and in other places. Two optimistic solutions are available: improve the character of public officials, and then improve their behaviour by better educating them about their obligations and by establishing controls over their conduct. Such solutions are loosely described as optimistic because both imply that ethical conduct can be improved without major alterations to democracy. If pressured enough, democracy can heal itself without a transformation. A third solution calls for substantial changes if public conduct is to be improved. In the eyes of many critics, modern democracy has deep flaws that lead to improper conduct. What is required is a democracy inspired and dominated by the norms of impartiality and fairness.

Before reviewing these approaches, several qualifications are necessary. First, the approaches are not mutually exclusive. Advocates of the first two—character improvement and rules—generally see merit in each others' positions and hence vary in their emphasis. And those who call for deeper democratic reforms also see clearer rules and better people as necessary but not sufficient conditions for ethical politics. Second, our emphasis on three approaches hides their often considerable intellectual diversity. Those who seek greater fairness and impartiality in modern democracy do so for different reasons.

A modern cliché is that good government demands fewer politicians and more statesmen. This assertion highlights a concern that modern politics has too few men and women of character. Unfortunately, we disagree about the meaning of integrity and character, where they are found in society and what combination of experience, education, and values makes a good public official. For example, our essays reveal that the present federal and Alberta governments and those in British Columbia under Social Credit stress that a good politician is a businessperson who sees government service as a public-spirited interlude from work in the private sector. This viewpoint is contested by those who worry about too-close links between government and business. For some, the businessperson as politician is the source of ethical problems, not its solution. Similarly, a feminist and a conservative, for different reasons, might argue that adulterers must never occupy important public offices. But they would probably disagree deeply about whether a decent public official must be a member of a traditional family. The latter example highlights differences in how we judge character. It also reveals how the modern debate about character in politics has degenerated to the notion that good character means abstinence from certain conventionally defined vices including philandering, excessive drinking, and possibly even smoking tobacco. A clean lifestyle thus reflects good character. The contemporary confusion between lifestyle and character moves us away from debate about other character traits that probably lead to ethical government when in abundant supply. And while our lists of character traits will vary, most will include genuine self-confidence, respect for the dissenting viewpoints of friends, colleagues, and opponents, and a capacity for deliberate thought about morally complex issues.

An obsession with character is myopic because it sees decision makers as individuals and downplays the often corrupting influence of organized political life.[22] Honest and intelligent public officials often commit serious wrongs as dictated by their organizational roles and in response to strong pressures exerted upon them by other actors. Public misconduct seldom results exclusively from the moral deficiencies of the leaders themselves. To paraphrase Jeffrey Simpson, the apples may be rotten, but because of flaws in their barrel or in the markets in which they trade.[23]

Another cliché is that morality cannot be legislated. Advocates of clearer and stricter rules for office holders acknowledge this truism and also recognize that situations will arise that are not covered by rules, however clear. But advocates of rules assume that ethical problems can be managed if intelligent people establish and communicate relevant and coherent standards of conduct. Rules are a necessary, if not sufficient, condition for the attainment of responsible public behaviour. Such an orientation to ethical conduct is often seen as rooted in negative assumptions about human nature. But 'ethics managers' seldom assume that public officials are inherently bad. On the contrary, they assume that humans are educable, that good behaviour can be taught, and that human conduct can be substantially improved through education. Their deepest conviction, one with Aristotelian roots and one echoed in Kenneth Kernaghan's chapter, is that good behaviour is learned. Sanctions are for the minority who are not good pupils.

In modern Canadian government, ethics management is the ascendant philosophy. While acknowledging the importance of character, governments are adopting new regimes of rules. As Kernaghan notes, Ontario is now the leader in this movement. Its ethics arsenal boasts strict controls over ministers, a legislated code of conduct for elected officials, a freedom of information and privacy law, strict electoral financing laws, and a commitment to extend such practices to the province's municipalities. Canadian governments are not yet marching to identical ethical drummers. But all are moving towards greater formal regulation of official conduct, albeit at different paces and in response to local traditions and circumstances. Proposals to develop codes of conduct for political parties attest to the contemporary vigour of the 'rules' approach.

American authors frequently observe that the extension and strengthening of 'ethics machinery' in the United States coincides with a continuing increase in allegations of misconduct. Having reviewed the post-Watergate proliferation of laws about political financing, conflict of interest, and access to information, Joel

L. Fleishman concluded, 'As each new regulation has gone into effect, it has seemed to spawn its own evasions which, at least to the ears of some, cry out for even more regulation.'[24] Such an observation focuses attention on the limitations of a rules approach. What does Carol Lewis mean when she concludes that ethics codes do less than everything and more than nothing?[25]

Most codes of conduct deal with financial conflicts of interest. Their salutary effects include the identification of certain activities as improper and the provision of a formal, public commitment by officials that they are vigilant about conflicts between private interests and public duties. We assume that democracy is improved by the education of officials, especially newcomers to public life, about the obligations of public office. Strong statutory codes of conduct can also shatter the view of a cozy élite that justifies misconduct on the basis that 'everyone does it'.

Like those who favour better public officials, advocates of rules promote regimes that stress individual actions and downplay the significance of organizational influences. As authors in this book note, serious public misconduct is more often organized and systemic than freelance and individual. Controversy also abounds about patronage and the private conduct of officials, areas that are not touched by codes of conduct. Moreover, both patronage and private conduct are examples of controversial areas where modern societies are deeply divided about standards. Can important areas of public life be easily regulated in the absence of a social consensus?

Without much thought to the consequences, Canadian governments are constructing ethics bureaucracies that, while not yet large, exert an important influence on the ethics agenda. Ethics, or more precisely, a concern with conflicts of interest, are being organized into politics and institutionalized. The provincial ethics commissioners are powerful people; clad in the legitimating armour of non-partisanship and neutrality, they pass judgement and offer opinions that shape citizens' views about democratic politics. To ask an ancient question, who controls the controllers? Is it always wise to remove ethical controversy from the hurly-burly of democratic politics to the serene offices of ethics commissioners?

The offices of ethics commissioners may exhibit 'mandate creep'—a steady expansion of the issues that concern them and the range of public institutions over which they aspire to hold sway. Or, armed with mandates to deal with conflict of interest, ethics commissioners may look narrowly upon their duty and thereby exert a bias towards the worrisome view that an ethical politician is one who avoids financial conflicts of interest. A modest, indeed minimal, standard for public office holders—a refusal to abuse office for personal financial gain—might become too important in our thinking only because its discussion is built into the machinery of government. Rules and the machinery for their enforcement have lives and influences of their own.

Consider for a moment several contemporary proposals designed to promote a more ethical Canadian democracy. One notion is that political parties and party leadership conventions must, if public trust is to be maintained, be regulated by codes of conduct and stricter rules about fundraising. Another idea is that political patronage is an offensive practice that must be restricted. A related notion, clearly presented in Ian Stewart's chapter, is that pork-barrelling is an unethical practice. Another set of ideas calls for electoral reform including proposals for publicly funded elections, restrictions on the content of parties' election advertising, and stricter controls on the publication of public opinion polls during campaigns. Occasionally, we hear that politicians are wrong to advance their constituents' interests before bureaucratic agencies or to urge employers to locate plants within their constituencies.

We are not arguing that these diverse proposals are correct or even widely advocated. But they have important common denominators. The reforms seek to eliminate or curtail contemporary government practices that are seen as anachronistic or unfair. They strive for a fairer allocation of public resources. And each reflects a distrust of, and disdain for, modern democratic politics. Probed more deeply, each reveals the idea that democratic politics is inherently corrupt and corrupting of those involved in it. The problem transcends the abuse of office for personal gain: public officials are driven by the institutions they inhabit, by the practices they employ, and by the company they keep to ignore the public interest and to respond to narrow concerns, once again variously defined. The problem is the system, not the quality of the officials or the rules that govern their conduct.

The view that democratic officials serve narrow—not broad—interests is an old one. Ironically, it finds resonance and strength in modern democracies as the Soviet Union disintegrates and its former components struggle to adapt democracy to their own conditions. Three different, intertwined, and sometimes inconsistent elements underpin contemporary criticisms of democratic life and government ethics. The first idea is that public officials are subservient to and dependent upon special interests. Public officials are not strong enough to resist narrow interests, with the result that the 'vox populi' is lost in the resulting clash. Too many compromises are made. The second idea is that competition for office leads to unseemly policy compromises and self-serving partisanship as professional politicians package themselves for electoral consumption. Implicit in this critique is the notion that their promises, despite rhetorical differentiation, are essentially the same and hollow. Government is debased by an excess of partisanship. It is unethical because its practitioners neither stand for nor pursue clear principles. Margaret Thatcher responded to both these views when she thundered in a memorable statement: 'I am not a consensus politician. . . . I am a *conviction* politician.'[26] Finally, we are reminded of the common assertion that public officials are 'only in it for themselves.' This cliché asserts that public officials have too much autonomy, not too little. Their decisions and behaviour are poor because they put institutional and personal interests, such as a lust for power, personal wealth, or an expansion of bureaucratic influence, ahead of their obligation to the commonweal. Although such ideas inform our contemporary concern with ethics, they also underpin perennial debates about democratic representation.

This brief tour of critiques of modern government brings us back to contemporary reforms. To summarize, modern reforms, however disparate in content or origin, advance a universal message. Democratic politics, to be ethical, demand changes that will enhance the autonomy of officials, cause them to be fairer, and diminish traditional partisanship in electoral politics, and certainly in government decision making. At a societal level, the reform zeal manifests itself in a rediscovered interest in the apparatus of direct democracy. It also powerfully manifests itself in proposals for the improvement of government. Witness, for example, the idea that elections and internal party politics should be governed by clear, fair rules. Notice also the wide discontent with such practices as patronage, pork-barrelling, and unregulated lobbying. In short, democratic politics must be cleansed of corrupting self-interest, narrow partisanship, and interest group dominance. In the emerging orthodoxy, a good public official, elected or appointed, is the guardian of a sacred trust—a public office. The vision revises our ideas about democratic politics. For one thing, the good democratic politician now resembles our idea of an excellent civil servant under cabinet government. That is, he or she is neutral, technically competent, and predictable in habit and decision.

A democracy of fairness, impartiality, and extraordinary standards of conduct is not a new desire. Writing in 1930, the American journalist Walter Lippmann argued that the idea of public office as a public trust was a utopian notion.[27] It might motivate the genuinely powerful, those who occupy the stratospheres of power, but it would never be accepted by the majority of public officials and political activists, for whom democratic government would remain a vehicle for acquiring a morsel of power, a bit of recognition, or maybe some camaraderie and a tiny sense of contribution to public affairs. Human nature as interpreted by Lippmann demanded that 'clean' politics be seen as a lofty ideal. The democratic sanitizers of the 1990s can also be criticized for advancing a simplistic view of government. Is it feasible to think of modern democracies as political systems where organized interests, as corrupters of the public interest, can be simply wished away? Are modern policy problems really better solved when public officials, sheltered from robust democratic debate, merely reflect their constituents' preferences (and prejudices)?

Maybe Lippmann is right to portray a democracy of fairness as utopian. Perhaps we are right to argue that many reforms are simplistic. But the harder question is whether a politics of impartiality is even a worthy ideal. What do impartiality and fairness mean? For many they imply a detached neutrality and the dominance of technical expertise in decision making. But is technocracy or bureaucracy superior to democracy? Does it not substitute the hidden biases of experts for the obvious ones of democratic politicians whose views, if nothing else, are generally known to us? Another question is whether democratic governments can be free from business influence. Corporate sway may be reduced by eliminating its financial contributions to elections or by restricting lobbying. But business's political power ultimately flows from its control over investment, especially in an era of economic restructuring. The idea that public officials can be shielded from this deeper form of 'undue influence' may dangerous if it leads citizens to misunderstand political power.

Where do we go from here?

The narrow debate about procedural ethics is ultimately about the future of representative democracy in Canada. The 'ethical fixers' may deny this, arguing that attracting better leaders, tightening controls over them, and educating them about good behaviour will restore trust and remove ethics from the agenda. But the denials ring hollow. Behind the calls for more controls on conflict of interest and patronage is public concern about the fairness of modern democracy. The same concern underlies the calls for an elected senate and free votes, referenda and the recall of elected officials as antidotes to governments that do not do what we want. The anxiety about democratic processes is heightened by governments' apparent inability to solve complex policy problems.

In the immediate future, we will see even more regulation of official conduct. Spurred on by stories of corruption, 'integrity fixers' will campaign for stricter rules, tighter enforcement by ethics guardians, and tougher sanctions for offenders. As officials struggle to stay ahead of the predacious instincts of the opposition and media, the real rules will become even more onerous than those that are legally endorsed. One will never be able to be too clean and, as a result, prudence will dictate that ministers, civic politicians, and tribal leaders spend more time anticipating the scandal potential of any personal mishap, political association, or official action. People will be left out of cabinets or excuse themselves from the exercise of certain responsibilities for fear that some past or present sin will be revealed and the public agenda and their careers will be highjacked by a purity purge. Might future Canadian governments be ethically bombarded to death?

A delightful future to contemplate is one in which public officials recognize the need to redefine the notions of public stewardship and civic virtue, to rethink the relationships between governors and citizens, and to discuss such matters in clear language. If there is a case for refurbishing contemporary liberal democracy, now is the time to make it. Instead of running for cover with every accusation and redefining political roles and practices in response to scandals, government leaders should encourage discourse on the merits of doing public business in different ways. Instead of merely reacting to criticism, leaders should spell out their ideas about the obligations of ministers, the merits of patronage, and the proper relationships between politicians, civil servants, and the public. For their part, citizens must examine these arguments and think carefully about alternatives before scorning the status quo. Such a dialogue would put ethics on the agenda in a new way. It would make the conduct of public business the subject of a continuing debate rather than a fleeting issue on which we pass hasty judgements before moving to the next problem. It would focus attention on our civic culture as a whole.[28]

Profound economic changes might move ethics off the public agenda in the longer term. If economic decline persists, one can envision a future in which governments adopt the practices of the presently more successful Pacific economies to be more effective. The ethically troubling aspects of this shift might include closer relationships between private firms, banks, trade unions, and government agencies. The secretive élite accommodation that would characterize such an economic strategy would be at odds with the frustrated calls for fairer government that now drive the ethics agenda.

An unstated assumption in the modern drive to reform government is that fairer government is more effective government. But might our interest in purer government erode if we come to agree that more secretive government (possibly riddled with conflicts of interest because of its close ties with business) will be more effective, especially in the area of economic management? Clean government might fall into disfavour if it cannot deliver the goods. Democratic electorates have often supported villains—amiable and otherwise—who get the job done.

Notes

1 John Sawatsky, *Mulroney: The Politics of Ambition* (Toronto: Macfarlane, Walter and Ross, 1991).

2 Mark Twain reminded us of our obligation to examine ethical controversy carefully when he stated: 'A lie travels around the world before honesty has a chance to put on its boots.' Cited in Paul H. Douglas, *Ethics in Government* (Cambridge, MA: Harvard University Press, 1952): 95.

3 In her chapter, Professor Sutherland refers to conflict of interest as 'patronage you give yourself'. But rather than thinking of it as a subset of patronage, conflict of interest may be the 'imperialist' concept, one that absorbs patronage.

4 *Victoria Times Colonist*, 18 Dec. 1992: A3.

5 For an overview of such arguments, see Kenneth Kernaghan and John Langford, *The Responsible Public Servant* (Halifax: Institute for Research on Public Policy and the Institute of Public Administration of Canada, 1990), especially ch. 2.

6 Bernard Williams, 'Politics and Moral Character', in S. Hampshire, ed., *Public and Private Morality* (Cambridge, UK: Cambridge University Press, 1978): 57.

7 For a statement of this thesis see Bayless Manning, 'The Purity Potlatch: Conflicts of Interests and Moral Escalation', in A. Heidenheimer, ed., *Political Corruption: Readings in Comparative Analysis* (New York: Holt, Rinehart and Winston, 1970): 307-13.

8 Carl Bernstein, 'Journalism and the Growth of the Idiot Culture', *Manchester Guardian Weekly*, 14 June 1992: 21.

9 For an excellent discussion see Alan C. Cairns, *Charter versus Federalism: The Dilemmas of Constitutional Reform* (Montreal and Kingston: McGill-Queen's University Press, 1992).

10 Gary Sturgess, 'Corruption—The Evolution of an Idea 1788-1988', in Scott Prasser,

R. Wear, and J. Nethercote, eds, *Corruption and Reform: the Fitzgerald Vision* (St Lucia: University of Queensland Press, 1990): 3.

11 Two helpful studies take an empirical approach to the establishment of the ethical values of Canadian public officials. See Michael Atkinson and Maureen Mancuso, 'Do We Need a Code of Conduct for Politicians? The Search for an Elite Political Culture of Corruption in Canada', *Canadian Journal of Political Science* 18 (1985): 459-80, and Frank Cassidy and Marilyn Gore, 'Ethics in Local Government: The Views of Municipal Administrators', *Optimum* 22 (1991/2): 44-53. For a discussion of the shortcomings of such research see P.J. Bergerson, *Ethics and Public Policy: An Annotated Bibliography* (New York: Garland, 1988).

12 For a good discussion of Acton's dictum, see A.R. Rogow and H.D. Laswell, *Power, Corruption and Rectitude* (Englewood Cliffs, NJ: Prentice-Hall, 1963).

13 For an overview, see C.A.J. Coady, 'Politics and the Problem of Dirty Hands', in Peter Singer, ed., *A Companion to Ethics* (Oxford: Basil Blackwell, 1991): 373-83.

14 Michael Walzer, 'Political Action: The Problem of Dirty Hands', *Philosophy and Public Affairs* 2 (1973): 174.

15 Dennis F. Thompson, *Political Ethics and Public Office* (Cambridge, MA: Harvard University Press, 1987): 4.

16 See Jeffrey Simpson, *Spoils of Power: The Politics of Patronage* (Toronto: HarperCollins, 1988): 16.

17 See, for example, J.C. Scott, *Comparative Political Corruption* (Englewood Cliffs, NJ: Prentice Hall, 1972).

18 See, for example, N.H. Leff, 'Economic Development Through Economic Corruption,' in M.U. Ekpo, ed., *Bureaucratic Corruption in Sub-Saharan Africa: Toward a Search for Causes and Consequences* (Washington, DC: University Press of America, 1979): 329-33.

19 On Canadian patronage, see Reginald Whitaker, 'Between Patronage and Bureaucracy: Democratic Politics in Transition', *Journal of Canadian Studies* 22 (1987): 55-71.

20 See Peter Jenkins, *Mrs Thatcher's Revolution* (London: Pan Books, 1989), especially 30-49.

21 James Q. Wilson, 'Corruption: The Shame of the States', in A. Heidenheimer, ed., *Political Corruption*: 298-306.

22 Thompson, *Political Ethics and Public Office*.

23 Jeffrey Simpson, *Spoils of Power*.

24 Joel L. Fleishman, 'Self Interest and Political Integrity', in J. Fleishman *et al.*, eds, *Public Duties: The Moral Obligations of Government Officials* (Cambridge, MA: Harvard University Press, 1981): 52-92.

25 Carol W. Lewis, *The Ethics Challenge In Public Service: A Problem Solving Guide* (San Francisco: Jossey-Bass, 1991): 140.

26 Jenkins, *Mrs Thatcher's Revolution*: 3. Emphasis in original.

27 Walter Lippmann, 'A Theory about Corruption', in Heidenheimer, ed., *Political Corruption*: 294-7.

28 For an elaboration, see Gilles Paquet, 'The Best Is the Enemy of the Good', *Optimum* 22 (1991-2): 7-15.

2

John W. Langford

Quasi-crimes and eager beavers

Public sector ethics in British Columbia

Governance in British Columbia has tended to disturb or titillate many observers over the years because its practitioners have often appeared indifferent to key procedural values associated with liberal democracy. In other words, B.C. politicians don't seem to give a fig about *how* the business of government is conducted. They focus, instead, on delivering the goods to their supporters (and all too often themselves) and damn the niceties. In a book on the first three years of the first Bill Bennett government, Stan Persky characterized this style of governance as quasi-crime, a term meant to cover 'a wide range of semi-legal pilfering, non-lethal backstabbing, and unspeakable acts with closeted skeletons, appropriate to the timid quasi-criminal imaginations of car dealers and other small businessmen'.[1] The notion of quasi-crime is a useful one because it focuses our attention on behaviour that is ethically questionable without being criminal. But Persky's definition is not wide enough to capture the full spectrum of the procedural abuses that have been commonplace in B.C. In a polity run by Social Credit governments for all but four of the last forty years, patronage, cronyism, conflict of interest, unfair or careless administration, secrecy, and invasion of privacy have been a normal part of government. At times, the ship of state has been awash in this wider notion of quasi-crime and the public seems to have been largely indifferent.

But the public mood may be changing. In October 1991, after sixteen straight years of Social Credit rule, the New Democratic Party was given the reins of power by the electorate. Moreover, the NDP was elected at least in part on its promise to provide 'good government'. Giving the NDP a substantial majority of seats in the legislature, elevating the long dormant Liberals to the official opposition, and reducing the Socreds to a rump group, the electorate appeared at last to be showing as much interest in *how* government business is done as *what* business it does. For its part, the new government began by sending strong messages to the public and the public service that the old ways of doing business were no longer acceptable.

This raises an important question, which this chapter cannot answer: namely, are we observing a sea change in B.C. politics and government that will see provincial affairs conducted with significantly more respect for widely accepted procedural values?[2] There are some promising signs, but it is simply too early to say. In this chapter I will try, first, to provide a feeling for the ethical culture that has dominated B.C. political and bureaucratic life over the last ten years. This contemporary time-frame was chosen because it provides the reader with glimpses of the last years of the lengthy Bill Bennett administration, the Bill Vander Zalm regime, the short Rita Johnston interregnum, and the first year of the Mike Harcourt government. I then suggest some noteworthy developments and trends reflected in the political and bureaucratic shenanigans of the past decade. Finally, I will examine the ethics regimes that have provided the legal and institutional boundaries within which politicians and public servants are supposed to operate, offering, in conclusion, some necessarily gloomy views on the effectiveness of the rule-making efforts to date and prospects for the future.

Is all this concern about unethical conduct warranted? Some observers of the B.C. scene are more amused than disturbed by the 'let's get it done' approach to governance, judging it to be peripheral to the real animating force of B.C. politics, the ideological divide between the Social Credit and New Democratic parties.[3] Such a dismissal is, in my view, undeserved. Ethical misconduct brought down the Vander Zalm government in 1991. More importantly, it has, particularly since the mid-1980s, fuelled a growing public cynicism about the political system, allowing the opposition and the media the latitude to disrupt the policy-making process at will with accusations or hints of misbehaviour by officials. In addition, this quasi-criminal political world has had a costly effect on the public service, creating what one ombudsman described as an 'eager beaver' culture in which public servants become accomplices of the politicians in 'results-oriented' government.[4] All of these developments, in turn, have led to the inevitable institutional initiatives designed to restore confidence in the processes of government. A habit of procedural abuse, public cynicism, and the distorting effects of new ethical regimes on the way governments do business are already a lasting legacy of ethical misconduct in the B.C. public sector.

Morality tales from the front lines

Instead of attempting to establish the ethical culture of the British Columbia provincial government through a detailed chronology of questionable behaviour over the last decade, I would like to tell a few stories. I believe that these morality tales illustrate key facets of the ethical climate and provide a useful, if intuitive, basis for an analysis both of the efforts to manage this culture (and its attendant behaviour) and its significance for the political and governmental system in B.C.

Most of these stories are well known to the citizens of B.C. All have been the subject of public reports or opinions by an inquiry commission, the ombudsman, or the conflict of interest commissioner. They have been chosen because they illustrate how elected and appointed officials (often in concert) have become caught up in a wide spectrum of ethical dilemmas in such areas as the use of confidential information, patronage, political neutrality, conflict of interest, and the uncharted territory of the relationship between private and public morality. Apologists might argue that these cases are the exception, and that their investigation by appropriate authorities proves that the system is working as it should. A quick glance at more detailed accounts of the last decade would dispatch that notion in a hurry.[5] For my part, thirteen years of classroom and workshop discussions with B.C. public servants make such a proposition almost laughable. These stories are no more or less strange than many others that could have been told. Some of these tales reflect the existence and strength of operational values that are at some distance from the ethical standards contemporary Canadian public officials—including those in B.C.—have publicly acknowledged to be appropriate. Others reflect the inability of public officials to keep up with rapidly shifting public and media expectations about how they should behave.

Political enemies and 'eager beavers'

Early in 1982, a complaint was made to the ombudsman that the minister's office of the Ministry of Human Resources, with the cooperation of ministry officials, was using the files of the Income Assistance Division of the ministry to gather information on five individuals involved in a welfare rights demonstration.[6] The complaint was precipitated by a leak from within the ministry to the individuals in question.

In the investigation that followed, the ombudsman discovered that the special assistant to the minister had asked the deputy minister by memorandum to discover if the five individuals were clients of the ministry. The deputy sent the request on—by memorandum again—to the coordinator of the Income Assistance Division. The coordinator initiated the search through the master list of income assistance recipients and then followed up with two telexes: the first to five district offices corresponding to the addresses of the individuals requesting any record of them, and the second extending the search to more than 150 district offices requesting records of information regarding financial assistance *or contact* with any of the five. After a further inquiry from the deputy, the coordinator sent back a summary of the financial information received on two of the individuals and stated that there was no record on the other three. The deputy sent the information directly to the minister.

During the ombudsman's inquiry, the special assistant to the minister insisted that the search request was provoked by an allegation of welfare fraud by the five that was received in the minister's office. However, the minister's office was unable to produce any record of the receipt of such an allegation and the special assistant had no recollection of how it was received or from whom. In addition, no mention was made of fraud in the memorandums that precipitated the search. Moreover, the ministry has established structures and procedures for social assistance fraud investigation that were ignored in this case. The only link between the five was their involvement in the rally on 21 November 1981. The request for a search came only five days after the rally, and the request listed the five individuals and their complete addresses.

The ombudsman summed up his concerns as follows:

> The Ministry's position is essentially that there is nothing wrong with the search as conducted. All we have here, according to the Ministry, is an eager beaver civil servant anxious to do a good job for his Deputy Minister. The eager beaver theory might explain the action taken by the MHR official and I have no grounds to think that there were other reasons to explain his conduct. However, his eagerness to please his Deputy Minister does not justify his trespass into the privacy of citizens by flashing their names on telexes into 150 MHR offices throughout the entire province. I am very concerned that such eager beaver civil servants are not imbued with any sensitivity to or respect for the privacy interests of citizens. I am even more concerned that senior officials in this Ministry do not appear to realize or appreciate how offensive this conduct is and, worst of all, that they appear inordinately preoccupied with the fact that another eager beaver public servant disclosed the memo to the victims of the information search. Throughout the entire search no one to whom the request was addressed ever seems to have asked: why do we want or need this information? Do we have a right or justification to conduct such an information search?[7]

Subsequent to the ombudsman's report, it was learned that this was not an isolated instance. Apparently, during this period, the minister's office expected and received the cooperation of ministry 'eager beavers' in efforts to identify and possibly neutralize other extra-parliamentary political opponents. Other incidents over the decade suggest that insensitivity to the privacy of citizens was not confined to one minister or ministry. For instance, the ombudsman was critical of the early 1987 efforts of the ministry of the attorney general to use a law firm and private investigators to infiltrate the operations of a prominent pro-choice group that had broken no laws.[8] The ombudsman, in another report, also expressed reservations about the way in which relevant ministries either used or planned to use criminal records to screen individuals working with vulnerable people such as children and the handicapped.[9]

These events justifiably raise concerns about the lack of importance that provincial politicians and public servants attach to the privacy of citizens. But they must also raise concerns about the professionalism and political neutrality of the public service. What happened to the convention that the role of public servants does not extend to being an accomplice of ministers in the sabotage of their 'enemies'? As the next two cases illustrate, political neutrality is not a particularly healthy concept in B.C.

The Premier's Office calling

In September 1986, the manager of the Knight Street Pub in Vancouver began the complex application process for a pub licence. That licence was granted by the ministry of labour and consumer affairs in May 1988. A complaint to the ombudsman that the neighbourhood referendum required by regulation had been improperly conducted led to a detailed investigation of the licensing process and disturbing revelations about patronage, the politicization of bureaucratic processes, the erosion of political neutrality, and the respect for fair procedure in the public service.[10]

The problem in this case centred around the activities of the general manager of the Liquor Control and Licensing Branch within the ministry. He was a career public servant who had been appointed to the position by the premier's office in November 1986, apparently without consultation with the minister or deputy.[11] The new general manager's previous position had been in the premier's office.

After the new general manager took over, the branch made a series of questionable moves. First, the branch provided the application with a pre-clearance, although it did not meet a number of key criteria for such status. A copy of the pre-clearance was sent to the owner of the property on which the pub would be situated. The owner, a close friend of the premier, had actively lobbied the branch regarding the application. Second, after a phone call from the premier's deputy minister, the general manager added a polling firm (DMS Ltd) owned and operated by the premier's 1986 leadership campaign chair to the list of firms considered eligible to conduct the required neighbourhood referendum. This firm subsequently was given the contract to do the referendum, although it had no previous experience in polling. Finally, the general manager ignored an early warning from a neighbour of the proposed pub that the referendum was not being done properly and approved the pub licence on the strength of the results of the poll.

In the end, the operators of the 'polling' firm pleaded guilty to a criminal charge of uttering a forged document and were fined. The investigation of the incident by the deputy minister of labour and consumer relations was shown by the ombudsman's subsequent inquiry to have ignored the procedural irregularities and to have failed to be 'thorough and exacting in the investigation of complaints'. The call by the premier's deputy minister to the general manager was described by the ombudsman as 'inappropriate political interference with administrative decision making'. The contention by the premier's deputy that the call (made after the owner of the pub site had called him to suggest that DMS be given the polling contract) was 'merely a show of support for a good guy, an on-side guy' and was 'in the nature of an inquiry and was not a direction' was given short shrift by the ombudsman, especially as the general manager viewed the 'inquiry' as an order. The ombudsman recorded without comment the amazing contention of the premier's deputy that responding to political approaches to him by contacting the relevant administrator and indicating support for a particular individual or company was the *raison d'être* of his office.[12] Finally, the manager of the branch was chastised by the ombudsman for allowing political considerations to influence his exercise of administrative discretion.[13]

Again, in this case, we see politicians and 'eager beaver' senior public servants working together to bend legally established and widely accepted rules of conduct. Here the objective is to ensure a flow of benefits to close friends of the premier. In the course of satisfying that objective, political neutrality takes another beating and virtually every rule and convention associated with the notion of administrative fairness is ignored.

Someone may be listening

This complicated story began with the revelation in September 1989 that the minister of tourism had, earlier that year, provided a large grant to a non-profit society in White Rock, B.C., on the condition that it purchase a recycling system from a company owned by his 1986 election campaign manager and a personal and family friend. The story broke in the media just after the first cheque for $138,532 was received by the society and passed through to the company. The minister resigned and the RCMP recommended to the attorney general's ministry that he be charged with criminal breach of trust. In February 1990, the attorney general announced that the ministry would not be pressing charges against the ex-minister despite an RCMP request that the decision not to lay charges be reviewed. Shortly after, the premier characterized the ex-minister's behaviour not as illegal or improper as much as 'overly generous because it was his constituency and he was the minister responsible'.[14]

This attempt to reward a party supporter and a friend might—on its own—have raised questions concerning the problematic interface between conflict of interest and patronage. The story is saved from being a prosaic case of patronage and corruption, however, by the events that followed.

In April 1990, to clear the air of suspicions about the administration of criminal justice, the attorney general asked the ombudsman to head a public inquiry into the government's decision not to lay charges against the ex-minister. In May, after the issue had become the subject of heated political debate for some months, the opposition justice critic commenced an unusual private prosecution against the ex-minister, retaining a Victoria criminal lawyer to deal with the prosecution. This private prosecution was dropped in late June. Not only would continuing the prosecution be expensive, but in the interim, the justice critic had been given tapes of car-phone conversations involving the attorney general, which provided the justice critic with the opportunity to accuse him of interfering in the administration of justice by working with officials and the media to embarrass the private prosecutor. The behaviour of the ex-minister of tourism was forgotten in a media-assisted frenzy of voyeurism provoked by the release of the taped conversations and the relationships they revealed between the attorney general and both his assistant deputy attorney general and a female TV reporter.

At this point the case became more interesting from an ethical perspective. Concern centred around four themes: privacy, the objective administration of criminal justice, the political neutrality of public servants, and the relevance of personal morality to public life.

Critics questioned, first, the propriety of releasing transcripts of phone conversations involving the attorney general that were surreptitiously recorded. Did this inappropriately violate his privacy? Opinion was divided. The ombudsman (writing as the inquiry commissioner) captured both sides of the argument, noting, on the one hand, that the 'unauthorized interception or disclosure of private communications is unlawful; it is also repugnant'; but, on the other hand, observing that the law does not necessarily protect private conversations 'where they are action oriented and the action is improper'. His view, on balance, was that the NDP justice critic had a 'sincere and understandable concern' that the attorney general's statements 'were action oriented and were intended to obstruct justice'.[15] In other words, privacy is important, but concern about obstruction of justice is more important.

The second concern centred around the role of the attorney general and the credibility of the criminal justice system. Neither the evidence of continuing contact between the assistant deputy attorney general and the minister of tourism's defence team nor the attorney general's efforts to embarrass the private prosecutor did much to inspire confidence that the administration of justice was untainted by partisan politics. The ombudsman's conclusion on the latter was that the dual role of the attorney general as a minister in the government and the chief law officer

> places severe constraints on the Attorney General. He or she must never allow partisan political actions to mix, or appear to mix, with the responsibility for the administration of justice. In this case, the political interest in countering earlier Opposition claims was an inappropriate mix of the roles because it related to a case that was proceeding before the criminal courts.[16]

Less prominently discussed in the media, but a provocative issue among public servants, was the apparent enthusiasm with which the assistant deputy attorney general provided derogatory information about the private prosecutor to his political master when it was evident that the latter would be using the information for partisan political purposes. Reflecting on the jocularity of the conversation, the ombudsman made the following observation:

> It is predictable that people who work closely together on a daily basis and who are professional contemporaries might become friendly and thus have such conversations. However, this must be measured against the importance of senior public administrators not being affected in their decisions and actions by partisan political considerations.[17]

It is an understatement to say that no trace of the convention of political neutrality is evident in the transcript of this conversation.

Finally, media discussion of the taped phone calls raised the spectre of the cross-border leak of the growing American preoccupation with the character, competence, and capacity of public officials. The conversations between the attorney general and the female TV reporter not only demonstrated the lengths to which he was prepared to go to get derogatory information on a perceived political opponent (the private prosecutor) to the media, but they strongly supported the thesis that the two parties to the conversation were more than passing acquaintances. Speculation about this relationship was a critical contextual factor in the media analysis of the attorney general's performance of his public duties. The premier never went any further in his public criticism of the attorney general than to allow that he was disappointed by his conduct. In the context of the emotional attachment of the Social Credit Party and the premier to the institution of the family, it remains an open question whether he was more disappointed by the attorney general's official actions, his criticism of the premier on one tape, or his private life.

Conflict in the garden

The controversy surrounding the 1990 sale of Fantasy Gardens was brought to a head by the publication of a report on the sale by the then acting conflict of interest commissioner, Ted Hughes.[18] This report, in turn, precipitated the departure of Bill Vander Zalm from the premiership in April 1991, and probably sealed the fate of the Social Credit Party in the election the following October.

The facts of the case are, for the most part, quite straightforward.[19] The premier took an active role in the sale of Fantasy Gardens, a religious theme park owned by his wife and himself, to Asiaworld (Canada), a company owned by Taiwanese businessman Tan Yu. The deal was facilitated by Faye Leung, a real estate agent whose frenetic monologues during taped phone conversations with the premier are now the stuff of political legend. During marathon negotiations between the principals in a Vancouver hotel suite that led to a deal being concluded early into the morning of 4 August 1990, Tan Yu gave the premier $20,000 in cash in a brown paper bag. The reasons for this transfer of funds have never been satisfactorily established. Over two weeks after the deal was concluded, the premier called the president of Petro-Canada to facilitate the sale to Asiaworld of a Petro-Canada property adjoining Fantasy Gardens. The premier also arranged a meeting on 6 September between Tan Yu, the premier's deputy minister, and the minister of finance to explore further investment by Tan Yu in B.C. Finally, the premier facilitated for Tan Yu—at Faye Leung's request—a luncheon at Government House on 6 September, and, on the evening of 7 September, attended, with other government officials, a reception for Tan Yu arranged again by Faye Leung.

Eventually, the now ex-premier was charged with criminal breach of trust and acquitted. A justice of the Supreme Court of B.C. concluded that:

While many of Vander Zalm's imputed activities as revealed by the evidence before me might be considered foolish, ill advised and in apparent or real conflict of interest or breach of ethics, for the reasons I have set out, I am unable to conclude from the totality of the evidence that it has been proven beyond a reasonable doubt that he committed a breach of trust in connection with the duties of his office by using his public office to assist or promote his personal and financial interest in the sale of the property known as Fantasy Gardens.[20]

The story of the sale of Fantasy Gardens and its raffish set of characters is noteworthy from an ethical perspective largely because the report on the sale by the then acting conflict of interest commissioner, Ted Hughes, raised some fascinating questions about the nature of conflict of interest. First, the report employed a broad definition of conflict, which was drawn from the Parker Commission inquiry into the activities of Sinclair Stevens.[21] This definition insists that a conflict exists not only at the point when a minister actually takes official action to forward his or her private interests, but earlier, when the minister 'has knowledge of a private economic interest that is sufficient to influence the exercise of his or her public duties and responsibilities'.[22] Using this definition makes it possible to accuse an office holder of being in conflict even though that individual has taken no *official* action to compromise the performance of his public duties or forward his own private economic interests. The acting commissioner never explained why this tougher definition was chosen over others (including the less demanding definition found in B.C.'s 1990 conflict of interest legislation), which might have led to more benign interpretations being placed on the premier's actions.[23]

The Hughes Report also upped the ante with respect to conflict of interest by suggesting that the mere ownership of a business by the premier automatically represented a potential conflict of interest, and implying that a prominent public official cannot carry on any private business (e.g., make a call to the head of Petro-Canada concerning the purchase of a property) without being in conflict. Finally, by construing official courtesies extended by the premier towards the purchaser of Fantasy Gardens as 'special privileges' and the 'red carpet treatment'—even when the courtesies were extended after the land deal was closed and such courtesies were regularly extended by the premier and other cabinet members to other individuals who had no business dealings with them—the Hughes Report created a standard of integrity that may be beyond the capacities of even the most saintly public official.[24]

The overall significance of the case from the perspective of this analysis is that (in common with the Sinclair Stevens case at the federal level) it suggests the extraordinary degree to which the concept of conflict of interest can be powerfully invoked even when the public official may not have misused his public office to enrich himself and may not have perverted the performance of his public duty in any significant way.

A year of living anxiously

Two incidents in the first year of the New Democrat administration illustrate the apprehension the new government felt about accusations of ethical misconduct. In both cases, the focus of concern was conflict of interest.

Immediately upon taking office in November 1991, the cabinet struggled over the propriety of some of its members participating in a decision to overturn Socred public service wage restraint legislation so that teachers could receive the full increases their unions had negotiated with school boards throughout the province. The problem was that a number of ministers were married to teachers or other public servants covered by the legislation. There was a potential, therefore, that they could benefit from the repeal of the legislation. On the other hand, repeal of the legislation had been a clear plank in the party's election platform, and the party had just won the election. Moreover, this was an action that would benefit a large class of people beyond those individuals related to cabinet ministers. The cabinet considered having the affected members withdraw when the issue was discussed, but faced the ludicrous prospect of having nearly half the cabinet leave the room. In the end, the matter was referred to the conflict of interest commissioner, who indicated that participation in the decision by the affected cabinet ministers would not, under the circumstances noted above, constitute a conflict. Yes, he argued, the decision to amend the guidelines and regulations enacted under the Compensation Fairness Act would enhance the private interests of some cabinet ministers, but their spouses represented a tiny proportion of the 300,000 public service employees to whom the legislation applied. The commissioner was satisfied that such a large group did comprise a 'broad class of electors', thereby allowing an exception under the prevailing conflict of interest legislation.[25]

Another case involved a decision by the minister of forests, in July 1992, to transfer a major forest licence from Westshore Terminals Ltd to Repap Carnaby Inc. The problem was that the minister was on a leave of absence from his position as a millwright at Skeena Cellulose Inc., another subsidiary of Repap Enterprises Inc. When the conflict of interest commissioner was formally asked by the cabinet for his opinion on the transfer, he indicated that a real conflict existed because the minister had to know that the decision to transfer the licence provided him with the opportunity to further his private interest. The premier accepted the commissioner's assessment without demur. The minister was suspended for ninety days, resulting in an estimated loss of $10,000 in ministerial salary.

The curious features of this case are not limited to the novelty of the penalty. The commissioner, in rendering his opinion, also indicated that in his view the minister's decision was *not* motivated by a private interest and that the transfer was *entirely* in the public interest. The transfer was widely applauded in the minister's own constituency, where serious layoffs would have occurred if it had not taken place. The minister had been on leave for over six years and had no intention of returning to his position. In fact, shortly after the licence transfer he gave up his position at Skeena Cellulose. His own union publicly denounced the transfer. Under these circumstances, critics of the commissioner's decision asked, how could the decision realistically be construed as an opportunity to further the minister's private interests? They also wanted to know what kind of action a B.C. forest minister could take that would not affect the fortunes of a large company like Repap one way or the other. The suspended minister wistfully concluded that: 'Someone else should have done it, not me. It could have been my deputy minister, and every cabinet minister has a back-up minister. But really, no other decision could have been made.'[26] One wonders if this kind of restrictive boundary around a minister's freedom to act is really what the designers of responsible cabinet government had in mind. Equally, one wonders whether the proponents of 'withdrawal' wouldn't be offended by the suspended minister's portrayal of recusal as an easily sidestepped irritant.

Trends and developments over the last decade

The latter cases show how politically charged a question public sector ethics has become in B.C., especially on the heels of an election fought by the NDP largely on the issue of open and honest government. Because the government has made integrity a major agenda item, promising 'good government' legislation on issues ranging from electoral reform to conflict of interest and freedom of information, it has become a sitting duck any time the opposition or the media find even the hint of wrongdoing. The election campaign, the years of Social Credit quasi-crime, and the persistent criticism of this misconduct by the NDP while in opposition have sensitized the media and the electorate to ethical misconduct as a central feature of the continuing political drama. Events that ten years ago would have attracted virtually no notice are front-page stories or lead items on the evening news. As a result, ministers are becoming overly sensitive, preferring to excuse themselves from situations that might raise an ethics question from the opposition or the media. The conflict of interest commissioner is now being asked to 'pre-clear' the involvement of more cautious ministers in certain discussions or decisions.

These are all indications that B.C. is moving from a province in which the electorate seemed largely indifferent to the means used by governments to get the job done to a jurisdiction waiting for the next elected or appointed official to appear in court or be shuffled off to the sidelines while the ombudsman, conflict of interest commissioner, or comptroller general investigates and files a report. For the foreseeable future, enhanced media and public sensitivity is bound to have the effect of driving the government off its substantive agenda every time a 'scandal' rears its head. In recent months, for instance, the government has been blind-sided by a tortuous tale involving accusations of mismanagement of constituency funds by government MLAs and misdirection of charity 'bingo' money to party coffers by a party fundraising organization. In addition, the government's appointment and contracting practices have regularly forced it to defend against patronage charges by the opposition, the media, and even its own supporters. The political costs of such attacks have been high even before the facts of the more complex cases have been clarified by quickly launched inquiries.

While any government whose political fortunes are tied to the probity of its members and supporting organizations deserves great sympathy, there are even more disturbing developments reflected in these morality tales. The first is that conflict of interest has become a 'monster' concept in B.C. political and governmental life. Conflict of interest has taken on the character of a code phrase, used indiscriminately to label virtually any behaviour perceived to be inappropriate. As a concept, it has swallowed up the notion of patronage, rendering completely invalid what in more innocent times was an acceptable part of political life—showing preference in jobs, contracts, and honours for one's political supporters.[27] It has been further bloated by the inflation of the meaning of private interest to include not only the financial assets and liabilities of the public office holder, but those of the official's spouse, family, friends, business associates, and even constituents, in the case of elected officials. At stake here is the capacity of the elected official to act on behalf of an ever-widening circle of citizens who in law or practice are being viewed as part of his or her personal entourage.

This capacity has been further reduced in B.C. by a recent ruling by the conflict of interest commissioner that ministers must not make personal representation on behalf of a constituent who is seeking remedy or redress from a commission, board, agency, or other tribunal of the government. The commissioner expressed the view that:

> A minister acting in such a way would always be seen as a minister of government and that is a position of responsibility that he or she cannot shed at will and it would be improper to appear in an advocacy role of this kind.[28]

In the quest for the elusive 'level playing field', the role of elected officials is changing dramatically in B.C.

But the impact of conflict of interest does not end here. The term, as both the public sector wage restraint and forest licence cases illustrate, has lost its capacity to discriminate between actions that may benefit the public official only and those that benefit the official as part of a large class of beneficiaries. The Fantasy Gardens case is a perfect example of the degree to which conflict of interest has become more focused on appearance and what used to be called potential conflict of interest than on misconduct in the form of purposeful action demonstrably at the expense of the public interest. In short, conflict of interest, unleashed as a cleansing agent, has become a tool of political terrorism in B.C., and ministers are beginning to act with commensurate caution.

The tale of the attorney general's taped conversations suggests that there is potential for the concept of conflict of interest to become an even larger monster.

In the United States, an endless catalogue of personal incapacities, negative characteristics, and incompetencies have been declared to be relevant to the performance of public duties by appointed and elected officials.[29] In effect, the 'smell test' extends the notion of personal interest to include factors such as sexual behaviour, substance abuse, and religious beliefs that might be seen to have relevance to the credibility, reliability, or judgement of the official. The 'politics of virtue'[30] have been placed on the menu in B.C. What remains to be seen is whether or not the opposition, the media, and the public will develop a lasting appetite for this kind of 'eruption of the private realm into the public'.[31]

Often overlooked among these fast-moving developments with respect to conflict of interest is the fact that ethical misconduct in the B.C. public sector has not been limited to such matters. While conflict of interest has been the headline-grabber over the last decade, politicized, unfair procedures, the misuse of confidential information, the invasion of the privacy of citizens, and lapses in accountability are far more common and undoubtedly represent more serious threats to the viability of democratic government. The latter represent fundamental attacks on bedrock values of our system of government, not merely petty efforts to divert state resources to decision makers or their supporters. Citizens are far more likely to be affected directly by such shortcomings, especially if they become embedded in the bureaucratic services that they confront daily.

Another important development reflected in the cases is the degree to which questionable behaviour over the preceding decade has not been limited to elected officials. In the context of demoralizing restraint and downsizing, the fundamental values of responsible public service have been challenged by politicization of the senior ranks, erratic and sometimes bizarre leadership from the office of the premier, blatant cronyism in the hiring of senior officials, and the emphasis placed on being a 'team player'. The result is that too many senior public servants have been pulled into the political game, prepared on too many occasions to assist their masters in their partisan schemes, help them out with shoddy 'investigations' when things go wrong, and even anticipate their inappropriate needs when they are not clearly articulated. Niceties such as established procedures for decision making, the maintenance of proper records, treating all candidates equally, and protecting the privacy of clients are quickly set aside in such a world. In this atmosphere, senior public servants have not generally seen it as their duty to insulate their employees from the inappropriate requests of politicians. It is very hard to stand up for anything when you are keeping your own head down, or trying to impress your minister or other more partisan colleagues that you are 'on side'. Lower down in the ranks of the public service, junior officials may only rarely be confronted directly with the need to be 'on side', but they learn the rules of the game from watching those above them. As we shall see shortly, efforts to build an ethical public service in an 'eager beaver' culture have come to little.

Managing the quasi-crime culture

Perhaps surprisingly, this record of frontier government has not been played out on a landscape devoid of rules. In common with other jurisdictions in Canada, most of the emphasis on rule-making has been in the area of conflict of interest.[32] Also in common with other jurisdictions, a small number of restrictions on the behaviour of MLAs have been in place for a considerable period. The Constitution Act prohibits members from carrying out business directly or indirectly with the provincial government. The Standing Orders of the Legislative Assembly have since 1892 prohibited MLAs from voting on matters in which they have a financial interest.

The first significant contemporary initiative in the management of 'quasi-crime' came in 1974 when the NDP government of Dave Barrett passed the Public Officials' Disclosure Act, committing itself to the innovative principle of public disclosure of personal financial interests as the best preventive measure against conflict of interest. The act was slightly amended and renamed (The Financial Disclosure Act) by the Socreds when they returned to power in 1975. It covered a wide range of public officials at the provincial and municipal levels, but at the provincial level it was only applied to MLAs. They were required to make a written disclosure of their financial interests semi-annually to the clerk of the legislative assembly. The clerk acted merely as a repository for disclosure reports, as the act made no provision for advice or interpretation. The reports were available to the media and the public. Failure to disclose was punishable by a fine up to $10,000 and financial gains made from undisclosed financial interests could be made payable to the government.[33]

By contemporary standards, the exposure of financial interests required by the Financial Disclosure Act was not particularly demanding. It did not, for instance, require the comprehensive reporting of the financial interests of spouses or dependent children. The rules for disclosure made it difficult for the observer to determine what kind of business a declared holding company was actually conducting. Oddly, conflict of interest was not defined or even alluded to directly in the legislation. In any event, the legislation did little to affect the operation of the quasi-crime culture in the late 1970s and through the mid-1980s. Responding to a round of scandals at the end of the Bennett premiership, the Socreds, now under the leadership of Bill Vander Zalm, actually 'made moral and ethical leadership the centrepiece of their 1986 election campaign'.[34] After winning the election, Vander Zalm announced in early 1987 a set of conflict of interest guidelines for ministers that were designed to enhance, but not replace, the Financial Disclosure Act. Under the guidelines, ministers were admonished to ensure that their ability to perform their public duties was not affected and did not appear to be affected by either financial interests of their own or their immediate family. Ministers could not hold directorships or offices in active corporations. Involvement in any business activities likely to pose a conflict and the use of confidential information for personal gain were forbidden. Ministers were obliged to withdraw from any decision in which they or their immediate family had a present or future (through an offer of employment) financial interest, except for decisions about their own remuneration or those in which their interest was shared in common with members of the public. Finally, after leaving office, ministers were forbidden to change sides on an issue or to represent an outside interest to government for six months where that minister had access to relevant information not available to the public. While the guidelines were— for B.C.—relatively restrictive (e.g., introducing controls over 'revolving-door' activities of ex-ministers), they were widely criticized by the opposition and the media because they were vague, lacked sanctions, and were administered by the premier.

Criticism escalated after a wave of conflict of interest scandals within the Vander Zalm cabinet.[35] The government responded by introducing conflict of interest legislation in the Legislative Assembly in July 1990.[36] Reflecting a hurried response, this bill was borrowed almost word for word from the legislation passed by the Ontario government in 1988. In fact, most of the changes in wording were focused on clauses designed to suppress the rights of the opposition to raise allegations of conflict of interest in the legislative assembly. Under pressure from the opposition and the media, the most significant of these limitations were expunged from the bill in the two days that elapsed between its introduction and passage.

In the end, the legislation represented a significant advance on the guidelines it replaced. Its major positive features included a clear definition of conflict of interest, more specific guidance with respect to behaviours that would and would not qualify as a conflict of interest, and a recognition of the need to exclude both actions on behalf of constituents *and* actions that provide benefit for the MLA as part of a wider public from the notion of conflict of interest. The legislation also established a one-year ban on 'revolving-door' abuses by ex-ministers. Its approach to enforcement focused on public disclosure of assets, liabilities, and business activities by MLAs, and an obligation on MLAs to disclose conflict and withdraw from decision making. The legislation also provided for administration by an independent conflict of interest commissioner and clear penalties for contravention of the act.

The legislation was not without its problematic aspects, however. It defined conflict of interest very narrowly, ignoring appearance of conflict, and limiting the concept of real conflict to situations in which a member actually makes a decision knowing that his or her interests could be served.[37] Members were only obligated to update their financial disclosure annually. Trust arrangements, widely criticized as ineffective in other jurisdictions, were introduced as a means of distancing an MLA from businesses retained while in office. Also, there were some weaknesses in the management of revolving-door abuses: the legislation did not insist on a lifetime ban on changing sides on an issue after leaving office, and it provided no explicit ban on ministers dealing with prospective employers while still in office. Finally, with the premier's guidelines still in place, uncertainty was created for cabinet ministers concerning the relationship between the guidelines and the new legislation.

With the passage and proclamation of the legislation, the appointment of an acting conflict of interest commissioner in December 1990,[38] and then the resignation of the premier in April 1991 on the heels of the acting commissioner's scathing report on the sale of Fantasy Gardens, the ethics agenda became the property of the NDP opposition. The Socreds did table an Access to Information and Protection of Privacy Act (Bill 12) in late June 1991, but in the run-up to the fall election it received little attention.

Exploiting the weakness of the government, the NDP had by 1990 made 'good government' a major plank in its election platform. The leader of the opposition promised to put in place the toughest conflict of interest rules in the country and turn the conflict of interest commissioner into the 'Maytag repairman'. But the real strength of the 'good government' package which emerged from the 1990 party convention was its recognition that ethical government involved more than the management of conflict of interest. The package represented a wide-ranging set of proposals and some draft legislation designed to create a fairer electoral process, enhance the role and performance of the legislature, and establish open, fair, and conflict-free administration.

Once in office, the NDP moved relatively swiftly on parts of the package. The premier did not follow the precedent of the Ontario NDP government and immediately strengthen existing legislation by creating rigorous conflict of interest guidelines for cabinet ministers and parliamentary assistants.[39] Instead, the government took some time to study the issue before introducing and passing amendments to the existing conflict legislation towards the end of the first session. Both moves reflected concern within the cabinet that adopting tougher and more explicit standards might prove problematic. What you gain in public approval of your new rigorous standards, you lose if your ministers and MLAs cannot meet the standards you have created.

The amendments to the Members' Conflict of Interest Act, which were tabled in the legislature and passed in June 1992, do toughen the regime borrowed from Ontario by the Socreds in some significant ways. The definition of conflict of interest has been broadened in two ways. First,

> a member has a conflict of interest when the member exercises an official power or performs an official duty or function in the execution of his or her office and at the same time knows that in the performance of the duty or function or in the exercise of the power there is an opportunity to further his or her private interest.[40]

Stripped of legalese, this means that a member doesn't have to have made a decision to be in conflict; just continuing to attend to job responsibilities when private interests could be affected is enough. Second, the amendments add the notion of apparent conflict of interest as a situation to be avoided. In addition to definition changes, the prohibition on cabinet members holding a directorship or office in any organization other than a social club, religious organizations, political party, or Crown corporation is made absolute rather than dependent on the member's judgement of the likelihood of a conflict emerging.[41] More transparency is introduced by obliging members to record publicly those instances in which they have withdrawn from the performance of their jobs because of a conflict or apparent conflict. Continuous upgrading of disclosure statements is now required instead of annual revision. Citizens, rather than only members, are given the right to complain to the conflict of interest commissioner about a member and get a ruling. Finally, the period during which cabinet members and their parliamentary secretaries are prohibited from making contracts or receiving benefits for themselves or for a party they represent is increased from twelve to twenty-four months after they cease to hold office.

All these amendments toughen the existing conflict of interest regime, but whether they create the promised 'toughest regime in Canada' is arguable. The Ontario guidelines for cabinet ministers and parliamentary assistants, for instance, prohibit the office holder from carrying on any private business, and place more onerous restrictions on the rights of the spouse or minor child of an office holder to be employed by the government or contract with it. The federal code forbids cabinet members and parliamentary secretaries from practising a profession. Quebec prohibits any speculation in land by cabinet ministers. The Nova Scotia regime allows conflict of interest complaints about a member to be made up to two years after the office holder has left office. Such potentially invidious comparisons aside, however, the amended conflict of interest regime is comprehensive, comprehensible, and strict.

The new government has acted with equal alacrity with respect to openness and the protection of privacy. In June 1992 it also enacted freedom of information and privacy legislation covering ministries, Crown corporations, and over 200 boards, commissions, and agencies, promising further legislation to cover municipal governments, school and hospital boards, colleges, universities, and self-regulating professional organizations.[42]

The government described the legislation as the most progressive in the country, and some of its features obviously set it apart from the earlier Socred proposals and similar regimes in other jurisdictions. For example, it has a narrower set of exemptions from the rule of openness in areas such as cabinet confidences, policy and legal advice, and law enforcement. It also creates shorter time limits than many jurisdictions for the whole access process (thirty days) and for keeping exempt information secret (e.g., ten years for policy advice). The act provides for mandatory disclosure of exempted information if it is clearly in the public interest, and addresses privacy issues such as computer matching, mailing lists, and genetic data. Finally, it provides the independent information and privacy commissioner with substantial powers to force agency heads to act, especially with respect to the protection of privacy.

On the other hand, the legislation does have its critics. They note, for example, that information affecting conservation and heritage protection can be kept secret; that exemptions related to information that would cause economic harm to the province, reveal trade secrets, or harm law enforcement are vaguely worded; and that some contemporary privacy issues (e.g., electronic monitoring of the workplace, AIDS confidentiality practices) are not addressed. It has also been argued that under the legislation, repetitious and systemic requests for information that disrupt the operation of government can be denied.[43]

The attorney general, in introducing the legislation, indicated a desire 'to create a "culture of openness" within government'. The accompanying press release talked of strengthening 'existing government safeguards for the privacy of personal information held in government records'.[44] These sentiments are being backed up by a well-funded implementation plan designed to transform the prevailing political and bureaucratic attitudes to information before the legislation is proclaimed in late 1993.[45] In the context of the indifference towards both privacy and openness that B.C. public officials have exhibited in recent years, this transition plan will have to achieve a total cultural change if it is to be effective in altering prevailing information practices.

Rules in an ethical vacuum

For an illustration of how little effect formal rules can have on the existing ethical culture, one need look no further than the sad case of the Standards of Conduct for Public Service Employees.[46] This ethics code, which was put into place in 1987, is one of the most progressive set of standards for public servants in Canada.[47] It begins by setting out some general standards of conduct and then goes on to deal in more detail with conflict of interest, confidentiality, public comment, outside remuneration, working relationships among public servants who are related or share the same household, and workplace behaviour. It sets down sanctions and places the responsibility for managing the code squarely on the deputy minister—all of this in an accessible pamphlet.

Not only does the code cover most of the key issues, but it is provocative from a substantive perspective. For example, it creates a positive obligation for a public servant to blow the whistle if an alleged contravention of the law, waste of public funds, or danger to public health or safety is not appropriately dealt with by superiors up to the deputy minister.[48] The standards for the involvement of public servants in political activity go a long way towards meeting contemporary concerns of civil libertarians and the courts by minimizing restrictions on public comment and partisan involvement. Moreover, the code deals comprehensively with conflict of interest, drawing attention to the corrosive effects of apparent conflict and the fact that conflicts can be created by non-financial personal interests. Its rules on outside remuneration—i.e., moonlighting—and personal relationships in the workplace are designed for modern realities. In the same vein, this code comes to grips in a progressive and refreshing way with sexual and personal harassment.

The problem is that the code has made almost no impact whatsoever on the ethical climate of the public service because most deputy ministers have done nothing to bring it to life in their ministries.[49] As a result, few public servants are familiar with the code, and standards of conduct continue to be communicated by example. In the context of our morality tales, this is hardly a prospect that inspires confidence.

Conclusion

Rules do not create an ethical culture in a large organization unless they are strongly rooted in the beliefs and attitudes of its leaders and employees. That is why the rhetorical flourishes of ministers, the conflict of interest commissioner, and some members of the press corps to the effect that recent legislative initiatives have turned the corner on conflict of interest, openness, and privacy have to be treated with some scepticism.[50] It is true that a government party made up largely of salaried professionals should be able to minimize the gross forms of quasi-crime that were the stock in trade of their small business predecessors. It is equally true that the passage of legislation that reduces the secrecy in which government business can be conducted should make it more difficult for politicians and bureaucrats to operate outside the pale of progressive information control practices. But, at the same time, the levers of patronage are being pulled with enthusiasm, the conventions of political neutrality remain under pressure, and technological advances are eroding the advantages of legally-mandated openness and privacy protection. It is also early innings for the new government. The ethics of governing politicians are only truly tested when they and their supporters grow used to the perquisites of power, the opposition and media turn nasty, and electoral defeat becomes a threat on the horizon.

If the ethical behaviour of politicians does show sustained improvement over time, one is entitled to inquire about the costs. Increasingly, ministers live in fear of ethical controversy and will do almost anything to avoid it—including asking other ministers to do their jobs for them. The tougher rules have distorted the notion of a truly responsible minister and made guardians such as the conflict of interest commissioner into the arbiters of good government. Far from being turned into the 'Maytag repairman', the conflict of interest commissioner has become a figure of almost papal grandeur on the B.C. political scene. His imprimatur is the only sure way to avoid a press scouring where conflict of interest is at issue. The commissioner, like the ombudsman, commands wide public respect, but there is no sign of that respect being transferred to politicians.

The bureaucratic ethical culture seems little affected by changes at the political level and it is far from clear what impact concerted efforts to transform aspects of that culture might have (in the management of information, for instance). This is a large, somewhat dispirited organization schooled by generations of Socred politicians, many of whom mistrusted bureaucrats and reacted viciously if they did not go along with their schemes. B.C.'s 'eager beavers' have lived through many 'reforms' that came to little at the end of the day. It will take more than legislation, codes of conduct, and 'happy talk' to alter the way they do business.

Notes

1 Stan Persky, *Son of Socred* (Vancouver: New Star Books, 1979): 158.
2 A stage of development that would in part be captured by Noel's concept of bureaucratic clientism. See S.J.R. Noel, 'Leadership and Clientism', in D.J. Bellamy *et al.*, eds, *The Provincial Political Systems* (Toronto: University of Toronto Press, 1977): 197-213.
3 See, for example, Jeffrey Simpson, *Spoils of Power: The Politics of Patronage* (Don Mills, Ont.: HarperCollins, 1988), ch. 15.
4 See Ombudsman of British Columbia, *Ombudsman Investigation of an Allegation of Improper Search for Information on Five Individuals on the Part of the Ministry of Human Resources*, Public Report: 2, March 1982.
5 Fuller chronological accounts of the crimes and misdemeanours of recent years can be found in: Graham Leslie, *Breach of Promise: Socred Ethics Under Vander Zalm* (Madeira Park, B.C.: Harbour Publishing, 1991); Allan Garr, *Tough Guy: Bill Bennett and the Taking of British Columbia* (Toronto: Key Porter, 1985); Stan Persky, *Fantasy Government* (Vancouver: New Star Books, 1989); and Stan Persky, *Son of Socred*.
6 Ombudsman of B.C., *Ombudsman Investigation of an Allegation of Improper Search*.
7 Ombudsman of B.C., *Ombudsman Investigation of an Allegation of Improper Search*: 25-6.
8 Ombudsman of B.C., *Abortion Clinic Investigation*, Public Report: 13, August 1988. See also Leslie, *Breach of Promise*: 162-4.
9 Ombudsman of B.C., *The Use of Criminal Record Checks to Screen Individuals Working With Vulnerable People*, Public Report: 5, April 1987.
10 Ombudsman of B.C., *An Investigation into the Licensing of the Knight Street Pub*, Public Report: 12, August 1988.
11 See Leslie, *Breach of Promise*: 80-1.
12 Ombudsman of B.C., *An Investigation into the Licensing*: 21-3.
13 Ombudsman of B.C., *An Investigation into the Licensing*: 25.
14 Leslie, *Breach of Promise*: 99.
15 Stephen Owen, *Discretion to Prosecute Inquiry: Commissioner's Report* (Victoria: Province of British Columbia, 1990) Vol. 1: 94.
16 Stephen Owen, *Discretion to Prosecute*: 95.
17 Stephen Owen, *Discretion to Prosecute*: 96.
18 E.N. Hughes, Q.C., *Report on the Sale of Fantasy Garden World Inc.* (Victoria: Queen's Printer, 1991). This report was done by Hughes at the request of the premier between February and late March 1991.
19 This account is based on the Hughes Report and information that emerged during the trial of the ex-premier for criminal breach of trust during May and June 1992.

20 Reasons for Judgment of the Honourable Chief Justice Campbell in H.M. the Queen vs. William Vander Zalm, Supreme Court of British Columbia, Vancouver, 25 June 1992: 37.

21 Commission of Inquiry into the Facts of Allegations of Conflict of Interest Concerning the Honourable Sinclair Stevens, *Final Report* (Ottawa: Supply and Services Canada, 1987).

22 Commission of Inquiry, *Final Report*: 35; Hughes, *Report on the Sale*: 52.

23 The conflict of interest guidelines and legislation referred to in this paragraph are explored more fully later in the chapter. For a more detailed discussion of definitions of conflict of interest, see John W. Langford, 'Conflict of Interest: What the hell is it?' *Optimum* 22,1 (1991-92): 28-33.

24 See especially Hughes, *Report on the Sale*: 52-61.

25 Commissioner of Conflict of Interest, *Annual Report: 1991-92*: 5-7

26 *Prince Rupert This Week*, 27 Sept. 1992: 1. See also *Victoria Times Colonist*, 18 Sept. 1992: A1.

27 For a discussion of the evolution of the notion of patronage in Canada, see Simpson, *Spoils of Power*.

28 Commissioner of Conflict of Interest, *Annual Report: 1991-92*: 8.

29 See Dennis F. Thompson, *Political Ethics and Public Office* (Cambridge: Harvard University Press, 1987), ch. 5.

30 See Suzanne Garment, *Scandal: The Politics of Mistrust in American Politics* (New York: Random House, 1991).

31 Anthony King, 'Sex, Money, and Power', in R. Hodder-Williams and J. Ceaser, eds, *Politics in Britain and the United States* (Durham, NC: Duke University Press, 1986): 187.

32 The analysis that follows ignores that part of the regime of rules confronted by all public office holders across the country; namely, the Criminal Code provisions relating to fraud, bribery, influence peddling, and breach of trust.

33 The early management of ethics in B.C. is documented more fully in Mark O. Ruttan, *Managing Conflicts of Interest: A Report Submitted in Partial Fulfilment of the Requirements for the Degree of MPA* (University of Victoria, 1989).

34 Leslie, *Breach of Promise*: 320.

35 By the time of the Vander Zalm departure in March 1991, eight cabinet ministers and the premier had resigned after charges of improprieties and mixing their private interests with the performance of their public duties. Again see Leslie, *Breach of Promise*, chs. 3 and 4.

36 Government of British Columbia, *Members' Conflict of Interest Act*, Fourth Session, Thirty-fourth Parliament, 1990.

37 See discussion of this issue in Langford (n.23 above): 28-30.

38 The acting commissioner, Ted Hughes, Q.C., was confirmed as the commissioner in May 1991.

39 See Government of Ontario, *Premier's Guidelines With Respect to Conflict of Interest*, 12 December 1990.

40 Government of British Columbia, *Members' Conflict of Interest Amendment Act, 1992*, First Session, Thirty-fifth Parliament, 1992, s.2.

41 This prohibition has caused headaches because it appears to bar ministers from holding directorships in organizations such as the Western Premiers' Transportation

Council or the Commonwealth Games Society—probably not what the drafters had in mind.

42 Government of British Columbia, *Freedom of Information and Protection of Privacy Act*, First Session, Thirty-fifth Parliament, 1992.

43 For contending views on the legislation, see Ken Rubin, 'Bill 50: "Better than" ain't best', *Victoria Times Colonist*, 2 June 1992: A5; and Murray Rankin, 'Adviser defends B.C. access bill', *Victoria Times Colonist*, 6 June 1992: A5.

44 Province of British Columbia, 'News Release', 22 May 1992.

45 See Information and Privacy Branch, Ministry of Government Services, *Transition Planning for Freedom of Information and Protection of Privacy*, 31 Aug. 1992.

46 Much of the analysis of the Standards of Conduct is drawn from John W. Langford, 'Out of the Code Closet', *Victoria Forum* (Fall 1989): 10-11.

47 Before 1987, the only explicit rules governing the behaviour of public servants were found in the Oath of Office and the Revenue Oath. These rules related to confidentiality, bribery, influence peddling, and the receipt of gifts.

48 The ninth master contract between the government and the B.C. Government Employees Union, negotiated in 1992, contains a clause designed to protect union employees who blow the whistle. No such protection exists at the management level.

49 I am aware of only two ministries that have made anything resembling a concerted effort to build an ethical framework for their employees based on the Standards of Conduct.

50 See, for example, Ted Hughes, 'A Most Honourable Profession', Speech to the Certified General Accountants Association of B.C. (7 April 1992); and Jim Hume, 'Conflict law curbs charges', *Victoria Times Colonist*, 3 June 1992: A5.

3

Tom Pocklington and Sarah Pocklington

Aboriginal political ethics

The inclusion in this book of a chapter on aboriginal political ethics is warranted by the special importance of aboriginal politics. Four main considerations contribute to this importance. First, it has become unmistakably clear to politically attentive Canadians that the overwhelming majority of aboriginal people do not want to be assimilated, culturally or politically, into either the French-speaking or the English-speaking part of what Natives often refer to as 'the mainstream society'. (Of course, this is not to say that Natives favour obstacles to their participation in mainstream society. Aboriginal leaders sometimes say that they want integration, but not assimilation.) Native people want their politics to be distinct. Second, both Natives and non-Natives have become increasingly aware that Canadian policy towards aboriginal people, starting long before Canada became a separate state, has involved persistent efforts to assimilate the Natives against their will and that, for this reason among others, Natives have been victims of deep injustices. Third, there began around 1970 an unprecedented escalation of Native political activity, generated in large part by the two factors we have noted already, and since then aboriginal political organizations have become more vociferous, tougher, and more sophisticated with each passing year. To a considerable extent, the special importance of aboriginal politics stems from the fact that Native political associations have made themselves forces to be reckoned with. Finally, much greater aboriginal political autonomy (commonly called Native self-government) now has a prominent place on the Canadian political agenda. As Cassidy and Bish, among others, have shown, Native political self-determination is evolving, gradually and without any master plan, in various ways in various parts of the country.[1] The governments of all the provinces and territories are now on record as favouring constitutional entrenchment of an 'inherent' right of aboriginal self-government. For all these reasons, aboriginal politics have assumed special importance. Accordingly, a survey of political ethics in a variety of jurisdictions would be seriously incomplete if it ignored Native perspectives, practices, and problems.

The thesis of this chapter is twofold. We maintain, first, that some of the central issues of political morality facing the Native people of Canada have deeper roots than is sometimes supposed. And second, we hold that at this deeper level the political-moral outlooks (and therefore some of the problems) of aboriginal and non-aboriginal Canadians are remarkably similar. However, before we begin to explain and defend these ideas, we need to briefly tackle three preliminary tasks. First we must defend a broad understanding of the concept of political morality (or political ethics; we use the terms 'ethics' and 'morality' synonymously). Our thesis that Native and non-Native political moralities converge at a deep level is quite uninteresting if political morality is understood narrowly as, say, the precepts that specify how public officials should carry out their duties. Second, we will discuss the major similarities and differences among aboriginal peoples. Moral precepts and the outlooks from which they stem can be understood and critically assessed only in reference to the actual circumstances in which they are applied. Moral judgement is a practical activity, and moral and political philosophy are the most practical spheres of philosophy. So we should take pains early in the game to avoid undue abstraction. Our final preliminary task, and our last step in filling in background, is to describe briefly the special legal provisions that apply to aboriginal office holders.

The concept of political morality

We noted earlier that our thesis that aboriginal and non-aboriginal political ethics tend to converge at a deep level presupposes a broad rather than a narrow understanding of 'political ethics'. A narrow understanding of political ethics is narrow in two ways. First, it sees political morality as referring exclusively to the conduct of office holders—politicians and civil servants. Political morality does not have to do at all with the conduct of 'ordinary' citizens. And it is narrow, second, because it understands political morality as confined to questions about public officials fulfilling or abusing their trust. In this view, which is widely (though not universally) accepted by students of public administration, the field of political ethics relates to the ability or inability of public officials to resist temptations to use their offices contrary to the public interest for personal gain, or for the advantage of their friends or allies. Reference to this view as a conception of 'political ethics' is something of a misnomer: a better label might be 'government ethics'.

In the alternative view, political ethics is conceived broadly in two ways. First, with regard to the activities of public officials, their conduct is subject to moral judgement not just because it is, or is not, narrowly self-seeking, but also because it does or does not promote praiseworthy programmes, policies, or practices. And second, this view is broader in that it covers the activities of all citizens, not just those of public officials. For example, public officials who prosecute an unjust war and citizens who support it are subject to condemnation on grounds of political ethics. But in the narrower view, only public officials can be culpable, and then only if they use their positions illegitimately to advance their own interests or those of their cronies.

The question whether political ethics should be construed narrowly or broadly is then really two questions. The first, which puts self-interest against praiseworthy policy, can be answered by looking at outcomes. In the most unlikely event that it were shown that good, just outcomes are most likely when public officials concentrate on feathering their own nests and those of their friends and patrons, surely we would have to commend this kind of self-interest. Above all, we condemn narrow self-interest because we think it tends to promote lousy outcomes. It follows that, in this respect, we should adopt the broad view of political ethics.[2]

The second question is this: Does political morality cover the conduct of all citizens, or only that of public officials? We cannot answer this question decisively, although the common opinion that acts and campaigns of political disobedience (such as civil disobedience, *coup d'état*, and revolution) are subject to moral evaluation suggests that the broad view is the right one here too. However, as far as the subjects of this chapter are concerned, there are strong reasons for adopting the broad view. Joseph Tussman has argued persuasively that in a democracy the citizen occupies something like an office. Like those we commonly refer to as public officials, democratic citizens have authority, rights, responsibilities, and duties, which are quite properly referred to as part of the democratic constitution.[3] Admittedly, it would be a mistake to push this similarity to the point where it blurred differences rather than revealed likenesses. But the similarity is surely sufficient that it would be perverse to claim that the conduct of paid public officials falls within the scope of political ethics while that of democratic citizens does not. This reasoning applies to Natives, who typically profess to be democrats, as much as non-Natives.

The aboriginal people of Canada

The Constitution Act of 1982 identifies the Canadian aboriginal people as 'the Indian, Inuit, and Métis peoples of Canada'.[4] As for enumerating the various aboriginal peoples, obstacles to accurate counting are so formidable that the best we can manage are reasonable estimates.[5] There are now about 525,000 registered Indians in Canada. Registered Indians (or, as they are sometimes called, status Indians) are people who are Indians by law, that is, according to the provisions and interpretation of the Indian Act. In Canada, it is quite possible for a person who regards himself or herself as an Indian, who is regarded by others (themselves uncontestably Indian) as an Indian, and who satisfies any and all 'ethnic' or 'racial' standards of Indianness, to fail to qualify legally as an Indian. For this reason there is a discrepancy between the number of registered Indians and the number of people who identify themselves as Indians. For example, according to the 1986 Census, which relied on self-identification, about 585,000 people regarded themselves as 'North American Indians'. This is about 60,000 more than the estimated number of registered Indians in 1992. This discrepancy is all the more striking because the registered Indian population increased significantly after 1986, not just because of a continuing high rate of fertility, but also because changes to the Indian Act significantly increased the number of people eligible for legal Indian status.

The 1981 Census found just over 25,000 Inuit. The 1986 Census, using different criteria of self-identification, found just over 36,000. The number is in any case quite small. Moreover, inaccuracies in estimating its size are not very consequential politically, since the Inuit constitute an overwhelming majority of the population in the High Arctic where almost all of them live. By far the greatest difficulty in estimating the size of the aboriginal population has to do with the Métis. In the 1981 Census, just over 98,000 people identified themselves as Métis. Perhaps mainly, again, due to different criteria of self-identification, in the 1986 Census the number rose to almost 152,000. But there is general agreement among thoughtful students that this figure is far too low. To mention only one important consideration, it is thought that persons of 'mixed blood' often identify themselves to census-takers by referring to the European rather than the Native side of their ancestry. Accordingly, writing in 1984, Michael Asch estimated the Indian and Métis populations at about 400,000 each, with the total Native population amounting to about 840,000.[6] And in 1986, Donald Purich estimated the status Indian population at 330,000, the Inuit at 25,000, and the Métis and non-status Indians (the latter being ethnically and culturally but not legally Indians) at 750,000, yielding a total aboriginal population of about 1,100,000.[7] If we surmise that Purich's estimate may have erred on the high side in 1986, a conservative estimate is that it is not far out of line now. If so, aboriginal people constitute about 3.5 per cent of Canada's population, and they are the fourth-largest ancestral group in the country, after British, French, and German.

Some similarities and differences among Native people
Judged by standard indicators of well-being, aboriginal people are the least advantaged group in Canada. Consider the following comparisons between status Indians (who are not worse off than other Native people) and the Canadian population as a whole.[8] The average life expectancy of Indians is well under fifty years, compared to nearly seventy for the population as a whole. The Indian infant mortality rate is double that of the entire population. Accidents, violence, and poisoning account for one-third of all Indian deaths, as compared with 9 per cent for the entire population. The Indian suicide rate is about three times the national average. Between 50 and 60 per cent of Indian deaths and illnesses are alcohol-related. The annual per capita income of status Indians is about one-third of the national average. Unemployment on Indian reserves is epidemic—often over 90 per cent. Over half the population of Indian reserves receives social assistance or welfare payments, compared with 6 per cent of the national population. About 80 per cent of working-age Indians have completed grade eight or

less, compared with about 37 per cent nationally; only 5 per cent of Indians, compared with 27 per cent of the population as a whole, have completed some post-secondary education. Native people constitute less than 4 per cent of the Canadian population but about 9 per cent of the inmate population of federal penitentiaries. Figures like these do not present a pretty picture. They are brought to life in the vivid portraits of degradation rendered in such works as Maria Campbell's *Halfbreed* and Anastasia Shkilnyk's *A Poison Stronger than Love: The Destruction of an Ojibwa Community*.

The many enviable qualities of Native people are not amenable to statistical presentation. For example, how could you quantify the practice of reacting to a seemingly hopeless situation with a wisecrack or even a long story about the sly trickster who ends up the victim of his own cleverness? Similarly, it would be next to impossible to document quantitatively the force of the norm of sharing in aboriginal communities. Sometimes elders lament the decline of the sharing ethic as their people adopt the ways of 'the white man'. Nevertheless, to most non-Natives, especially those of European heritage, the extent to which aboriginal people share their good fortune, be it the fruit of a successful hunting trip in the High Arctic or a big win at bingo in Regina, is sure to be surprising. Another remarkable feature of aboriginal collectivities is the relative absence of stratification by age. The view that children should be seen but not heard is foreign to aboriginal peoples. As well, old folks are typically seen as valued members of the community, rather than ripe for isolation in the old age home; 'elders' are honoured as the community's main source of wisdom on spiritual and secular matters. More than anything else, the non-aboriginal observer is likely to be struck by the pervasiveness and power of kinship ties in Native collectivities. We may have difficulty even grasping the notion, 'my sister-in-law's cousin's son'. But if we were Native, we would understand the relationship, we would know the person, and we would believe that we should care for him or her more than our next-door neighbours (if they were not relatives). It is almost impossible to overstate the influence of kinship among aboriginal people (including the political influence, which we will discuss later).

While bearing in mind the characteristics of aboriginal people, it is also important to be aware that they are by no means a homogeneous group. Indians, in particular are the most diverse of the aboriginal groups. We have noted one aspect of this diversity already, namely, that some people who identify themselves as Indians are not legally Indians (that is, they are not registered or status Indians). But there are also significant cultural and linguistic differences among registered Indians. For example, Cree is by far the most common Native language, but it is spoken by fewer than one-third of Canadian Indians. And there are four major dialects of Cree. Turning to culture more broadly, Michael Asch suggests perceptively that it is useful to think of the term 'Indian' as equivalent to the term 'European', and the various groups that comprise its constituent members as analogous, in terms of their inter-group differences, to the various nations of Europe.[9] Some Indian reserves are populous, close to cities, and have many members who are familiar with the ways of non-Natives. The Six Nations Reserve, for example, the most populous in Canada, is near the city of Brantford. Other reserves in remote areas have tiny populations, and hardly interact at all with non-Natives. Most of the Indian bands in Canada are quite small. There are around 600 bands with over 2,000 reserves (most bands have more than one reserve). Some registered Indians are covered by treaties, but others are not; in fact, only about half of Canada is covered by treaties. Some Indian groups covered by treaties do not have reserves (the Lubicon Cree of Alberta, for example), while others (as on Vancouver Island) have reserves but no treaties. Our purpose is to emphasize the crucial point that the Indian population is very diverse.

If the Indians are the most diverse of the aboriginal peoples, the Inuit are the least. But even here it is essential not to equate similarity with homogeneity. Asch suggests that, just as Indians may be regarded as analogous to Europeans, the Inuit may be thought of as analogous to Scandinavians.

The degree of diversity among the Métis depends on how you define them. Sometimes the term is used broadly to refer to all people of mixed Indian and non-Indian ancestry, in which case they are immensely diverse, including a high proportion of Canadians of partial French or British descent whose families have a long history on this continent. More commonly, 'Métis' is used to refer to descendants of the Métis of Red River, who live mostly in the prairie provinces and the Northwest Territories, but also in smaller numbers in northwest Ontario and parts of British Columbia. Even by this narrower definition, there is still plenty of room for disagreement as to the diversity of the Métis population, because there is much disagreement about the point at which intermarriage with non-Natives or adoption of non-Native ways disqualifies a person of 'mixed blood' as genuinely Métis. In any case, the Métis population is quite heterogeneous. Some speak an Indian language fluently, follow ancient religious practices, and gain their livelihood through such traditional practices as hunting, fishing, and gathering. Others are unilingual English-speaking urbanites who are immersed in the market economy. This leads us to our final comment about the diversity of aboriginal people. It has been estimated that over 30 per cent of Indian people live in urban centres.[10] The figure is undoubtedly higher for Métis. In discussions about the political situation or prospects of aboriginal people, it is essential to avoid supposing either that they are overwhelmingly rural or that they all have a collective land base on which they might some day govern themselves in splendid isolation.

Legislating morality

All the issues of political ethics discussed in other chapters of this book are present to some degree in aboriginal associations. For example, allegations of corruption and conflict of interest are at least as common to addicts of politics, in Native as in non-Native collectivities. Most Native people are not governed by special legally enforceable standards of ethical conduct, because most of them do not have special legal status. As for laws governing political ethics, the position of a majority of Natives is the same as that of non-Natives. Special legislation applies only to Indians who live on reserves[11] (who are, by any reckoning, outnumbered by the aggregate of Inuit, Métis, and off-reserve Indians), and this legislation consists of only a few short provisions of the Indian Act. Not surprisingly, then, law does not address the most significant or the most interesting issues of political ethics facing aboriginal groups. However, the legal provisions do warrant some attention here, not only for the sake of establishing continuity with the other chapters, but also because a brief look at the law (not only what it contains but also what it omits) reveals some important peculiarities of Native politics.

One begins to get a feel for the special situation of status Indian politicians from a reading of the relevant provisions of the Indian Act. Section 78 of that act specifies that the office of band chief or councillor becomes vacant when the person who holds that office is convicted of an indictable offence [Subsection (2)(a)(i)]. This is an odd provision for at least two reasons. First, it allows no one, least of all the electorate, any opportunity to discriminate among indictable offences as to their severity or their relevance to the convicted official's ability to fulfil the duties of office. While indictable offences are all serious, it is far from obvious that a councillor who took a club to some boys who were harassing her daughter should be automatically dismissed from office, especially if this were a first offence.[12] It certainly seems that this case should be distinguished from that of the councillor who is convicted of forgery for the third time. And second, this section remains on the books even though a less Draconian Nova Scotia law was declared unconstitutional in 1987 (it limited disqualification to legislators convicted of indictable offences punishable by imprisonment for a maximum of more than five years).[13]

But if that provision is questionable on account of its prohibiting the exercise of discretion, subsequent provisions are disturbing because the discretion they permit is almost unlimited. Subsection (2)(b)(i) provides that the office of band chief or councillor becomes vacant if the minister of Indian Affairs declares that '*in his opinion* [emphasis ours] the person who holds that office is unfit to continue in office by reason of his having been convicted of an offence'. Moreover, if the minister of Indian Affairs disqualifies a chief or councillor on the ground that, *in the minister's opinion*, the official was 'guilty, in connection with an election, of corrupt practice, accepting a bribe, dishonesty or malfeasance', then the minister may take the further step of declaring the disqualified official ineligible to be a candidate again for a period not exceeding six years [Subsection (3)].[14] Even if surpassingly meticulous records were readily available on the use of these extraordinary powers, which they are not, they could not reveal the extent (if any) to which the powers have been used by officers of the Department of Indian Affairs to intimidate or manipulate chiefs and councillors. Who has not committed a legal offence? (Note that the wording does not require that the offence be a criminal one; a parking offence would do.) And how many politicians are *absolutely* beyond reach of someone's *opinion* that they are guilty of some dishonesty 'in connection with' an election? (Note that there is no requirement that the dishonesty be substantial or that the opinion be substantiated.) Presumably, if the minister thinks that the candidate knowingly promised more than he or she could deliver, that could count as sufficient dishonesty in connection with an election for purposes of the Indian Act.

These provisions of the Indian Act (which are the only ones that deal specifically with ethical standards for office holders) illustrate in a particular context a general fact about the lives of status Indians, namely, that they are subject to an extraordinary degree of control by the federal government. It is striking that the most severe provision—the one stating conditions for automatic dismissal from office—is the *least* disturbing. The far more questionable provisions are those that permit the minister of Indian Affairs (which of course means agents of the minister) to decide, within indefinitely elastic boundaries, whether and when an office holder has sinned grievously enough to warrant removal from office. Quite apart from general concerns about paternalism that are raised by these provisions, the provisions are disturbing because of the extent to which they permit arbitrary (hence illiberal) and irresponsible (hence undemocratic) conduct on the part of officials of a senior government in relation to a junior one. A provincial bill that allowed a minister of municipal affairs such arbitrary control over city officials would undoubtedly (and rightly) provoke outrage.

From legality to morality

It is striking that the Indian Act contains no mention of the phrase 'conflict of interest', given that conflict of interest is often regarded nowadays as *the* moral vice of Canadian public officials. Perhaps the reason for this omission is that the Indian Act has traditionally both reflected and helped enforce an understanding of Indians as wards of the state. Moreover, even though genuinely Indian government has become increasingly a fact of life on the reserves in the past couple of decades,[15] few Indian governments have developed formal, written codes of conduct relating to conflict of interest. This is not to say that conflict of interest is not an important matter of political ethics for Native people, who condemn as righteously as anyone else those on government payrolls who use their positions for personal benefit contrary to justice or the common good. However, for a variety of reasons 'conflict of interest' has limited utility for exploring matters of political ethics. For one thing, the term 'interest' is one of the loosest in the vocabulary of political science. Consider the confusion that can arise because there are two very different senses in which a person can be said to have an interest in something (Bell Telephone, for example). In one sense, I have an interest in Bell in case the practices, personnel, or policies of the company attract my attention. But in the other sense I have an interest in the company only if I have some kind of material stake in it—as an employee, for example, or a shareholder. For another thing, the very notion of a conflict of interest is ethically loaded. Commonly, we do not say that Smith is in a situation of conflict of interest and then go on to ask whether that is a good thing (although we might find some conflicts of interest worse than others). Conflicts of interest are generally understood, by Natives as much as by non-Natives, to be states of affairs that politicians and civil servants should avoid. Consequently, the ethical question about conflict of interest becomes a definitional one: Which alleged situations of conflict of interest really warrant that label? Transforming moral questions into definitional questions is a bad idea because it eliminates the central question of *why* conduct is right or wrong. Finally, as John W. Langford has pointed out, in recent years in Canada the very concept of 'conflict of interest' has fallen victim to a sort of conceptual imperialism, such that it is difficult to discern either its outer boundaries or its purpose.[16] Of course, raising doubts about the utility of the notion of conflict of interest is not to deny that moral conflicts are important politically. We maintain that aboriginal politicians frequently face dilemmas far more serious than conflicts of *interest*, namely, conflicts of *obligation*. Furthermore, conflicts of obligation often give rise to genuine moral dilemmas, and these are very interesting indeed. As we shall see, exploration of these dilemmas reveals that they have roots in two competing conceptions of a healthy socio-political order. Moreover, this exploration leads us to a deeper understanding of one important source of controversy concerning political ethics in non-aboriginal Canada.

Moral dilemmas

The toughest moral problems are genuine moral dilemmas, that is, situations in which an agent is confronted with a choice between two lines of action, both of which are profoundly unwelcome. No matter which line of action the agent pursues he will feel deep regret, and, typically, he will be blamed for wrongdoing by people whose respect he values. The term 'moral dilemma' is often used loosely to cover a wide range of moral conflicts. Our claim that 'genuine' moral dilemmas are the toughest moral problems rests on, and only makes sense in connection with, a narrow and semi-technical sense of the term 'dilemma'.

What, then, do we regard as moral dilemmas? We take them to be moral conflicts that have three characteristics. First, the alternatives from which the agent must choose are moral rules or principles. There is no moral dilemma when one of the alternatives is moral and the other is not, or when one of the alternatives is a principle ('Never inflict needless pain') and the other is some other kind of moral consideration ('Courage is the most important moral virtue'). Second, it is not obvious which of the alternatives is weightier, as when the choice is between keeping an appointment to meet someone for coffee and saving a life. And third, the agent would feel regret no matter which of the alternatives he or she chooses. Moral dilemmas involve tough choices, and the moral agent would feel some remorse for rejecting one of the alternatives, even if he or she believes the choice of the other alternative was right.[17] Are there genuine moral dilemmas in political life? Of course there are. Consider, for example, the sizeable number of Progressive Conservative candidates who were elected to Parliament in 1984, having committed themselves to abide by the wishes of the majority of their constituents, knowing the majority favoured the return of the death penalty, but who subsequently came to believe that capital punishment is a violation of the right to life. The example is manifestly political, and it exhibits all three elements of a moral dilemma. First, there is a conflict between moral principles: 'Always keep commitments' and 'Do not violate the right to life'. Second, neither of the principles is obviously weightier than the other. (The temptation to suppose that the right to life is certainly weightier should be relieved by reflection on such examples as the abortion controversy, the right of self-defence, and the idea of a just war.) And finally, a conscientious MP would feel some remorse no matter how he or she decided. Even if it is on balance justified, the breaking of a solemn commitment or the violation of the right to life is an occasion for moral regret.

Native office holders, elected or appointed, face moral dilemmas incessantly. Most aboriginal people are members of extended families which are commonly (and, it is believed, ideally) closely knit. A person is deemed to owe to kin not only special affection but also partiality. That is, given scarce goods to distribute, he or she is expected to think first of relatives. Moreover, he or she experiences this expectation not merely as a cultural norm imposed by others (what may be called the perspective of the anthropologist) but as an obligation (the perspective of the participant). For example, if he is an Indian band councillor, and if the band has in its possession two new houses this year, and if one of the several eligible applicants is his sister-in-law's son, the course of duty is clear: nepotism is obligatory. But he has a competing duty, that is, to distribute benefits without prejudice according to objective standards of need or merit. A house cannot be allocated to the sister-in-law's son, unless he happens to be entitled to it because of greater need than other applicants: nepotism is impermissible. So a Native office holder confronts a moral dilemma whenever his duty to allocate benefits to relatives conflicts with his duty to allocate benefits according to an objective standard of entitlement.

There are two attractive ways of misunderstanding this sort of dilemma, and it is important to avoid them. One sort of misunderstanding sees only the kinship duty as authentic (because indigenous and traditional), and that the 'dispassionate' duty is illegitimate (because imposed by Europeans). We doubt that Natives require the help of Europeans to rise above the narrowest kind of parochialism. Most aboriginal people accept a morality in which there is a duty of partiality to kinfolk and a duty of adherence to objective standards. No amount of explaining how this morality came into being, or lamenting its arrival, can establish that one kind of duty is more legitimate or binding than the other. Questions about the soundness or otherwise of moral standards are moral, not anthropological, questions.

The other way of misunderstanding the conflict of duties is to regard the parochial obligations as occupying an earlier, and lower, stage in the evolution of human morality than the objective ones. In this view, familial moral considerations are vestiges of the tribal past, superseded by the impersonality of 'higher moralities' which require that everyone be treated as an end or as an equal candidate for satisfaction of desire. This view misrepresents both aboriginal and non-aboriginal moralities. In regard to favouritism, it ignores the fact that nepotism is widespread in non-Native society. The characteristic of nepotism in Native collectivities is that it is for the most part openly political, that is, it is a matter of office holders favouring kinfolk. In non-Native society nepotism occurs mainly in what we call, revealingly, the *private* sector. If the managers of capitalist enterprises bestow favours on their relatives, well, that may be a bit unsavoury, but it is their own business, not a matter of political ethics. So it is not that Natives practise nepotism while non-Natives don't. Natives usually practise nepotism in the political sphere, and it is usually seen as morally problematic. When non-Natives do it, it is usually in the 'private sector', and it is usually seen as a matter of personal preference rather than morality. It takes little reflection to see the parochial influence in non-Native morality as well. For example, we conveniently ignore the moral implications of the fact that we think it *right* that the mayor of Edmonton should put the interests of Edmontonians ahead of the interests of Haligonians, that Quebec politicians are not deeply concerned that Newfoundlanders should become *maîtres chez eux*, and that the minister of external affairs does not pledge to treat Kenyans and Austrians as generously as Canadians.

When we understand the dilemmas faced by the aboriginal office holder, we see them unromantically (that is, we do not see aboriginal moral agents as pale shadows of their fully communal ancestors) and without condescension (we do not see them as struggling upwards from a parochial morality to a morality of principles). Does this mean that we see no difference in this regard between the aboriginal and the non-aboriginal office holder? In regard to what we may call the 'basic structure' of political morality there is, we believe, little difference. Aboriginal and non-aboriginal political moralities alike contain both parochial and universal elements. However, in what we may call the 'experiential structure' of political morality there is a striking difference. Native office holders (and their constituents) experience the parochial aspect of morality as precepts that command their attention and compete with universal precepts. For non-aboriginals, in contrast, the parochial principles are unspoken, if not unconscious, so that non-aboriginal office holders can suppose they act only on universal principles. Thus, it is not surprising that aboriginal office holders face genuine moral dilemmas regularly, non-aboriginals only occasionally.

We suggest that this feature of Native political ethics has deep roots, which tap into two competing conceptions of political association. The familial/parochial precepts that generate nepotism, we submit, are nourished by a conception of polity that is evoked by terms like 'solidarity', 'civic friendship', and 'community'.[18] The universalistic precepts, in contrast, stem from a political ideal that stresses personal autonomy. The one conception is 'collectivist', the other 'individualist'. These conceptions, and the relationships between them, will be examined more fully as we see how they shape other major issues of political ethics in aboriginal collectivities.

Individual and collective rights

The central cluster of issues of the 1990s for aboriginal people in Canada is aboriginal self-government. Interestingly (and, as we shall argue, deceptively), issues concerning self-government have been expressed in the language of rights. One of the most controversial of these issues pits individual rights against collective rights. Most politically attentive Canadians became aware of this as an issue when Ovide Mercredi, Grand Chief of the Assembly of First Nations (the national organization of registered Indians), objected to the proposal of the government of Canada that a constitutionally entrenched right to aboriginal self-government should be subject to the Canadian Charter of Rights and Freedoms. His objection was based partly on the principle that an 'inherent' right to aboriginal self-government could not be qualified by the constitutional provisions of another (and not superior) jurisdiction. But it was also based on the proposition that the Charter conflicts with aboriginal belief in the priority of collective over individual rights. As the Constitutional Secretariat of the Assembly of First Nations put it: 'Subjecting the right to the Charter clearly goes against one of the primary tenets of aboriginal culture: collective rights are more important than individual rights.'[19] This way of putting the matter ostensibly raises a question of political ethics: With what justification do the members of one polity impose their standards and practices on the members of another? Needless to say, this matter is a particularly sensitive one among aboriginal peoples, simply because their political history in the years since contact has been a history of forced subjection to alien standards and practices. The issue became less clear (and more interesting) when the Native Women's Association of Canada vociferously expressed its view that Native governments should be subject to the Charter, because male-dominated Native governments could not be trusted to provide equal protection for women.[20] Subsequently, it was widely reported that numerous residents of Indian reserves feared that the introduction of self-government without Charter protections might expand the opportunity of reserve political élites to oppress 'ordinary' residents.[21] Moreover, it will be surprising if urban Indians, non-status Indians, and Métis who live among non-Natives are eager to waive Charter protections.

But is it true that an issue of political ethics arises out of a conflict between (aboriginal) collective rights and (non-aboriginal) individual rights? As a preliminary point, we suppose for the sake of argument that there is no problem with the notion of a collective right to self-government. There seems to be no conceptual barrier in the way of assigning rights to collectivities.[22] And the right to self-government seems to be a particularly strong candidate for the status of a collective right. It has yet to be established, however, and it seems wrong to maintain that recognition of a collective right to self-government is incompatible with protection of the sorts of individual rights named in the Charter. Indeed, respect for many of those rights (albeit not necessarily by way of a charter) is surely essential to the functioning of a government that is both democratic and liberal. And if any Native leaders foresee the establishment of aboriginal regimes that are undemocratic or illiberal, they have not said so. Does this mean that Native leaders who affirm the priority of collective over individual rights are apologists for the aboriginal élites that are sure to be, at least in the short run, the main beneficiaries of self-government?

We think not. Aboriginal people who condemn the Charter in the name of collective rights and those who applaud it in the name of individual rights implicitly invoke competing conceptions of an admirable political regime. Moreover, these conceptions are the same ones that we found behind the opposition between parochial and universal duties. Regimes that emphasize the protection of individual rights uphold a vision of the good society as one that protects and fosters personal autonomy. A regime that protects basic individual rights effectively enables one 'to decide the terms of one's own life for oneself'.[23] Effective individual rights protect one against the incursions of both vicious oppressors and unduly solicitous paternalists. On the other hand, loving care for individual rights has a way of turning into an obsession. Then rights function less to promote self-fulfilment than to encourage the excessive fractiousness, egoism, litigiousness, and disregard of the common good that many see as characteristic of American life and as increasingly prevalent in Canada. We suggest that a major concern of Natives who insist on the priority of collective over individual rights is to condemn these excesses. Such condemnation frequently invokes a competing conception of a good society, a conception that has a claim to be sanctified by the traditions of aboriginal communities. For one thing, many Native communities traditionally made their public decisions by 'consensus', rather than by more adversarial procedures like bargaining or majority rule. As well, there is a powerful and continuing Native tradition of sharing, the extent of which is only hinted at by dramatic manifestations like the west coast potlatch and the prairie giveaway. This perspective is not aptly expressed by the term 'collective rights', which evokes precisely the adversarial sort of relationship that is found wanting.[24] It is better, as before, to characterize the perspective, loosely, with labels like 'communitarian' and 'collectivist'. The central question now is: Can the two perspectives be reconciled? It is obvious (as the example of Native women attests) that it is important to respect individual rights, and obvious also (as exemplified by the extravagant emphasis on rights and the distressing inattention to family policy in the abortion controversy in the United States and Canada[25]) that there can be an unhealthy infatuation with rights. As the abortion example shows, the reconciliation of the two perspectives is not important only for Native people. Indeed, the conflict between these two perspectives (designated in the literature as 'liberalism' and 'communitarianism') has been one of the major concerns of English-language political philosophy during the last decade.[26]

Membership and political morality

A major issue of political ethics for aboriginal political collectives (in practice, primarily aboriginal political leaders) has to do with the criteria for membership in such collectives. Until recently, the most striking expression of the moral problems connected to the membership issue was a provision of the Indian Act that specified that an Indian woman who married a non-Indian man immediately lost her Indian status (as did any of her children fathered by a non-Indian). This loss of Indian status was not a loss merely of the relatively few legal advantages that attach to being legally an Indian, such as immunity to taxation on income earned on a reserve. A woman who 'married out' could also be prohibited from visiting the reserve on which she was born, even to attend her sister's wedding or her father's funeral. We do not mean to suggest that many, let alone most, band councils acted so heartlessly, but we do personally know women who were forbidden to enter their old reserves for precisely the purposes we mentioned. We also know women who were assured that permission would not be given for them to be buried in the reserve graveyard alongside their kinfolk.[27]

In 1985, in a piece of enlightened social legislation rare for it, the Mulroney government eliminated the blatant sexual discrimination in the Indian Act. Bill C-31, still the popular name of the anti-discrimination provisions even though they are now embedded in law, received royal assent in 1985. This legislation permitted disenfranchised women and their children to reacquire Indian status. The victory was not won easily. Several Indian leaders, predominantly male, especially on the prairies, went so far as to threaten violence if the bill became law. One leader even hinted ominously about another Wounded Knee.[28] The current situation regarding membership is that the federal government—in effect, Indian Affairs—decides who is a registered Indian. Since all Indians are legally entitled to certain special health and education benefits, Indian status is no trivial advantage. However, the 1985 legislation gave bands some control over their own membership; bands can establish their own rules for membership by majority vote. The practical upshot of this provision is that bands can establish membership criteria that are very welcoming towards 'C-31 Indians', or they can set criteria that virtually exclude them. There is no legal requirement that Indian bands make public either their membership criteria or the number of 'C-31s' who have satisfied the criteria. However, according to our usually reliable sources, most bands have not erred on the side of generosity.

Nevertheless, it would be a mistake to jump to the conclusion that on this matter Indian leaders deserve strong moral condemnation. For one thing, many reserves are already overcrowded. (This is part of the explanation for the continuing migration of Indians from reserves to the cities.) As well, the number of reinstated Indians wishing to return to the reserves has far exceeded estimates made when the elimination of statutory sexual discrimination was contemplated, and this has exacerbated the problem of overcrowding. In addition, some bands in

Alberta are oil-rich and regularly award their members sizeable royalty cheques. Many members of these bands fear an influx of residents whose interest in returning to the reserve is exclusively economic. For yet another, the federal government has been unwilling to increase payments to the reserves sufficiently to enable bands to accommodate immigration without reducing services. Finally, many Indians maintain that the authority of Native collectivities to determine their own membership is an important part of the movement towards Native self-government. Part of the resistance to welcoming reinstated Indians into the bands simply expresses defiance of federal government paternalism.

The issue of membership has been at least as divisive on the only Métis land base in Canada, the eight Métis settlements of northern Alberta. Two related matters in particular have generated moral dispute. These disputes can be understood in the light of four background considerations:

• the area of the Métis settlements is huge (about 1.25 million acres, which is almost as much land as all the Indian reserves in Alberta combined);
• the settlements were set aside for the use of *all* the Métis of Alberta (who number, by conservative estimates, over 100,000 people);
• there is a waiting list of applicants for membership in the settlements;
• there is ample room on each settlement for much more housing.

In spite of these facts, the total population of the eight settlements is under 5,000, and it is kept so low by the controversial policies of several of the settlement councils. The first, and less inflammatory, of these policies prohibits the allocation of land far from all-weather roads. Most residents of the settlements seem to believe that this policy is justified on the ground that, whatever they might promise in advance, sooner rather than later settlers located far from roads would complain bitterly (with some justification) about the inequitable hardships they faced. A sizeable minority rejects this opinion, holding that it is wrong to withhold land from Métis who want it. There are, we believe, two reasons why the prevailing policy is not seen as a major matter of political ethics. The first is that the matter of occupancy of land insofar as it concerns only judgements about convenience is seen as properly falling within the jurisdiction of the elected settlement councils, even by those who dislike the current policy. The second is that those who oppose the current policy see it as misguided, or at worst ungenerous, but not *unjust*. In particular, they do not see it as discriminating for or against leading extended families. For our own part, we find this line of argument far from compelling. Métis settlement politicians have shown extraordinary political ingenuity during the past decade. It is hard to believe that they could not devise procedures that would defuse complaints from settlers who had to wait for certain amenities.

The second matter relating to membership that has provoked moral conflict in Alberta Métis settlements is the policy of freezing membership levels in order to leave large tracts of settlement land in a more or less natural state. A majority of residents supports this policy on the ground that a Métis way of life requires extensive areas of uncultivated land for hunting, fishing, gathering, and simply communing with nature. But a vociferous minority regards the policy as ungenerous and unjust. It is ungenerous, they believe, because it denies opportunities to members of one of the most disadvantaged groups in the country. And it is unjust because it discriminates in favour of the dwindling number of Métis who choose to live in the traditional way.

Behind the particular disputes among Native people about membership lies a very general question of political ethics: Do they have the unconstrained moral right to determine the basis of membership in their collectivities? One's immediate response to this question is likely to be, of course they have this right. If they don't, who does? And if the right is not unconstrained, who is entitled to constrain it? However, further reflection brings to light two considerations that cast doubt on this easy answer. The less important, though certainly not inconsequential, consideration is that the Native people of Canada are Canadian citizens. Moreover, the Constitution Act states explicitly that the federal government is responsible for Indians and land reserved for the Indians. It is highly doubtful, therefore, either as a matter of law or as a matter of morality, that the government of Canada would be justified in allowing any people who are eligible for Indian status under Canadian law to be denied the benefits of that status, regardless of the breadth or depth of support for such a policy among Indians. A similar line of argument would show that neither the federal nor the provincial governments are entitled to allow Inuit or Métis people to disadvantage any of their number through the use of discriminatory membership provisions.[29]

Perhaps the problem sketched above could be resolved by political stratagems, such as providing compensation to Native victims of membership discrimination. But there is a second consideration that casts doubt on the proposition that Native collectivities have an unconstrained moral right to determine their own membership. Most existing and contemplated standards for membership in Native collectivities are racist. Since the enactment of Bill C-31, for example, for a person to be considered for membership in an Indian band it is now essential that he or she be deemed 'genuinely' Indian. Since there is a compelling moral case against racism (widely recognized, for obvious reasons, by Native people), there is similarly a case against most existing and proposed criteria for membership in Native groups, and thereby against the proposition that aboriginal groups have an unconstrained right to determine their own memberships. The solution to this problem is not difficult. All that is required is that the candidate for membership in a Native collectivity identify, and be recognized by existing members as identifying, with the history and culture of that collectivity.[30] Such a rule is not racist, and at the same time it does not invite an avalanche of applications for membership in aboriginal groups.

However, there are those who would find even a rule of this sort objectionable from the standpoint of political ethics, as incompatible with fundamental principles of liberal democracy. Limiting membership in a political group to those who not only share certain beliefs and attitudes and accept certain norms but also are certified by others as meeting standards of conformity seems to be profoundly at odds with the pluralism and egalitarianism central to liberal democracy. But we want to suggest once again that the issue here is not unique to Native people, and that it relates to the tension between individualism and collectivism that we have already encountered.

The most obvious non-aboriginal counterpart to aboriginal debates about criteria for membership is the debate about immigration policy. However, debates about immigration policy are not usually confrontations between two irreconcilably opposed views, the one individualist and the other collectivist. With regard to immigration, most of us are both individualists and collectivists. The debate therefore concerns the relative weight that should be assigned to each. Almost all of us are collectivists in that we think that both the size and the composition of groups of immigrants should be related to the well-being (especially the economic well-being) of those who are already Canadian citizens, and also in that we think that immigrants should be capable of being assimilated into Canadian society. But many of us are also individualists with regard to immigration policy. For example, we oppose the idea that 'assimilability' should be used as an excuse for racial discrimination. As well, we think that humanitarian considerations, such as the provision of a haven for political refugees, should play a part in our immigration policy. Some of us emphasize collectivist considerations (especially by stressing the importance of assimilability); others place greater emphasis on individualistic considerations (by exhibiting more willingness to welcome refugees). The point is that the parameters of the debate are both individualist *and* collectivist.

Concerns about conditions of membership are also evident in the education policies of all the provinces and territories. In this realm, too, there is both a tension and mutual reinforcement between individualist and collectivist tendencies. Official school curricula in all jurisdictions attempt to reduce the likelihood that students may develop illiberal and anti-democratic attitudes and convictions. As a matter of policy, a significant part of public education is supposed to inculcate in students 'good citizenship', which means, primarily, adherence to liberal and democratic norms. No doubt there is a certain tension here, in that some parents and educators favour greater emphasis on the liberal (individualist) norms and others on the democratic (collectivist) ones. But neither side favours one to the exclusion of the other. Under different circumstances, it would be essential to elaborate and defend at length these comments about immigration and education policy. For present purposes, however, enough has been said to support the two main points about aboriginal and non-aboriginal political ethics we set out to establish in this section: first, that attention to the issue of membership does not reveal major differences between the two groups; and second, that the terms of this issue, like the others discussed in this chapter, can be traced to competing conceptions of the good life, which are appropriately described as individualistic and collectivistic.

The ethics of consensus and representation

A final issue of aboriginal political ethics is the relationship between political leaders and their constituents. As we noted earlier, many Native communities traditionally made at least some of their public decisions by consensus rather than by more adversarial procedures like bargaining or majority rule. The term 'consensus' is notoriously vague. At the extreme, a consensual decision rule would specify (1) that all members of the community must be consulted, (2) in regard to all matters of community concern, and (3) that all decisions must be unanimous (that is, each member has a veto). But it is appropriate to label 'highly consensual' political communities that approximate this rule. For example, the rule that all members must be consulted on recognizably important matters, with a requirement of near-unanimity, would obviously count as highly consensual. The same could be said of all rules that were very demanding in regard to the three relevant variables: the proportion of community members who must be consulted, the range of issues on which they must be consulted, and the nearness to unanimity required for decision. This, at any rate, is our concern: political communities with highly consensual decision rules.

There are many Native collectivities in Canada in which conventional political morality specifies a highly consensual decision rule. The moral conception underlying this rule is that there is a common good, so that the proper task is to find an agreeable way of pursuing it. This contrasts with the basis of adversary rules, like majoritarianism, which concentrate on the protection of interests. Attachment to consensus as a decision rule is characteristic of the Dene people of the Northwest Territories. According to Dene elders, before contact with Europeans the Dene, who lived in small hunter-gatherer bands, operated under a quite strict form of consensus. All band members had the opportunity to speak their minds. The job of the chief, who was usually an elder, was to help band members reach agreement through discussion. And there was great reluctance to override any member's opinion. The emphasis on consensus, it was understood, did not preclude inequalities of influence on decisions. For example, when the issue of where to hunt was raised, usually the advice of the most skilled hunter was accepted. However, neither the chief nor the skilled hunter was deemed to have the authority to impose decisions.[31]

Today, the Dene continue to follow the traditional rituals of consensus at their national assemblies, which occur once or twice a year. The twenty-five community chiefs, as well as a number of delegates (mainly band council members), are given the opportunity to speak on all matters. Motions are presented only if it is evident that there is strong support for a particular proposal. As a result, even though the assemblies formally operate under simple majority rule, the actual practice ensures that proposals succeed only if they have very wide support. Moreover, if this support is not forthcoming, the issue is often left until the next assembly. This allows the chiefs time to discuss the issue with their communities, so the requirement of a significant degree of consensus is extended to the community level. Discussion at the community level is usually accomplished in an informal manner, because formal community meetings tend to have a low turnout. The chiefs and councillors try to talk to as many people as possible. Several chiefs run local businesses, such as a gas station or video rental store, which enables them to chat with a considerable range of people in a casual environment. And many residents make it a practice to drop by the band council office occasionally for an exchange of views. The Dene are visibly attempting to adhere to a consensual style of decision making, and it is clear that they succeed to some degree. The same is true, though typically to a lesser degree, of many Native collectivities south of the sixtieth parallel.

But there are circumstances in which it is very difficult for a political leader to remain faithful to the practice of consensus. If the leader believes in the consensus rule, but also believes that the time has come to break it, he or she faces a problem of political ethics. This situation was faced more than once by James Wah-Shee, the first elected president of the Indian Brotherhood of the Northwest Territories (later the Dene Nation). Wah-Shee was strongly committed to upholding traditional Dene ways of reaching decisions by consensus. However, he encountered a number of obstacles to acting on his convictions. These included the structure of the Brotherhood's constitution, which endorsed hierarchical principles antithetical to Dene political custom; severe obstacles to effective communication between Dene communities and the head office (education, language, distance, and expense) which left the Dene ill-equipped to make sound decisions due to an insufficient understanding of issues; widespread lack of understanding of the Canadian political system as a result of limited encounters with it; and the length of time it often took to reach consensus on an issue.

Although he tried to conform to traditional leadership customs and to educate people about the various issues, Wah-Shee increasingly assumed a highly directive role within the Brotherhood. He presented himself (not without justification) as an expert on issues about which other people had little knowledge, and thereby induced the Dene to endorse his ideas even though a majority of them were confused and hesitant to make a decision. He usually chaired the general assemblies, and careful reading of the proceedings suggest that he played a prominent role in steering the discussions and decisions in directions he thought wise.[32]

Difficulties in reconciling the demands of consensus with those of representation eventually led to the ouster of Wah-Shee as president of the Brotherhood. In the early years of his presidency, there was consensus among Dene leaders (including Wah-Shee) that the territorial government of the NWT should be boycotted because it was not a Dene government. Over time, however, Wah-Shee began to recognize that the territorial government was gaining more control over the daily lives of Dene people as a result of the federal government's initiative to devolve powers to territorial agencies. He also came to believe that an effective strategy for gaining power was to encourage Dene people to sit on the territorial council. Among other things, this would allow a Native bloc to ensure that their common interests were not overlooked. Wah-Shee gained a seat on the territorial council himself and urged other Dene to do so. However, some fellow members of the executive of the Indian Brotherhood, as well as a number of community chiefs, felt that his violation of the consensus against participating in the territorial government was seriously wrong. The ensuing debate among Dene leaders, inside and outside the Assembly, which involved both politicians and elders, revealed some deep disagreements about the ethical standing of the consensus rule and the ethics of leadership. Ranked on one side were those who were adamant in their conviction that consensus was the right way, not just because it was the Dene way, but because it was the only way to recognize the equality of the people. On the other side were those who believed that it is sometimes right for leaders, who (should) possess special knowledge and insight into the exigencies of external relations, to act on their own judgement. Similar debates about the scope and limits of consensus are common in other Native collectivities.

Belief in consensus as a decision rule obviously rests on a vision of a good political system. The central feature of this vision is that there is a common good, not just a range of competing individual or group interests. When the objective is to resolve conflict among competing interests an adversary rule, such as majority rule, is most appropriate. A consensual rule presupposes that people agree on the ends of the association, for otherwise the requirement of consensus would result in endless deadlock. Also presupposed by a consensual rule is the belief that the people are willing and able to agree on effective and morally defensible means to the agreed ends. If the people did not possess these qualities, consensus would result in adoption of policies that were impractical, or immoral, or both. It is evident that the Dene, as well as many other aboriginal groups in Canada, do believe that they have a common good and that the people usually can be relied on to find it. This political vision, and the beliefs that accompany it, are profoundly collectivistic. However, as we have seen, collectivism does not reign unchallenged. Although there is virtual unanimity within Native communities on the existence, if not the content, of a common good (differences of opinion about the virtues of 'our culture' are not generally welcomed), many Native politicians and elders maintain (and others deny) that there are circumstances in which it is morally permissible, or even obligatory, for leaders to exercise their own judgement about what will promote the common good in the long term.

Throughout this chapter we have drawn attention to the similarities in political ethics prominent in Native and non-Native communities. But we must be careful not to push a good thesis too far. In the Canadian political system, majority rule (or, more realistically, 'minorities rule') is the norm. Political leaders are expected to exercise their best judgement. Now and then (as recently under the banner of the Reform Party) there are calls for representatives to engage in more frequent and more widespread popular consultation, and even for governments to hold occasional referendums. But this is a long way from support for decision making by consensus. A consensual decision rule lacks support because the political vision that sustains it lacks support. For the most part, Canadians believe that politics is about competing interests, not common goods. And they do not believe that they or their fellow citizens are willing or able choose effective and morally defensible means to such ends as are agreed upon: that is a job for experts. But although support for consensus, and for the underlying vision that supports it, are rare in 'mainstream' Canadian politics, they are not absent altogether. In fact they are alive and well in some religious associations (for example, the Quakers), academic departments (my own during the past decade for example), self-help groups (such as Alcoholics Anonymous), and small communities.[33] Moreover, it may not be too much to hope that, just as Native groups have come to see that when there are serious collisions of interest, adversary decision making is more appropriate than consensual, the rest of us may come to see that we are better served by consensus than by majoritarianism when our interests coincide. It is far from obvious that such matters as homelessness, violence against women, the growth of adolescent gangs in the inner cities, sexual abuse of children, and poverty among the elderly should be understood as involving conflicting interests, to be addressed by the usual assumptions and techniques of adversary, representative democracy.

Conclusion

The main thesis of this chapter is stated in two propositions. The first is that, beneath the surface, there is less difference between the political ethics of aboriginal and non-aboriginal people in Canada than is often supposed. The second is that the underlying similarity of the two outlooks centres around the incorporation of, and tension between, individualist and collectivist conceptions of a good political order. If this thesis is correct, it is unlikely that there will be any major change in the basic terms of aboriginal political ethics in Canada in the foreseeable future. Changes are likely to be relatively small, incremental movements, sometimes towards the individualist side, sometimes towards the collectivist.

But to say that changes are likely to be small and incremental is not to say that they will be trivial. If, as seems almost certain, the principal thrust of aboriginal politics in Canada in the next several years continues to be a movement towards Native self-government, regardless of the recent defeat of the Charlottetown Accord, one might expect that most change is likely to run in a collectivistic, if not tribalistic, direction. Within limits, that expectation is reasonable. Under the rubric of collective rights, Native collectivities—especially those with a land base —are likely to implement policies and programs that are intended to promote the common good rather than individual autonomy. For example, some communities will probably initiate far-reaching preventive health care schemes, including in some cases local prohibition of alcohol. And some communities may attempt to kick-start economic development by relying on extended families for the recruitment and discipline of workers. As well, there is sure to be much more use of collectivist decision-making procedures. In particular, many communities are sure to revitalize or invent techniques to involve some sort of 'consensus'.

However, it would be a serious mistake to underestimate the strength of individualist moral conceptions in Native groups. A significant element of moral individualism in most Native cultures predated the arrival of Europeans. After all, Native communities were never ant hills. Moral individualism has been promoted by incessant efforts to assimilate aboriginal people into mainstream culture. And it has been fortified above all by the sheer numerical dominance of non-Natives, not just in education, communication, and propaganda, but also in powerful local socializing agencies like minor hockey associations and union halls. Moreover, there are overtly political forces affecting Native people that militate in favour of individualist political ethics. As aboriginal communities become increasingly self-governing, inevitably they will adopt not only the functions but also the structure and ethos of the bureaucracies they replace. And, as is well known, bureaucracies are far more hospitable to the dispassionate treatment of individuals according to universalist rules than to the recognition of favoured families and respect for collective rights. Furthermore, under regimes of increased Native political self-determination there are sure to be vociferous demands that Native politicians and bureaucrats adopt codes of ethics not less stringent than those of other Canadian governments. Finally, it is likely that Native people disadvantaged, or at least rendered very vulnerable, by de-emphasizing individual rights (for example, women, Métis, and urban Indians) will act as a counterweight to those who push too hard in a communitarian direction.

Nonetheless, arguments for excessive steps in a collectivist direction seem to us to be the principal threat within aboriginal political ethics in the near future. Two main factors account for this threat. First, within Native communities there has developed a major gap between an élite of politicians and managers with a high level of education, assertiveness, and political savvy and 'rank and file' members most of whom are lamentably short of these qualities. And second, most members of aboriginal collectivities, including those who are not politically attentive in the usual sense, increasingly take pride in their distinctiveness from other Canadians. These two factors, combined with powerful notions like 'collective rights' and 'consensus', provide members of Native élites opportunities to dominate, if not to oppress, the less advantaged members of their collectivities. In other words, as the aboriginal élites increasingly possess resources that enable them to influence the masses, and as the masses increasingly endorse political ideologies that disparage dissent, the threat grows that the élites will dominate the masses.

In the foreseeable future, neither individualist nor collectivist political ethics are likely to achieve hegemony in aboriginal communities (or, for that matter, in non-aboriginal jurisdictions). It is reasonable to hope, without an excess of wishful thinking, that both Natives and non-Natives will soon recognize more openly, and discuss more thoughtfully, the proper place of individualist and collectivist elements in their political and moral outlooks and practices.

Notes

1 Frank Cassidy and Robert L. Bish, *Indian Government: Its Meaning in Practice* (Lantzville, B.C.: Oolichan Books, 1989).

2 Thus our understanding of the scope of political ethics is heavily dependent on our view of the nature of ethics generally. We think ethics have mainly to do with outcomes.

3 See Joseph Tussman, *Obligation and the Body Politic* (New York: Oxford University Press, 1960), especially ch. 4.

4 Constitution Act, 1982, 35(2). This marked the first time the Inuit and Métis had been given explicit constitutional recognition. 'Indians and land reserved for the Indians' was designated as an exclusive power of the federal government in section 91 of the Constitution Act of 1867. However, constitutional recognition was especially important for the Métis, since the Inuit had long been assimilated with the Indians for major governmental purposes, whereas the Métis, constitutionally, were not differentiated from non-Native Canadian citizens.

5 Difficulties with the 1981 Census are discussed in Michael Asch, *Home and Native Land* (Toronto: Methuen, 1984): 3-4. For reasons unconnected to the competence or industriousness of Statistics Canada, the estimates of aboriginal populations in the 1986 Census are even less reliable. The results of the 1991 Census in regard to aboriginal peoples will not be released until late in 1993.

6 Asch, *Home and Native Land*: 2-3.

7 Donald Purich, *Our Land* (Toronto: Lorimer, 1986): 34.

8 The figures presented here are taken from James Frideres, *Native People in Canada: Contemporary Conflicts* (Scarborough, Ont.: Prentice-Hall, 1983), ch. 6.

9 Asch, *Home and Native Land*: 4.

10 Purich, *Native People in Canada*: 35

11 The statement in the text is a slight oversimplification. As the example (so far the only example) of the Métis settlements in Alberta shows, it is possible for the federal or provincial governments to create special governments for Native people (i.e., not necessarily registered Indians) to which apply special laws regarding political ethics. This could be very important if the movement towards Native self-government eventually leads to the creation of non-territorial governments (e.g., for urban Natives).

12 That assault is an indictable offence only if prosecuted by the Crown does not affect our main point.

13 The text, and a brief discussion, of this law may be found in the Halifax *Chronicle-Herald*, 31 Oct. 1986: 10. For the finding of the trial division of the Nova Scotia Supreme Court, see the *Chronicle-Herald*, 7 Jan. 1987: 1. We thank Ian Stewart for drawing the Nova Scotia events to our attention.

14 References to the Indian Act are from Donna Lea Hawley, *The Annotated Indian Act* (Toronto: Carswell, 1990): 90. There were similar provisions in the Alberta Métis Betterment Act, which governed the Alberta Métis settlements from 1938 to 1991.

15 See Cassidy and Bish, *Indian Government*.

16 John W. Langford, 'Conflict of interest: what the hell is it?', *Optimum* 22: 28-33.

17 The deepest recent thinking about situations of this kind can be found in the writings of Bernard Williams. See, in particular, his brilliant and humane essay, 'Ethical

Consistency', in Williams, *Problems of the Self* (Cambridge: Cambridge University Press, 1973), ch. 11. Judith Jarvis Thomson makes some interesting comments about Williams and some of his critics in *The Realm of Rights* (Cambridge, Mass.: Harvard University Press, 1990): 83-5.

18 We use the word 'community' with what we believe are still its common connotations, even though it has been debased by journalists, who use it to applaud batches of people they like ('the business community') or believe should be treated better ('the gay community'). In their lexicon there is of course no 'trade union community' or 'smoker community'.

19 Constitutional Secretariat, Assembly of First Nations, '"Sharing Canada's Future"— An Analysis From a First Nations Perspective', *Micmac-Maliseet Nations News*, November 1991: 34.

20 'Native women to challenge proposal on aboriginal rights', *Globe and Mail*, 17 Jan. 1992: A6.

21 In interviews with residents of two Alberta Métis settlements Tom Pocklington found that a majority of respondents expressed this sort of fear of self-government. See Pocklington, *The Government and Politics of the Alberta Métis Settlements* (Regina: Canadian Plains Research Center, 1991): 110-13.

22 See L.W. Sumner, *The Moral Foundation of Rights* (New York: Oxford University Press, 1987): 209-10; Carl Wellman, *A Theory of Rights* (Totowa, N.J.: Rowman & Allanheld, 1985): 193-4.

23 The phrasing is Don Carmichael's. See Don Carmichael, Tom Pocklington, and Greg Pyrcz, *Democracy and Rights in Canada* (Toronto: Harcourt Brace Jovanovich, 1991): 204. It is interesting that Carmichael finds the master expression of this conception in Hobbes.

24 Carl Wellman maintains, rightly in our view, that 'rights are asserted or denied only when two parties are, or at least could be imagined to be, in conflict, for the language of rights is essentially adversarial'. See Wellman, *A Theory of Rights*: 10.

25 See Rainer Knopff and F.L. Morton, *Charter Politics* (Toronto: Nelson Canada, 1992): 223-4, for a discussion of the extraordinarily narrow and legalistic character of abortion politics in the United States and Canada.

26 An excellent collection of essays relating to this conflict is Nancy Rosenblum, ed., *Liberalism and the Moral Life* (Cambridge, Mass.: Harvard University Press, 1989).

27 The standard justification offered for the imposition of such harsh measures was that the women 'knew what they were doing' when they chose to marry non-Indian men.

28 See Donald Purich, *Our Land: Native Rights in Canada* (Toronto: Lorimer, 1986): 138.

29 For an interesting, radical discussion of the implications of group membership for citizenship in a liberal democracy, see Iris Marion Young, 'Polity and Group Difference: A Critique of the Ideal of Universal Citizenship', in Cass R. Sundstein, ed., *Feminism and Political Theory* (Chicago: University of Chicago Press, 1990): 117-41.

30 The Alberta Métis settlements came close to adopting this position. In a 1982 pamphlet entitled *Métisism* they said: 'We are opposed to the use of narrow racial criteria to define the Metis people. . . . We accept as Métis any person of mixed Indian and non-Indian ancestry who identifies as Métis.' Quoted in Pocklington, *Goverment and Politics*: 140.

31 This description is based on interviews with Dene politicians and elders in Yellowknife, Fort Simpson, and Fort Good Hope, conducted by Sarah Pocklington July

and August, 1990. See also Dene Nation, *Denendeh* (Yellowknife: The Dene Nation, 1984): 11-12.

32 See Indian Brotherhood of the NWT, *Minutes of the Second Joint General Assembly*, 18-23 July 1975, Fort Simpson; *General Assembly*, 1-6 Dec. 1975, Fort Rae.

33 For evidence on this point in regard to the United States, as well as for a discussion of the nature and limits of consensus, see Jane J. Mansbridge, *Beyond Adversary Democracy* (Chicago: University of Chicago Press, 1983).

Jacques Bourgault and Stéphane Dion

4

Public sector ethics in Quebec

The contrasting society

Quebec's distinctiveness in public sector ethics is not immediately obvious. As elsewhere, controls have been progressively tightened to better combat unethical behaviour. The late 1970s saw several governments in Canada adopt codes of ethics and legal texts that were more stringent than those previously employed.[1] In this respect, Quebec took action at the same time as other governments.

But Quebec was unique in the scope of its change. It is difficult to find another Western government that, between 1960 and 1980, changed its approach to public sector ethics so dramatically. The government of Maurice Duplessis may not have been the most corrupt regime in North America. But it certainly had entrenched systems of patronage, cronyism, and pork-barrelling. At the same time, it is difficult to find a government more rigorous, energetic, and motivated in its fight against patronage and conflict of interest than the Parti Québécois under René Lévesque.

In the 1980s, Quebec's ethical rigour receded somewhat, making its codes of ethics more like those of other Canadian jurisdictions.

The contrast between Duplessis and Lévesque is striking. We examine this unusual evolution and illustrate how, with respect to patronage and conflict of interest, Quebec moved from extreme tolerance to unparalleled rigour in only two decades, before ending up with rules that are comparable to those of other Canadian governments.

This chapter stresses two classic issues of public sector ethics—conflict of interest and patronage. We will consider the period 1867 to 1992, with particular attention to the Duplessis era (1936-39 and 1944-60), the Lévesque era (1976-85), and the Bourassa governments (1970-76 and 1985-92). The word 'patronage' is used in its general sense of partisan favouritism in the allocation of jobs, contracts, and various government grants, permits, and subsidies. It refers to an action or a decision providing a benefit to a person or a group and taken in consideration of a party's interest or a party member's interest more than the intrinsic quality or competence of its beneficiary. In our perspective, such ethical issues as due process, fairness, the misuse of information and lying for the public interest are beyond the scope of this chapter.

Traditional Quebec: the era of tolerance

Political patronage, influence-peddling, corrupt voting practices, favouritism towards constituencies that voted for the 'right' side, the manipulation of the civil service for partisan purposes, the steering of contracts to friends—traditional Quebec's tolerance for these specific political practices has been pointed out so often that it is unnecessary to describe them in detail.[2] Of course, this tolerance was by no means the sole privilege of Quebec, contrary to what one might think after reading the often quoted paper by Pierre Elliott Trudeau.[3] It was Newfoundland, not Quebec, that received the lowest marks from Jeffrey Simpson in his history of Canadian patronage.[4] Nonetheless, his picture of Quebec is not flattering.[5] James Iain Gow, an historian of the Quebec public service, describes how patronage, scandals, and corruption characterized, to varying degrees, every Quebec government up to 1960.[6] Vincent Lemieux and Raymond Hudon have catalogued 2,884 allegations of patronage mentioned in newspapers between 1944 and 1972, with the highest number recorded between 1952 and 1962; it was not until the 1960s that the number of such cases fell significantly.[7]

This leads us to wonder what type of government ethics existed under such a system. We answer this question by pointing out a basic difference between ethical standards that aimed to *justify* patronage and contrary ones that limit its scope. Since no explicitly comparative study is available, we cannot easily assess the extent to which Quebec's traditional patterns of corruption and patronage differed from those prevailing in other provinces. At the very least, patronage and corruption in Quebec were justified and explained in different terms.

Patronage in Quebec, as elsewhere, was usually justified as a way to humanize the public service, a sort of kindness for those less fortunate, a way of validating recognition of people and their needs and as an antidote to bureaucracy. This philanthropic, anti-bureaucratic argument was frequently advanced in traditional Quebec.[8] Duplessis was a master of anti-bureaucratic rhetoric.[9] Without doubt, many ministers and senior officials believed that they were serving the public good by dispensing government favours here and there to little people they knew or to a specific village. The common distinction between 'small' patronage, which benefits the 'little people', and 'big' patronage, which benefits big shots, comes to mind. Of course, 'small' patronage became a convenient justification for the large-scale practice of 'big' patronage, as small jobs given to election workers were played up to make people forget the major contracts awarded to big contributors to the electoral fund.

That patronage was likened to a type of social service explains why, from 1867 to 1936, purges of the civil service and mass departures following changes in government did not occur. Each governing party filled the public service with its supporters and election workers, but also allowed the supporters of the preceding regime to remain. This was because employment in the public sector was considered a type of welfare.[10] Widespread purges did, however, follow the 1936 and 1939 changes in government.[11]

This social conception of patronage found favour in a land where the economy was weak and the francophone population was economically inferior. As Ralph Heintzman wrote, 'To a people whose provincial economy was less developed than those of some adjacent regions and who were at a serious economic disadvantage even at home, the patronage system remained an important economic tool.'[12] In the civil service, employees were badly paid, prompting them to look for alternative sources of revenue. Many civil servants had a second job, and having a sideline did not necessarily put a civil servant in a conflict of interest, as the two jobs may not have had anything in common; but the practice created a zone 'where the office, the car and the materials supplied by the government were used for the second job'.[13]

The human and philanthropic argument advanced in defence of patronage took easy root in a society under the firm grip of traditional Catholicism.[14] The Catholic religion supplies a powerful representational model of patronage, wherein a believer selects a saint to serve as an intermediary to attain God's blessing. In traditional Quebec the premier, ministers, and MNAs were often compared to good fathers.

Another weapon in the arsenal of justifications for patronage was nationalism. This gave an historical context to the idea that the provincial government had a personal, protective, and specific responsibility towards each child of the people. The government's benevolent little patronage was essentially directed at the majority population in the electoral district, especially in rural areas. As for big patronage, although it led to enormous concessions for largely English-speaking businesses, one result was an increase in the number of French-speaking millionaire entrepreneurs, according to one such millionaire.[15] The idea of promoting French-Canadians in the English-speaking business community was a convenient pretext for several ministers, including Premier Taschereau, to serve on a number of corporate boards of directors, creating a cosy corporate-political relationship.[16] Impersonal and bureaucratic procedures for allocating public subsidies were denounced as foreign, English methods.[17] The very idea of establishing rigorous public tendering for government contracts, or statutory rather than discretionary rules for awarding government subsidies, to municipalities and school boards was denounced as a method inspired by the federal government and thus foreign to Quebec.[18]

However, various nationalist intellectuals—Henri Bourassa being the most famous of them—denounced the traditional system of patronage and corruption as a national disgrace, an obstacle to the economic and cultural development of French-Canadians, and a betrayal of the province to large English-speaking companies.[19] Critical nationalist thinking was, however, marginal until the Quiet

Revolution, when nationalism stopped being a justification for patronage and began to be used against it.

Identifying patronage with social charity and national solidarity encouraged greater tolerance for it. Two other norms had a similar influence, although rather than justifying patronage they simply made it difficult to denounce. The ethics of loyalty or professional discretion that made up the moral code of numerous civil servants[20] were inhibitory norms. With no statutes to protect them from the caprices of those in power, government employees were not inclined to be independent. Some civil servants came to terms with their precarious context by finding personal satisfaction in following whoever was in power regardless of the orders given. A book by Alfred Hardy, who was *directeur général des achats* (director general for purchasing) for two decades under Duplessis and Godbout strikingly illustrates this point of view.[21] With numerous details and no embarrassment, Hardy explains the system of kickbacks under which the awarding of government contracts was an opportunity to stock the secret slush fund of the party in power, both under the Liberals and the Union Nationale. He describes how government materials and employee work hours were used for partisan or private purposes by ministers and senior officials, and how the media and journalists had their palms greased in exchange for silence. That his department was a cog in a corrupt system does not seem to present a moral problem for this bureaucrat; in any event, his book gives no evidence of a battle with his conscience. On the contrary, he boasts of always having served the party in power, throwing out indignantly those who suggested he turn to treason. One day a Liberal organizer asked him for secrets to incriminate the Union Nationale; in exchange, the go-between promised Hardy's position would be assured in case of a change in government. His reply was scathing:

'Get out, you stinking rat, get out of my sight,' I cried as I pushed him towards the door. 'I've got a message for the gang of Godbout cronies who sent you to test the waters. You can tell them that loyalty still exists even if your god-damned gang doesn't seem to know the meaning of the word.'[22]

A respect for privacy and the prudishness of the era provided the other inhibitory norm that encouraged silence on certain activities of the élite. There were some things—primarily sexual matters—that good taste did not allow the public to know. A remarkable example is found in Hardy's book: he notes how lavish contracts were awarded to a business belonging to the family of one of Duplessis's mistresses. During the budget review, the Liberal opposition hinted at the matter by mentioning that the premier seemed to be encouraging 'a member of his court'. Far from denying the accusation, Duplessis counter-attacked with the tone of one whose privacy has been violated: 'That's right, I did tell the Purchasing Manager to award some contracts to a very close friend that I want to encourage. I'm the Premier and that's my business.' Hardy concludes: 'Fearing no doubt that they had stepped on a banana peel by raising the subject of his private life, the Opposition ceased its attack and the budget was passed unanimously.'[23]

Finally, patronage fed on partisan battles. They were its driving force. Patronage was perpetuated by the spiral it created, the intrigues of one side being used as alibis for the intrigues of the other. Each side gave itself absolution by saying that its adversary would only do worse, given the chance. For example, Alfred Hardy, who dedicates his book in memory of Duplessis, bases his defence on the allegation that the Taschereau and Godbout administrations were just as corrupt as that of 'Le Chef'. Patronage thrived on the battles between parties and, by stirring up these battles, created a vicious circle. Indeed, dependence on the favouritism of the party in power sustained a deep devotion to partisan politics: 'The Québécois had to identify himself openly with the party of his choice in order to be in a position to profit from the system when his party came to power.'[24]

Various themes justified patronage in traditional Quebec. However, there were contrary norms that limited its scope. The notion of conflict of interest was certainly flexible, but since Confederation measures had been taken to prevent it. For example, the Legislature Act of 1888 forbade those who held well-paid offices in the governments of Quebec, Canada, or other provinces to be legislators. Article 139 established that anyone who had directly or indirectly entered into a contract with the province could not sit or vote as a legislator. An exception was made for corporate stockholders as long as their contracts did not involve the construction of public works. All offenders would lose their seats and incur a fine of $1000 per day that they remained sitting in Parliament (Article 140). These provisions were carried over into the various Acts that followed until the 1982 act that tightened the rules. Bribery and influence-peddling were prohibited in 1915 in accordance with the Criminal Code's existing provisions.[25] It forbade legislators to accept, directly or indirectly, any reward concerning any matter submitted, or going to be submitted, to Parliament. This provision remains in effect.

As for bureaucrats, the first report of the Civil Service Commission in 1868 contained a guideline calling for integrity, dedication to work, and discretion.[26] In 1869, the law forbade land officers to purchase land within their territories without the permission of the Lieutenant-Governor-in-Council.[27] Bureaucrats were also obliged to take various oaths pledging loyalty, honesty, and discretion in the performance of their duties, with the understanding that breaches would mean dismissal.

Such laws were sometimes ignored in practice. A striking example was the Civil Service Board. Created in 1868, its purpose was to protect the merit system from political interference. In practice, it was ineffective and weak, and was abolished in 1926.[28] The Civil Service Commission was resurrected by Premier Godbout in 1943, but in 1945 Duplessis appointed one of his men to head it, so that it was unable to protect the merit system from patronage.[29] Nonetheless, a legal framework was a sign of disapproval of conflict of interest and favouritism.

This legal disapproval was not merely an official cover: it was also shared in large part by various sectors of society. Lemieux and Hudon have catalogued 1,471 statements of opinion on the subject of patronage in various media between 1944 and 1972. Nearly 90 per cent of them expressed disapproval. The percentage of favourable statements never exceeded 19 per cent, a height reached during the years 1944 to 1948. This percentage declined steadily, and starting in 1970 respondents were nearly unanimous in decrying patronage. Even during the height of the Duplessis regime, many commentators viewed patronage critically; positive opinions were from the newspaper of the party in power.[30]

Patronage was denounced under the two themes of injustice and poor administration: it was unfair because it forced the citizens to see services to which they were entitled as favours; it was harmful because it wasted public funds.[31]

Disapproval of patronage and conflict of interest is also reflected in the defeat of three premiers (Ouimet in 1874, Mercier in 1891, and Taschereau in 1936) as a result of scandals. The defeat of the Union Nationale in 1960 was preceded by the so-called public morality campaign of 1956-60 led by people such as Laurendeau, Laporte, Dion, and O'Neil, and the magazine *Cité libre*.[32] *Le Devoir*'s revelation of the natural gas affair in 1958 marked the height of this morality campaign, when certain ministers, MNAs, and civil servants were reproached for reaping personal gain from selling Hydro-Québec's natural gas network to a private company whose stock they held. Like Duplessis in 1936, Jean Lesage campaigned in 1960 on a promise to end corrupt politics. Corruption was often a major theme of election campaigns in Quebec.[33]

A final sign that patronage was something of a disgrace is found in an implicit political norm of the era: it was important that the head of the government not be personally sullied by the corruption that surrounded him. The fate of the Taschereau administration was sealed by accusations of nepotism aimed at the premier's family. Duplessis's personal popularity was largely based on his image as a disinterested and devoted father. Personal enrichment was obviously not what 'Le Chef' was after, as he died heavily in debt. But had he acted otherwise, had he shown the same eagerness to use politics to line his pockets as some of his ministers and senior officials, he would have lost his popularity. His asceticism contrasted sharply with the corruption of his entourage and this contrast fascinated his supporters.[34]

Traditionally, Quebec has exhibited contradictory ethical norms. Various forms of patronage and conflict of interest were largely rejected as venal practices. But in other ways there was extreme tolerance in likening patronage to a form of social charity and national protection, making it difficult for anyone to denounce it without appearing to lack loyalty, *savoir-vivre*, or realism.

The result of these contradictory attitudes was that patronage was widely practised, but also commonly denounced, especially during elections. Campaigns to denounce patronage helped bring down some governments. And there were limits that could not be overstepped in the use of partisan favouritism, nepotism, and corruption. The most important of these limits was that the head of the government himself must not be corrupt. It is hard to say to what extent this mixture of contradictory values was peculiar to Quebec. A striking resemblance exists, for example, between Duplessis and the infamous Richard J. Daley, mayor of Chicago from 1955 to 1976. Like 'Le Chef', Daley always emerged as the hero of the piece because charges of corruption never touched him personally.[35]

How does one explain this dialectic of patronage, this love-hate relationship? The open, systematic recourse to patronage and corruption stimulated the very forces that fought it. Ralph Heintzman notes that entrenched patronage produces great cynicism towards politics and politicians: 'The knowledge that all government programmes and spending would be exploited for patronage purposes prompted a corresponding distrust of politics.'[36] One could argue that this general cynicism, which leads to a type of fatalism, a feeling of resignation, and an inborn mistrust of the government and politics in general, is broken up by sudden calls for purity, for politics free of partisan favouritism. Opposition parties stir up such aspirations, but perpetuate the system themselves once in power.

The 1960s and the Quiet Revolution produced a different, more bureaucratic government where patronage was less important. The groundwork for change was laid in the structural changes that transformed postwar Quebec: urbanization, sustained economic growth, a growing public sector, and the advent of electronic media (radio and television) that lay beyond the control of political parties.[37] There is a complex debate about if, how, and why 'modernization' alters the ethical climate. Such a debate extends beyond the scope of this chapter, but one thing is clear: by modernizing, Quebec gave itself new ethical standards more in line with bureaucratic and impersonal norms.

Favouritism and conflict of interest in contemporary Quebec: the rigour of René Lévesque

Jean Lesage ran his 1960 election campaign by promising to eliminate fraud and to establish a politically neutral civil service like the one in Ottawa. The Liberals quickly took measures to battle patronage and corruption, starting with the Salvas Commission of Inquiry created in October 1960 to examine the Union Nationale administration, and culminating in the 1965 Civil Service Act, which strengthened the Public Service Commission and its ability to enforce merit. Article 56 established for the first time that no one could use intimidation or threats to force a civil servant to participate in partisan politics. Civil servants received the right to strike. A legal framework was put in place to prevent the civil service from being an emanation of the party in power. Another major reform was the Election Act of 1963, which imposed ceilings on party and candidate expenditures during election campaigns. A system of public tenders was instituted, affecting the way that government contracts were awarded.

A decline in patronage damaged the electoral machine of the Liberal Party. It is one reason for the Lesage government's defeat in 1966. One study showed that the most active Liberal militants and organizers listed this change as the fourth major cause of the defeat. Patronage was apparently ended too quickly, without those involved being educated politically, so that many election organizers saw its disappearance as a lack of gratitude on the part of the party. In the same way, MNAs disappointed their electors by being less able to procure specific benefits for them.[38] And yet the number of favours asked of the administration by government MNAs was still relatively high during the sixties.[39]

Logically, when the party founded by Maurice Duplessis returned to power in 1966, patronage should have returned with a vengeance. However, the Union Nationale administration (1966-70) maintained the reformist course, notably by increasing the regulatory power of the government and by adding new administrative rules that limited the discretionary power of elected officials and civil servants.[40] A good example is the law creating the Civil Service Department in 1969, which specified the powers of all the relevant actors. The Union Nationale continued the fight against patronage, especially because the premier, Daniel Johnson, who had been accused of conflict of interest when he had been one of Duplessis's ministers, wanted to avoid accusations of corruption.[41] Furthermore, it would have been difficult to reinstate the Duplessis system in its entirety, given the unionization of the public sector, new contracting procedures in key departments, the introduction of competitive entrance examinations for the civil service, ceilings on party spending, and the other Liberal reforms.

In particular, the Union Nationale toughened the rules against conflict of interest with respect to civil servants: all professionals had henceforth to practise their professions solely on behalf of the government,[42] in accordance with the rule in force since 1965 for deputy ministers.[43]

Quebec's political practices changed dramatically during the sixties. Lemieux and Hudon note a clear decline of patronage in this period.[44] However, a decline in patronage does not mean it was eliminated, especially when the initial number of cases was so high: allegations of patronage and corruption were often brought to public attention.[45] There was even an increase in the number of such allegations during Robert Bourassa's first administration (1970-3). An example was the Paragon Ltd episode. Paragon was a company that received numerous government contracts while the premier's wife and his brother-in-law, Claude Simard, the minister of tourism, were among its stockholders. The commissions of inquiry on the devastation at James Bay (the Cliche Commission) and on organized crime revealed that contracts were often awarded without tenders. The Liberal Party was accused of financing its electoral fund through the Société des Alcools du Québec and Loto-Québec. Even the Chair of the Public Service Commission—whose mandate is to fight patronage—was forced to resign after the Cliche Commission revealed that he received his position after promising the premier's office that a union would be given special government recognition to help it to expand its membership.[46]

Premier Bourassa reacted strongly to such allegations of corruption. In 1974, he enacted the first modern code of ethics in Quebec, which required civil servants to refuse favours likely to affect their independence and impartiality, and to disclose to the Civil Service Commission, in writing, interests held by their spouses or children that could put them in a conflict of interest.[47] 'If the Commission deems that an actual or possible situation of conflicting interests exists, it must report that fact to the Prime Minister in the case of a deputy-head, or to the head of the Department as well as to the Minister of the Civil Service in the case of another member of the Civil Service, and indicate the measures it deems necessary to be taken in each case.' In addition, Bourassa issued firm directives to his ministers—probably the strictest in all of Canada—about conflict of interest. Henceforth, ministers and their families could no longer do business with the government either personally or through a third party. The Executive Council Department Act forbade ministers to be directors or administrators in commercial, industrial, or financial corporations. These directives were enacted just before the Liberals' defeat in 1976, hence it is not known whether Bourassa's government would have respected them. The rules were enacted too late to cleanse the Liberals in the eyes of the electorate. Honesty in government was a major theme in the Parti Québécois campaign and played a large part in defeating Bourassa in 1976.[48]

The Parti Québécois did not even wait to take power before setting clear policies about conflict of interest. In 1975 in Baie-Comeau, it put together a rigorous code of ethics that included MNAs and senior party officials. This code of ethics, written while in opposition, was combined with the rules left behind by the Liberals. Additionally, Lévesque enacted his own code for ministers. He issued these directives at the meeting of the Executive Council on 12 January 1977, and presented them to the National Assembly on 16 March. 'We did our best to close any doors that may have remained', Lévesque declared before the Assembly.[49] These directives contained the following major provisions.

Public disclosure. Ministers had to make full disclosure of financial interests held in any profit-oriented organizations by themselves, their spouses, and minor children. They had to give a complete account of any real estate owned by themselves and their immediate family, with the exception of houses or apartments for residential use. They were also obliged to identify all creditors for personal debts above $2,000 and to indicate the balance due when it exceeded $20,000.

Limits to business property. The first provision was self-evident: ministers had to cease all business or commercial professional activities that could be a source of conflict of interest. Ministers also had to terminate activities that could prevent them from devoting all their time to their duties. Finally, ministers and their immediate families had to divest themselves, within sixty days, of holdings in companies that were traded on the stock market. The same restrictions applied to land: ministers and their immediate families were forbidden to engage in land speculation or to acquire interest in real property in Quebec or in a real estate development company doing business in Quebec.

Ban on conducting business with the government. Ministers had to see to it that companies in which they held an interest, or in which their immediate families worked or held an interest, either personally or through a third party, refrained from making deals with the government: in other words, did not provide goods or services or receive money in the form of loans or subsidies. 'The government' was defined as the government of Quebec, its departments, agencies, and corporations. The only exceptions were those transactions with the government deemed necessary for the public good, provided that the Parliamentary Committee of Financial Commitments was notified of the details.

The opportunities for a minister and his family to remain in business were limited: the company's stock could not be traded on the market, it could not do business with the government, and it could only produce goods or services that were not related to the duties of the minister. The minister could not devote time to such private business and had to reveal its existence. The premier was responsible for interpreting the directives.

It is doubtful whether such strict directives concerning ministers have ever been adopted elsewhere. They were maintained by the Parti Québécois government from 1976 to 1985, undergoing only one major modification: in July 1981, a directive established that only ministers, not their immediate families, were obliged to divest themselves of interests in a company listed on the stock exchange. Spouses and children could keep such stock, but ministers still had to file yearly declarations of such family interests and avoid transactions with the government.

The Parti Québécois government also toughened the rules governing MNAs. Up to that time, an MNA who was a corporate stockholder could obtain a contract from the government if the contract had nothing to do with public works. Once An Act Respecting the National Assembly was passed in 1982, such deals could only be made if the amount invested by the MNA in the business and the circumstances surrounding the making of the deal were such that there was no collusion or undue influence (Article 65). In addition, the 1982 act included a public disclosure provision for MNAs: an MNA with a direct, personal financial interest in a matter submitted to Parliament for consideration had to publicly declare this interest if he wished to take part in debates or vote (Article 62). The act also created the position of a jurisconsult, appointed by a two-thirds majority of the National Assembly, who was in charge of providing confidential advice to MNAs who requested guidance about conflicts of interest (Article 74). The act even declared that the office of MNA was incompatible with membership on a municipal council, a school board, or a board of school trustees (Article 57).

For civil servants, new standards of conduct and discipline were established by regulation on 8 March 1979. They went further than those enacted by Bourassa in 1974. Henceforth, civil servants had to refuse all favours, regardless of their origin, not merely those 'of a nature which affect [their] independence or impartiality'. The same standards were basically repeated in Order-in-Council 577-85 issued on 27 March 1985.[50]

An Act to Govern the Financing of Political Parties and to Amend the Election Act, adopted in 1977, is evidence of the same strong desire to change political practices.[51] The goal was to eliminate secret funds through which contributors could bargain their support to a party. The act forced political parties to publish their financial statements. Contributions could no longer come from companies, only from individuals, and they became tax deductible. Moreover, an individual's contribution was limited to $3,000 a year. Donations over $100 had to be disclosed. Party as well as candidate contributions and expenses were subject to a ceiling during elections. Nowhere in the world had such a demanding system been instituted.[52] This system reflected a desire to free politics of the influence of money.

Another important initiative was the installation in 1977 of the Inventory of Services Providers. Made up of seven sub-directories, this system, nicknamed '*Rosalie*', was aimed at limiting arbitrary practices and favouritism in the selection of suppliers by using computers and more neutral rules for awarding contracts. The government's twenty-five departments and fifty-eight of its agencies were automatically subject to this system.[53]

Three factors explain the PQ's exceptional rigour with regard to money, patronage, and conflict of interest. The first was the lack of ties between the Parti Québécois candidates elected in 1976, who were, by and large, employees from the public sector and intellectuals,[54] and the business world, which was alarmed by its social-democrat and sovereigntist tendencies. As few ministers and MNAs were in business anyway, it was easy to impose strict standards upon them and their families. One minister from that era, who owned part of a publishing house, confided in an interview that he received no sympathy from his colleagues for the hardships he and his family endured because of the severe rules. In fact, because other difficult cases arose over the years, Lévesque eventually allowed the immediate family to keep stock traded on the market. A notable case was that of Pauline Marois, a minister during the PQ's second term, whose husband owned stock in a number of public companies.[55]

Unable to enter the world of business, the Parti Québécois lived off the contributions of its members. Therefore, outlawing corporate contributions to election campaigns and party funds did not really harm it. But the new law forced the PQ's opponents, parties traditionally tied to the business world, to completely rethink their fundraising methods.

Although removed from the business world, the membership of the Parti Québécois was close to the civil service and trade unions. This was a second factor explaining the PQ's determination to establish strict rules against political favouritism. Throughout the 1960s and 1970s the civil service and trade unions were in the forefront of the fight against patronage and political favouritism.[56] Long left without any real statutory protection and at the mercy of those in power, Quebec public sector employees saw their lot improve dramatically in the 1960s. They obtained a right to unionize, bargain, and strike more generous than that generally found elsewhere in the Western world.[57] They were in an excellent position from which to fight arbitrary interference by elected officials in the determination of their jobs, the control of their careers, and the content of their work.

That a party close to the civil service should narrow the acceptable limits of political favouritism is not surprising. In Saskatchewan, for example, the election of the CCF in 1944 triggered a vast reform in favour of the merit system.[58] If these parties appoint leaders sympathetic to their ideas to the upper civil service, they take care, more than other parties, to remove these positions from the classified service.[59]

The economic recession forced the Parti Québécois to slash salaries in the civil service and limit the right to strike. However, the PQ also gave civil servants the right to participate more freely in politics. In this respect, Quebec civil servants have come a long way. Before the PQ's election, all members of the civil service were obliged, during federal or provincial elections, to abstain from partisan political activities unless they were running as candidates. The Civil Service Acts of 1979 and 1983 changed all that. Civil servants could now be members of a political party, attend political meetings, contribute to political parties or candidates running for office, obtain leave without pay if running for office or acting as the official representative of a candidate in a provincial election, and if elected, get their civil service jobs back at the same classification, or even a higher classification if the experience they gained in politics justified it. These political rights are limited only by the usual clauses enforcing political neutrality in the performance of one's duties and an obligation to be appropriately reserved when publicly expressing one's opinions. Within these limits, the 1983 act authorizes nearly all forms of political activity, although a recent case indicates that civil servants cannot be party fundraisers without putting themselves in a conflict of interest situation.[60] What is more, the Parti Québécois eliminated the bridges that allowed members of ministers' office staffs to be integrated into the public service. The Lévesque government granted civil servants the right to engage in most political activities and reduced the capacity of elected officials to interfere with civil servants.

Here lies another major contrast in the evolution of public sector ethics in Quebec: the fact that two opposing trends occurred simultaneously. On the one hand, there was a shift from tolerance to rigour in the treatment of patronage and conflict of interest; on the other hand, there was a shift from extreme rigour to great tolerance with respect to the political and union rights of civil servants. Once again, the originality of the phenomenon lies not in its existence—it has happened elsewhere—but in its extent: few governments have liberalized the political and union rights of civil servants to such a large degree.

The third factor that explains the PQ's rigour about patronage and conflict of interest is its nationalism. National solidarity was used to justify the patronage and conflict of interest in traditional Quebec. It was thus important for Lévesque to show that his nationalism rejected past practices. For Lévesque, the corruption and paternalism of the Duplessis era reflected the colonialism that had slowed Quebec's evolution towards emancipation. In fact, Lévesque wanted to construct a fully developed modern state, one led by a government that inspired the full confidence of its citizens. Allegations of corruption had contributed to the fall of the Liberal government in 1976; henceforth, a clear and irreproachable government ethic would make Quebeckers fully confident of their ability to govern themselves. A clean state is a long-term investment for a separatist government.

Lévesque's personality was largely responsible for this 'sanitary' orientation of the Parti Québécois. His charisma was based on an image of integrity. In his memoirs, no adjective is too harsh for Duplessis's practices. The civil service before the Quiet Revolution was 'an arbitrary lottery'. The police force 'was rotten to the core'. Contracts awarded to friends could have devoured the entire budget. Secret electoral funds were 'the Augean stables'.[61] As premier, Lévesque made ethical politics his top priority. 'Of all the reforms we were able to push through, this is the one I will always be the proudest of', he wrote in reference to An Act to Govern the Financing of Political Parties and to Amend the Election Act.[62] It would be difficult to find another head of state who attached greater importance in his memoirs to the ideal of government integrity. The high marks that René Lévesque gave his government on this score are unequivocal:

> Above all, and this had never been seen either, in every corner of the administration, we had been incorruptible right down the line. . . . we had really done a big housecleaning job and had come out of it with clean hands.[63]

In power, the PQ experienced few scandals about money and conflict of interest. We found only a benevolence towards nationalist movements and festivals, a questionable contract awarded to a friend of the PQ for the renovation of public housing,[64] and the pitiful resignation of Claude Charron, a PQ minister caught shoplifting a coat.[65] This does not prove beyond doubt that the Parti Québécois government never acted unethically on financial issues. But the public record suggests a conflict-free and ethical administration. Very little contrary evidence is available.

Significantly, the PQ's most memorable scandal—the Claude Morin affair—was primarily a matter of political and police intrigue, not economic misconduct. The facts are well known. In 1974, when he was a prominent member of the Parti Québécois, then the official opposition, Morin agreed to regular secret meetings with an RCMP agent. He was paid approximately $400 for each meeting. When these facts were revealed by the media in 1992, Morin claimed he never gave the RCMP any information that could have damaged the PQ or the Quebec government; on the contrary, he obtained information from his contact that was useful to the sovereigntist cause. He maintained that he told René Lévesque about it at the time, a story that other sources have contradicted. As for the money he received from the RCMP, Morin said he gave it to charity and the Parti Québécois electoral fund.[66] In general, the media and PQ spokespersons refused to believe that the former minister, the architect of the 1980 referendum strategy, could have been a federalist spy. But at the same time, they denounced him for a terrible lack of judgement in dealing with a secret service.[67]

The Morin affair, where the achievement of the PQ's primary goal was in direct competition with the party's underlying ethical principles, is an interesting case for the study of government ethics. It shows how a single event may involve several kinds of ethical conflicts. Did Morin endanger the sovereignty and the integrity of his government? Did he lack discretion concerning cabinet discussion? Was he disloyal to party members? Perhaps most importantly, should one ever engage in dubious practices to better serve the cause? Morin built his defence on the idea that sovereigntists must not act like innocents, 'political hippies', in the face of Ottawa's 'low blows' and the RCMP's illegal practices. He maintained that because of these strategic considerations, René Lévesque fully accepted his actions at the time. The former premier did, after all, describe Morin in his memoirs as a 'tireless and sharp-witted journeyman constantly on guard against traps Ottawa might be laying for us'.[68] But other sources claim that the ex-premier was so shattered to learn that his star minister had taken money from the RCMP that he demanded Morin's resignation.[69] In any event, in 1992 the PQ rejected Morin's defence. His activities were denounced by many prominent péquistes, some of whom demanded his expulsion. The party wanted to return 'the tainted money' Morin had donated to it between 1975 and 1977. When he sent back the money, the party gave it to charity.[70]

After eight years in power, the PQ had changed historic practices of patronage in Quebec.[71] Did the Liberals' return to power in 1985 endanger this accomplishment?

Favouritism and conflict of interest in contemporary Quebec: easing the restrictions

As if to send a reassuring signal, Premier Robert Bourassa was anxious that one of his first directives, issued 12 December 1985, concern ethics: all gifts or presents worth more than $35 henceforth had to be given back to the donor, or else donated to the public purse.

Bourassa was indeed eager to reinforce this assurance. He remembered 1976, when allegations of corruption tarnished his government. But his party was much closer to the business world than the PQ, and several of his potential ministers had shares in firms. It would have been difficult to subject them to rules as strict as those in effect under the Parti Québécois. Bourassa therefore decided to ease certain restrictions, and did so in a directive to members of the Executive Council issued 10 April 1986. This directive was similar to that issued by the PQ, with two significant changes:

Limits to business property. Ministers who did not want to divest themselves of their interests in public companies had another option: hand over their stock to a proxy to be administered in a blind trust. In blind trusts, ministers could not exert influence on investment decisions. They could only withdraw their funds or add to them. Ministers were not obliged to disclose their stock holdings.

Ban on conducting business with the government. This rule, which was very strict under the Parti Québécois, now had an exception. The ban on conducting business with the government was lifted for ministers and their immediate families, if their share of a private business did not exceed 5 per cent of the capital, if the circumstances surrounding the deal were such that in all likelihood there was no collusion or undue influence, if the minister involved had nothing to do with the decision to make the deal, and if the deal was made in accordance with normal tendering procedures.

Another Bourassa initiative was to request a study on *Rosalie*, the automated system for awarding contracts established by the PQ. Presented in August 1986, this report concluded that the *Rosalie* system was too awkward and inflexible and that it required a number of changes. It was recommended that the government allow itself a greater number of exceptions rather than systematically turning to the computerized central directory.[72] These changes were denounced by the PQ opposition.

As for the code of ethics for civil servants, the Liberals maintained the framework put in place by the Parti Québécois. They tried to better promote the code so that civil servants were familiar with the rules and understood them. In 1990 the Department of the Executive Council distributed the document entitled 'Ethics in the Quebec Public Service' to its senior officials, executives, and civil servants. This document endeavours to explain what is permissible and what is prohibited conduct. It notes that conflict of interest and the appearance of conflict of interest must be avoided.

Bourassa's primary changes therefore involved a loosening of ministerial rules about conflict of interest. This easing of restrictions was criticized by the PQ opposition and the media. In particular, it was deplored that ministers were no longer obliged to divulge their stock holdings. Occurring in the midst of privatization, these changes caused anxiety that ministers might favour firms in which they held stock. In 1990, seventeen ministers, including the premier, owned stock in companies traded on the stock exchange.[73] Such ties with the business world are in stark contrast with the more distant relations that prevailed under the Parti Québécois, and help explain the parties' different approaches to financial conflicts of interest.

Bourassa was very anxious to dismiss allegations of corruption against his government. The flurry of scandals that hit the federal Conservatives and some other provincial governments—notably Nova Scotia and British Columbia—did not appear in Quebec. But there were more scandals than there had been under the Parti Québécois. Two ministers were disgraced and doubts were raised about the fairness of tendering.

In one incident, the solicitor general, Gérard Latulippe, resigned in 1989. The press and the opposition accused him of maintaining contractual ties with several law firms and receiving nearly $85,000 in legal fees, while the law firms he was involved with harvested government contracts. Commenting on his rotten luck, the former minister gave a veritable *cri du coeur* that said a lot about the uneasiness of some cabinet members with regard to the new rules concerning ethics: 'I honestly wonder who in our society could be interested in politics when every day there is the risk of being found guilty by association.'[74] And what happened to Latulippe? The MNA resigned his seat on 14 June 1989, 'to take up other professional challenges'.[75] Bourassa had appointed him Quebec's delegate-general in Mexico.

The second affair did not end in a resignation, but seriously embarrassed the minister in charge of mines, Raymond Savoie. When he was appointed, Savoie declared that he and his wife had liquidated their entire portfolio of mining stock. Yet it turned out that his spouse had held on to some shares in her family's company and that the company had received over $300,000 in government contracts and subsidies, some of which were awarded without tender. However, the shares in question apparently did not surpass the 5 per cent limit set forth in the directives issued by Bourassa, and the company was the only firm capable of providing the equipment needed. In addition, the minister affirmed that he got rid of the stock as soon as he learned of its existence. The ways in which the government and the opposition commented on this affair clearly illustrate their different philosophies. 'When you decide to go into politics, you must also decide to stop doing business for a while', maintained Jacques Brassard, the PQ MNA from Lac-Saint-Jean. 'We can't limit politics to bachelors and orphans', commented Robert Bourassa ironically.[76]

The most important affair was that which called in question the rules for awarding government contracts. During the 1989 election campaign, *La Presse* and the PQ accused the Liberal government and Hydro-Québec of having organized a system of favouritism to benefit friends of the Liberal Party. They produced lists of major contracts that had been given, without tender, to businesses that were allegedly tied to the Liberal Party.[77] The ex-treasurer of the Liberal Party, Tommy d'Errico, was apparently an important link in the network of favouritism.[78] In addition, the Chair of the Agricultural Land Protection Commission, Pierre-Luc Blain, was suspected of having favoured a Liberal Party financier by authorizing a zoning change that raised the value of the financier's land.

Once re-elected, Bourassa went to lengths to nip allegations of corruption in the bud. He created a committee to study the awarding of government contracts. To strengthen the credibility of this committee, he appointed as its chair Louis Bernard, former secretary-general under the Parti Québécois, and a man well known for his ties to the PQ. After six months of study, the committee produced a report listing some forty recommendations, directed primarily at tightening controls on the selection committees that chose firms. On the whole, however, the report was positive. It said Quebec's system of awarding contracts compared favourably with contemporary practices elsewhere.[79]

Matters of agricultural zoning have challenged the integrity of the government. In 1991, a commissioner on the Agricultural Land Protection Commission, Gaston Meunier, had to wait six months to have his contract renewed just when he had to render decisions concerning applications formulated by leaders in the Liberal Party.[80] In 1992, two senators and a financier linked to the Liberal Party obtained, under questionable criteria, an advantageous change in the zoning of their land on the island of Laval.

We can conclude, therefore, that there were more scandals under the Liberals than under the Parti Québécois, but that there has been no return to systematic favouritism and patronage.

Conclusion

Comparative studies confirm that definitions of ethical issues vary substantially from one country to another and from one government to another.[81] Quebec's originality lies in its history of striking contrasts. Nowhere else has a government moved so quickly—in barely twenty years—from one extreme to the other, from systematic patronage and widespread conflicts of interest to a rigorous regime of controls over official behaviour.

Nationalism is a key factor in shaping Quebec's changing approach to government ethics. The nationalist aspect of patronage is specific to Quebec, and parallels cannot easily be drawn between Quebeckers and the American big city 'bosses' who flourished in cities with large numbers of immigrants.[82] Duplessis used nationalism to support his system of government, but Lévesque did the same in his battle to purify Quebec politics. Duplessis invoked the collective identity of French-Canadians to justify his favouritism. With Lévesque, purification was undertaken in the name of bringing a nation into the modern world.

In 1985, the return to power of the Liberals—a party with close ties to business—meant that Quebec's approach to government ethics lost some of its originality. The rules were relaxed and thus became more similar to those found elsewhere. Gone is the time when ministers could not own stock traded on the market or hold shares in businesses with government contracts. Practices that are common elsewhere, such as the use of blind trusts and the right to do business with the government within certain restrictions, are now in force in Quebec.

What about the future? The next major issue may be the relationship between the government and its top bureaucrats and advisers in the aftermath of the 1992 referendum campaign. We now know the impact of the intentional and unintentional revelations by Premier Bourassa's close advisers on his campaign. First, a private conversation between deputy minister of Canadian affairs Diane Wilhelmy and Bourassa's constitutional adviser André Tremblay, over

Tremblay's cellular phone, was recorded and sent to the media. In the conversation, both senior advisers complained that Bourassa had 'caved in' during the negotiations. Wilhelmy's lawyers tried to prevent the publication of the conversation by requesting an injunction. But this was a poor strategy since the conversation was published outside Quebec. Second, André Tremblay's confidential talk to a commission of the Quebec Chamber of Commerce was also published. Tremblay said that Bourassa was so tired at one point in the negotiations that he was unable to speak in English. Third, confidential reports written during the negotiations were published by the magazine *L'Actualité*. A leak allowed *L'Actualité* to get its hands on explosive documents showing that Bourassa's close advisers did not support his compromises in pursuit of a constitutional agreement. Leaders of the 'No' forces used these revelations to challenge Bourassa's credibility during the contentious referendum campaign.

A common view was that this succession of indiscretions and leaks was unacceptable but explainable. It was explainable by the considerable gap between Bourassa's positions before the negotiations and their outcomes. For example, his own party's constitutional platform, the Allaire Report, requested twenty-two exclusive jurisdictions for the Quebec government, but the Charlottetown Accord provided only a modest devolution of powers to the provinces. Some advisers got the impression that they had been mocked by Premier Bourassa. They were unable to refrain from expressing their frustration.[83]

These events raise issues about the role of a permanent, non-partisan senior civil service. Some observers blamed Bourassa for retaining, as key constitutional advisers, officials appointed under the Parti Québécois. Usually, the reverse happens: premiers are blamed for politicizing the bureaucracy by filling top positions with partisan or political appointees. Bourassa was criticized for just this practice a few years before the referendum.[84] In the search for an equilibrium between the goverment's concern to work in confidence with advisers who share its view and the need to maintain a professional and neutral civil service, one may expect the debate to continue.

This episode may also focus debate on 'whistle-blowing', an issue that has seldom been debated in Quebec. The civil service code of ethics says that if a public servant is given an order that goes against his conscience, he must inform his superiors and, if possible, be relieved. An example is that of a Crown prosecutor who asked not to take part in proceedings against people accused of illegal abortions because he himself supported abortion.[85]

Until now, Quebec's ethical agenda has not been extended far beyond the perennial questions of conflict of interest and patronage. There is very little scrutiny in Quebec of the private lives of public officials. Quebeckers are reluctant to probe officials' private lives. A recent exception is the case of Robert Dutil, minister for family mattters, who was living in a family commune that advocated values conflicting with the family policies that his government wished to promote. This led the premier to move him to another department.[86]

The most pressing matter for the 1990s is post-employment mobility, which is also largely unexplored territory in Quebec. Current rules apply to current politicians and civil servants, and do limit their career opportunities after leaving public employment. The civil service code of ethics says that any civil servant who negotiates with a firm to settle a litigious matter in the name of the government *and* to secure future employment at the firm is in conflict of interest.[87] But nothing is said of post-employment conduct *per se*.

This situation reveals another contrast in Quebec's path in public sector ethics: the contrast between the detailed and demanding rules about various conflicts of interest and the vacuum about the regulation of post-employment mobility. A Quebec minister or senior civil servant can now leave the government to work for a private firm with no legal restrictions whatsoever, even if he uses confidential information gleaned when working for the government to benefit the firm. This raises concerns about the government's impartiality, the use of information, and favouritism among élites. An unfair access to important information may be given to private firms or groups. The lack of regulation may encourage officials to act, while in office, so that people in government or the private sector will be indebted to them.

Quebec has no post-employment restrictions similar to those used in the United States since 1978, where there is a lifetime ban on all representational activities in which former officials have been involved in 'personally and substantially'. A two-year ban also exists for matters over which an official has exercised a general administrative authority without having been involved personally and substantially. Similar restrictions apply in France, with no more practical success than in the United States.[88] In Canada, the federal, Ontario, Manitoba, British Columbia, and Alberta governments employ restrictions inspired by the American example.[89]

Recent scandals involving ex-officials have drawn attention to ethical problems created by the links between the élite of the public and private sectors in Quebec.[90] Mario Bertrand, Premier Bourassa's chief of staff for five years, became vice-president of the Steinberg grocery chain after playing a major role in the transaction by which the Caisse de dépôt, a large Quebec government corporation managing public insurance funds, gave businessman Michel Gaucher the money to buy Steinberg. Another noteworthy case was that of Pierre Fortier, who, as a minister, helped put through a law that was very favourable to the Mouvement Desjardins, a Quebec bank, and then went on to head one of the Mouvement's major subsidiaries. Critics can easily interpret such appointments as rewards for a job well done for the private sector employer while the individual was a public official. The appearance of conflict of interest might prompt a debate on the need to regulate the movement of officials between the public and private sectors.

This issue is likely to become salient at a time when 'Quebec Inc.' is a popular concept. That is the idea that a compact élite enables Quebec to foster cooperation, and to cope with international competition. But this potential strength may become a weakness if close ties between former politicians and business lead to ethically contentious relationships and practices.

Notes

The authors are indebted to Léon Dion, James Iain Gow, John W. Langford, Vincent Lemieux, Louis Massicotte, Sharon Sutherland, and Allan J. Tupper for comments on an earlier version of this paper, and to Louis Clavet, Bernard Gauthier, André Larocque, and Edith Skewes-Cox for their contributions at various stages of research.

1 Kenneth Kernaghan and David Siegel, *Public Administration in Canada: A Text* (Toronto: Methuen, 1987): 451-62; Michael Starr and Mitchell Sharp, *L'éthique dans le secteur public: Rapport du groupe de travail sur les conflits d'intérêts* (Ottawa: Ministre des Approvisionnements et Services Canada, 1984): 118-54.

2 For a short review, see Léon Dion, *Les intellectuels au temps de Duplessis*, Part I, chapter IV, section 10: 'Favoritisme' (Québec: Presses de l'Université Laval, forthcoming).

3 Pierre Elliott Trudeau, 'Some Obstacles to Democracy in Quebec', *Canadian Journal of Economics and Political Science* 24 (1958): 297-311.

4 Jeffrey Simpson, *Spoils of Power: The Politics of Patronage* (Toronto: HarperCollins, 1988): 146.

5 Ibid.: 195-216.

6 James Iain Gow, *Histoire de l'administration publique québécoise, 1867-1970* (Montréal: Presses de l'Université de Montréal, 1986).

7 Vincent Lemieux and Raymond Hudon, *Patronage et politique au Québec: 1944-1972* (Montréal: Boréal, 1975): 40.

8 Ibid.: 123-5.

9 Ralph Heintzman, 'The Political Culture of Quebec, 1840-1960', *Canadian Journal of Political Science* 16 (1983): 33.

10 Gow, *Administration publique*: 71-2.

11 Lemieux and Hudon, *Patronage et publique*: 136-40.

12 Heintzman: 16.

13 Gow, *Administration publique*: 292; also 72 (our translation).

14 Lemieux and Hudon, *Patronage et politique*: 156.

15 Quoted in Mario Cardinal, Vincent Lemieux, and Florian Sauvageau, *Si l'Union nationale m'était comptée . . .* (Montréal: Boréal, 1978): 185.

16 Simpson, *Spoils of Power*: 203.

17 Heintzman, *Political Culture*: 15; Trudeau (above, n.3): 301.

18 Lemieux and Hudon, *Patronage et politique*: 129-30.

19 Simpson, *Spoils of Power*: 204.

20 Roch Bolduc, 'Les questions d'éthique dans les années 1980', *Administration publique du Canada* 24 (1981): 201.

21 Alfred Hardy, *Patronage et patroneux* (Montréal: Éditions de l'homme, 1979).

22 Ibid.: 44 (our translation).

23 Ibid.: 122 (our translation).

24 Heintzman, *Political Culture*: 17.

25 See the *Legislature Act*, SRQ 1925, C-3, art. 75.

26 Jacques Bourgault, *Les administrateurs d'Etat des ministères du Gouvernement du Québec. 1867-1985* (manuscript, Paris: Institut d'études politiques de Paris, 1985): 157.

27 Gow, *Administration publique*: 73 (our translation).

28 Ibid.: 154.

29 Ibid.: 274-7; Howard A. Scarrow, 'Civil Service Commissions in the Canadian Provinces', *The Journal of Politics* 19 (1957): 241-2.
30 Lemieux and Hudon, *Patronage et politique*: 123.
31 Ibid.: 134-5.
32 Ibid.: 134; Pierre Laporte, 'Les élections ne se font pas avec des prières', *Le Devoir*, a series of articles published in October and November 1956; André Laurendeau, 'La politique provinciale', *Le Devoir*, a series of articles published in July and August 1956; Gérard Dion and Louis O'Neil, *Le Devoir*, a series of articles published in July and August 1956.
33 Gow, *Administration publique*: 170.
34 Hardy, *Patronage et patroneux*.
35 John M. Allswang, 'Richard J. Daley: America's Last Boss', in Paul M. Green and Melvin G. Hochi, eds, *The Mayors. The Chicago Political Tradition* (Carbondale and Edwardsville: Southern Illinois University Press, 1987): 161-2.
36 Heintzman, *Political Culture*: 18.
37 Ibid.: 38
38 Michel Lévesque, 'Historiographie des causes de la défaite du Parti libéral du Québec lors de l'élection du 5 juin 1966', in Robert Comeau, Michel Lévesque, and Yves Bélanger, eds, *Daniel Johnson: rêve d'égalité et projet d'indépendance* (Québec: Presses de l'Université du Québec, 1991): 131-4.
39 André Gélinas, *Les parlementaires et l'administration au Québec* (Québec: Presses de l'Université Laval, 1969): 194-5.
40 Gow, *Administration publique*: 325.
41 Cardinal, Lemieux, and Sauvageau, *Si l'Union nationale m'était comptée . . .* : 117; Vincent Lemieux, 'Un parti en rémission: l'Union nationale sous Daniel Johnson', in Robert Comeau, Michel Lévesque, et Yves Bélanger, eds, *Daniel Johnson: rêve d'égalité et projet d'indépendance* (Québec: Presses de l'Université du Québec, 1991): 109-21.
42 *Civil Service Act* 1969, art. 65b; Marcel Masse, 'Pourquoi un ministère de la Fonction publique?', in James Iain Gow, *Administration publique québécoise. Textes et documents* (Montréal: Beauchemin, 1970).
43 *Civil Service Act*, 1965, art. 19.
44 Lemieux and Hudon, *Patronage et politique*: 53.
45 Gow, *Administration publique*: 325.
46 Louis-Gilles Francoeur, 'Le Président de la fonction publique Yvon Saindon a été promu par persuasion', *Le Soleil*, 24 Jan. 1975: 1.
47 Regulation 74-317, under the *Civil Service Act*, S.Q. 1965, ch. 14.
48 Maurice Pinard and Richard Hamilton, 'The Parti Québécois Comes to Power: An Analysis of the 1976 Québec Election', *Canadian Journal of Political Science* 11 (1978): 739-75.
49 Quebec, National Assembly, *Debates*, 9 March 1977: 160 (our translation).
50 For a detailed description of the obligations of Quebec civil servants, see René Dussault and Louis Borgeat, *Administrative Law: A Treatise*, 2nd ed., vol. 2 (Toronto: Carswell, 1988): 123-37.
51 Louis Massicotte, 'Party Financing in Quebec. An Analysis of the Financial Reports of Parties 1977-79', in F. Leslie Seidle, ed., *Provincial Party and Election Finance in Canada*, Royal Commission on Electoral Reform and Party Financing and Canada Communication Group, vol. 3 (Toronto and Oxford: Dundurn Press, 1991): 3-38.

52 Robert Boily, *Le financement des partis politiques et des candidats dans nos sociétés démocratiques* (manuscript, Montréal: Université de Montréal, 1990).

53 Rapport Pominville, *Rosalie et les fournisseurs* (Québec: Les Publications du Québec, 1986): 17-18.

54 Jean-Pierre Beaud, 'Hiérarchie partisane et sélection sociale: l'exemple du Parti québécois', in Vincent Lemieux, ed., *Personnel et partis politiques au Québec* (Montréal: Boréal, 1982): 229-52.

55 See the declaration in the House of the PQ MNA from Saint-Jean, 29 April 1986, Commission permanente de l'Assemblée nationale: CL-167.

56 Gow, *Administration publique*: 318-19; Evelyn Gagnon, 'Jean Marchand, au Conseil central des syndicats de Québec: Le patronage mène au salaire de "crève-faim" des fonctionnaires', *Le Devoir*, 6 May 1963: 1; François Trépanier, 'Nous poursuivrons le gouvernement s'il ne met pas fin au 'patronage'—le syndicat des fonctionnaires', *La Presse*, 29 Oct. 1966: 2; Jean-Luc Duguay, 'Un foyer de patronage et de pots-de-vin? Le syndicat des fonctionnaires demande une enquête publique sur le ministère des transports', *Le Devoir*, 27 Aug. 1970: 1.

57 Rapport Martin-Bouchard, *Rapport de la Commission d'étude et de consultation sur la révision du régime des négociations collectives dans les secteurs public et parapublic* (Québec: Bibliothèque nationale du Québec, 1978).

58 Scarrow (above, n.29): 245.

59 Jacques Bourgault and Stéphane Dion, 'Haute fonction publique et changement de gouvernement au Québec. Le cas des sous-ministres en titre (1976-1989)', *Politique* 19 (1991): 82-106; Seymour Martin Lipset, *Agrarian Socialism: The Cooperative Commonwealth Federation in Saskatchewan* (Berkeley: University of California Press, 1950).

60 Denis Lessard, 'Louis Bernard estime que le cas Alepin constitue un conflit d'intérêts', *La Presse*, 8 Feb. 1990: B1.

61 René Lévesque, *Memoirs* (Toronto: McClelland & Stewart, 1986): 163, 286.

62 Ibid.: 286.

63 Ibid.: 316

64 Ibid.: 316.

65 Claude Charron, *Désobéir* (Montréal: VLB, 1983).

66 Claude Morin, 'Moi, Claude Morin, informateur de la GRC', *Le Devoir*, 8 May 1992: B-8.

67 Raymond Giroux, 'C'est dur pour le moral', *Le Soleil*, 9 May 1992: A20; Gilles Lesage, 'Qui joue avec le feu s'y brûle', *Le Devoir*, 9 May 1992: A10; Pierre O'Neil, 'Parizeau blâme Claude Morin. Le président du PQ reproche à l'ex-ministre d'avoir accepté l'argent de la GRC', *Le Devoir*, 9 May 1992: A1.

68 Lévesque, *Memoirs*: 300.

69 Normand Provencher, 'Selon Jean-Roch Boivin, ancien chef de Cabinet de René Lévesque, Claude Morin n'a pas eu le choix de démissionner', *Le Soleil*, 15 May 1992: A4; Michel Venne, 'Un proche de Lévesque dément la version de Morin: Lévesque a demandé sa démission en 1981 à cause de ses liens avec la GRC', *Le Devoir*, 14 May 1992: A1.

70 Gilles Normand, 'Le PQ verse à une oeuvre de charité l'argent de la GRC qu'il a reçu de Claude Morin', *La Presse*, 19 June 1992: A9.

71 Simpson, *Spoils of Power*: 196.

72 Rapport Pominville: 135-46.

73 Normand Delisle, 'Raymond Savoie ignorait les intérêts financiers de sa famille', *Le Devoir*, 10 Sept. 1990: A2.

74 *Debates*, 22 Oct. 1987: 9212 (our translation).

75 *Debates*, 14 June 1989: 6673 (our translation).

76 Bernard Descôteaux, 'Le PQ reproche à Bourassa sa tolérance excessive: il serait trop indulgent en matière de conflits d'intérêts', *Le Devoir*, 16 Sept. 1988: 3; André Forgues, 'Entorse à la directive sur les conflits d'intérêts par le ministre Savoie: Brassard déplore l'indulgence abusive de Bourassa', *Le Soleil*, 16 Sept. 1988: A8.

77 Pierre Gravel, 'Après le réseau d'Errico, le réseau Bibeau: le PQ accuse le conseiller de Bourassa d'être au coeur d'un système de favoritisme lié à Hydro', *La Presse*, 20 Sept. 1989: B1.

78 André Pépin and Denis Lessard, 'Tommy d'Errico a violé le code d'éthique du PLQ, quoi qu'en dise Robert Bourassa', *La Presse*, 28 June 1989: A1.

79 Rapport Bernard, *L'efficacité dans la transparence. Rapport du groupe de travail sur les processus d'octroi de contrats du gouvernement* (Québec: Publications du Québec, 1990): 51.

80 Réjean Lacombe, 'Commission de protection du territoire agricole: Gaston Meunier demeure commissaire', *Le Soleil*, 28 Aug. 1992: B3.

81 John A. Rohr, 'Ethical Issues in French Public Administration: A Comparative Study', *Public Administration Review* 51 (1991): 283-97; Andrew Stark, 'Public-Sector Conflict of Interest at the Federal Level in Canada and the U.S.: Differences in Understanding and Approach', *Public Administration Review*, forthcoming.

82 Vincent Lemieux, *Le patronage politique: une étude comparative* (Québec: Presses de l'Université Laval, 1977): 154.

83 Lysiane Gagnon, 'Des faits troublants', *La Presse*, 20 Oct. 1992: B3.

84 Bourgault and Dion (above, n.59).

85 Québec, Ministère du Conseil exécutif, *L'éthique dans la fonction publique québécoise* 1990: 24.

86 Jacques Dumais, 'Malgré son adhésion à la Cité écologique de l'ère du Verseau, Dutil réfute les allégations de conflit d'intérêts', *Le Soleil*, 6 Oct. 1988: A8.

87 Québec, Ministère du Conseil exécutif: 28.

88 Rohr (above, n.81): 285-7.

89 John W. Langford, 'Moonlighting and Mobility', *Canadian Public Administration* 34 (1991): 62-72.

90 Lysiane Gagnon, 'Retour d'ascenseur', *La Presse*, 3 Feb. 1990: B3.

5

Ian Stewart

Despoiling the public sector?

The case of Nova Scotia

'Ethics dominated Nova Scotia politics in 1988.'[1] So read the year-end headline in the Halifax *Chronicle-Herald*. In a province where public sector corruption has long been regarded as an unpleasant, but inevitable, fact of political life, such a summation might seem surprising. Nevertheless, even by Nova Scotian standards, 1988 was a particularly scandal-ridden year for Premier John Buchanan's long-serving Conservative administration. One cabinet minister was forced to resign amid charges of influence-peddling, while two others were accused of misleading the legislature. Two more Tory MLAs were found guilty in the courts, one of improperly releasing confidential information and the second of cheating on expense accounts. As a backdrop, Nova Scotians were treated almost daily to a royal commission's revelations of improprieties in the provincial justice system. Nevertheless, Nova Scotia voters dutifully went to the polls in September 1988 and re-elected the Tory government (albeit with a reduced majority). Even leaving aside the usual difficulties in psephological interpretation, this colossal indifference to a litany of ethical shortcomings might have been taken as definitive confirmation that 'anything goes' in Nova Scotia political life. Such a conclusion, however, might well have been unwarranted; it now appears that Nova Scotia's public sector ethics are entering a period of transition. Two years after his final electoral triumph, Premier Buchanan was forced from office in disgrace and was succeeded by Donald Cameron, a man apparently dedicated to cleaning up at least some aspects of the province's politics. However, Cameron's Conservatives were defeated by the Liberals in the 1993 provincial general election. The new premier John Savage is also committed to achieving higher ethical standards in government. Nova Scotia thus serves as a fascinating laboratory in which to test both the limits and potentialities of political leadership.

Students of Nova Scotia politics speak with a single voice when discussing the corruption of that province's public sector. As far back as the pre-Confederation era, states Murray Beck, Nova Scotia politics has been dominated by a struggle between 'the Ins and the Outs', a struggle 'for place, power, and the spoils of

90

office'.[2] Other observers echo Beck's words; Rand Dyck notes, for example, that one might have expected a 'greater degree of political sophistication and morality in Nova Scotia than in other Atlantic provinces but this does not appear to be the case', and that 'there is frequent evidence of political patronage and corruption'.[3] In a similar vein, Jeffrey Simpson asserts that in Nova Scotia 'the rush for spoils' has overwhelmed any 'isolated expressions of dissent',[4] while Peter Kavanagh describes provincial voters as 'open to moral suasion, patronage, hoodwinking or a combination thereof'.[5] Clearly, there exists a conventional wisdom about the nature of Nova Scotia politics, a conventional wisdom that stresses that the central political question is not 'Whose vision of the good will prevail?', but rather 'Who gets the swag?'.

Before highlighting the ethical issues that have dominated Nova Scotia politics over the last decade, some conceptual clarification is required. In one sense, there is an ethical component to every decision (and non-decision) of the state; no policy exists in an ethical vacuum. This article, however, will not consider the ethics of Nova Scotia's health care system, forest management programs, and so on. Nor will it address the wider ethical implications of the existing liberal-democratic regime. Instead, we shall concentrate our attention on the conduct of political and bureaucratic actors that is either manifestly or potentially corrupt. Admittedly, there are countless definitions of political corruption in the literature. Here, we will be using the term broadly. All office holders have a fiduciary relationship with the public; therefore, any violation of that public interest for any special advantage (whether material, partisan, or otherwise) will be deemed to be corrupt.[6]

Some problems remain, of course. Neither 'public interest' nor 'special advantage' are as self-explanatory as might be hoped. Many public interests exist; which specific public interests are office holders compelled to advance? Is it corrupt behaviour, for example, if ministers of the Crown vigorously pursue the particular interest of their constituency or their region?[7] Nor is it always possible to disentangle the public interest from special advantage. It is hardly surprising that office holders (especially those who have been elected to their posts) have much in common with their constituents. A largely agricultural district may well send a farmer to the legislature. Can that representative legitimately advance his or her constituents' interests when, by so doing, his or her private interests are simultaneously being advanced? Some observers take a hard line on this question. 'The public interest', asserts Jean-Pierre Kingsley, 'could be abused equally where the private interests of an office holder coincide with the public interest so as to mesh together, with the result that in serving the public purpose the individual benefits privately as well.'[8] Others, however, consider such a strict interpretation to be impractical. As United States Senator Robert Kerr once noted: 'If everyone abstained on the grounds of personal interest, I doubt if you could get a quorum in the United States Senate on any subject.'[9] One final conundrum is worthy of note. Most liberal democracies permit the private funding of aspirants for elected office. This means, however, that while it is universally regarded as corrupt for a businessman to give money to a civil servant, 'the same amount of money given to a politician's campaign fund may "buy" just as much influence over government decisions, but [be deemed to be] quite proper.'[10] There are some obvious parallels between the two scenarios; are they both, therefore, corrupt?

Some analysts have responded to these complexities by rejecting a simple dichotomy between corrupt and non-corrupt. Arnold Heidenheimer, for instance, speaks of corruption as being either black, grey, or white,[11] while Peters and Welch introduce a number of conditions that permit them to isolate 'gradients of corruption'.[12] While not denigrating their efforts, it is apparent that such conceptual finery is not especially relevant to the present analysis. Those in other jurisdictions may well profit from considering, for example, the dubious propriety of moonlighting by public sector employees.[13] By traditional Nova Scotian standards, however, such an activity is relatively innocuous, and to expend resources on its regulation would be akin to searching for a can of insect repellant while trapped in a burning elevator. Over the past decade, in short, the Nova Scotia public sector has been bedevilled by behaviour that *all* would agree was corrupt.

In the subsequent discussion, we will discuss seven different types of corrupt conduct. Three of these (patronage, pork-barrelling, and petty electoral corruption) are intimately linked to partisanship, while two of them (fraud and the improper use of confidential information) are more individualistic. Two final forms of corrupt behaviour (influence-peddling and conflict of interest) can be, but are not necessarily, rooted in the operation of party politics. The breadth of corrupt conduct that will be outlined in the succeeding pages should serve to confirm that, at least until very recently, ethical standards were remarkably low in the Nova Scotia public sector.

Patronage

Patronage, defined herein as the giving of employment, grants, contracts, and other government perquisites on the basis of partisan affiliation, has a long history in Nova Scotia. From Joseph Howe on, provincial governments have deemed it appropriate to reward their friends and punish their enemies. As a result, elections have taken on a special significance in Nova Scotia; for many citizens, their short-term material circumstances have hung in the balance on voting day. Those who have had the good foresight or the good fortune to support the winning party have had the opportunity to be employed as game wardens, liquor store employees, highway workers, gravel haulers, and so on; those lacking in political acumen or luck have been shut out. Opposition parties may have railed against these undemocratic practices, but their subsequent behaviour in office has suggested that envy, rather than moral outrage, underlay their complaints.

Are such practices corrupt, at least as we have defined the term? Clearly, parties employ patronage in order to secure a 'special advantage'; by so doing, must they compromise 'the public interest'? In a few isolated instances, perhaps not. If, for example, a vacancy occurs in the public sector through normal means (such as retirement), there is no discernible impact on the public interest if, among two or more equally qualified candidates, a known supporter of the governing party is selected. At least in Nova Scotia, however, patronage politics have traditionally run much deeper than this. Vacancies have been *created* in order that there can be *partisan* hirings *irrespective* of qualifications. Such a system must breed injustice, instability, and fear and cannot, therefore, be construed as being in the public interest.

The effectiveness of patronage is, of course, open to dispute. Unless the spoils are widely distributed, there is always the risk that patronage politics will alienate more electors than it satisfies. Nevertheless, it is worth noting the relative longevity of most Nova Scotia governments; on only five occasions since 1882, in fact, has an incumbent administration been defeated at the polls.

Inevitably, the complexities associated with administering a range of highly technical government programs has undercut some of the worst features of the spoils system. Agronomists, social workers, marine biologists, and the like cannot be hired and fired on the basis of partisanship. In fact, David Bellamy has gone so far as to conclude that there is now 'less utilization of patronage in Nova Scotia than elsewhere in the region' and that 'the provincial bureaucracy is largely staffed through the operation of the merit principle'.[14] A more systematic analysis of civil service hiring, however, belies Bellamy's contentions. The Civil Service Commission may screen potential job applicants, but Management Board, an Executive Council committee responsible for overseeing the government's internal operations, has been omnipresent, and the final recommendation on hiring has come from the relevant minister's office, a recommendation that the Commission has invariably accepted. Such a procedure, as J.K. Love notes, has left 'room for a good deal of political influence'.[15] In fact, Love maintains not only that the Nova Scotia Civil Service Commission has been the weakest in the Atlantic region but also that, since 1979, it has 'lost any claim to independence'.[16]

Premier John Buchanan's twelve-year stewardship confirms Love's analysis. Immediately upon winning office in 1978, the Conservatives fired 26 of 35 highway superintendents, as well as 76 of 216 supervisors, changed the ad agency for the provincial tourism department and the legal account for Nova Scotia Power Corporation, and began to make partisan appointments at all levels of the justice system.[17] From Finance Minister Greg Kerr allegedly screening all seasonal workers at a provincially-backed theme park[18] to Policy Board chair Terry Donahoe punctuating a search for a new provincial ombudsman with the remark there was nothing wrong with appointing qualified 'political friends' to such postings,[19] it seemed that no job was too small or too large to escape from the network of patronage appointments. When it briefly appeared that the Buchanan administration might be defeated in the 1988 provincial election, a host of mid-campaign appointments to government boards and commissions ensued.[20] To assert that, by 1990, there was not a single prominent Conservative who had not received some measure of government largesse would be rash. To demonstrate otherwise, however, would be difficult.

Table 1 Road construction expenditures by proportion of Government members per county (1959-88)

		Proportion of Government members per county		
Road construction expenditures		*None of the county's MLAs are in the governing party*	*Some of the county's MLAs are in the governing party*	*All of the county's MLAs are in the governing party*
Lowest	1.	30.9	12.4	17.4
	2.	26.8	19.5	17.0
	3.	25.8	14.2	20.7
	4.	12.4	27.4	20.4
Highest	5.	4.1	26.5	24.4
N*		97	113	270

Lambda = .07

* The total number of cases is 480 (that is, the annual data on road construction expenditures is included for each of the sixteen non-metropolitan counties of Nova Scotia over a 30-year period).

Source: Bruce Beaton, 'Potholes and Patronage: An Empirical Analysis', unpublished Honours thesis, Acadia University, 1992: 8.

Pork-barrelling

Unlike patronage, pork-barrelling cannot be targeted exclusively to party supporters; the indivisible nature of most public works (roads, wharves, and the like) renders them accessible to political opponents as well. Nevertheless, the practice of disproportionately concentrating such blessings in ridings held by government members of the legislature (or pork-barrelling, as it is commonly known) can still serve as a potent weapon of political advantage. Rewarding constituencies, rather than individuals on a partisan basis, favours relatively more political supporters than opponents, and provides government MLAs, but not their opposition counterparts, with impressive re-election portfolios. Pork-barrelling may, at times, be justified when there exists a coincidental, and fortuitous, overlap between the interests of the party and those of the public. In the long run, however, the spending of public monies on a basis that is not consistently linked to a criterion of public need must be injurious to the public interest.

Accusations of pork-barrelling have been a staple of Nova Scotia politics virtually since Confederation. In March 1985, for example, Opposition leader Vince MacLean charged that each Conservative cabinet minister and rural backbencher had access to one hundred thousand dollars for discretionary spending from the budget of the Department of Transportation.[21] Such charges, however, have been difficult to substantiate and some observers have claimed to detect a gradual decline in pork-barrelling. Hence, Murray Beck asserted in 1978 that 'the vast increase in highway expenditures has permitted—indeed, almost obliged—the government of the day to let its political opponents share in the benefits.'[22]

Unfortunately, a thorough analysis of Department of Transportation budgets between 1959 and 1988 does not support Beck's contention. While no public records have been kept of provincial road expenditures at the constituency level, this data has been maintained for each Nova Scotia county. Removing the urban (and, therefore, idiosyncratic) Cape Breton County and Halifax County from the discussion leaves sixteen counties, each with either one, two, or three provincial constituencies inside their boundaries.[23] As Table 1 reveals, there has been a clear relationship over the thirty-year period between the presence of at least some government MLAs and the extent of provincial road construction expenditures. Only 4.1 per cent of those counties that were entirely controlled by opposition MLAs were in the highest quintile of construction spending; the corresponding figure for the remaining counties was 25 per cent. Nor has this relationship varied significantly by county population, by county size, by party in office, or over time (although it has been strongest in the year immediately prior to an election). The relationship is not linear, since those counties that have some government MLAs seem to do as well as those that are entirely controlled by the dominant party, but it is unmistakable and, by most ethical standards, unconscionable. Beaton concludes his analysis of the matter by contrasting voting in provincial elections with betting on horse races:

> One makes the bet or fills out the ballot, and is a clear financial winner or loser when the race is over. Only in elections, however, is there such a strong material incentive to bet on the favourite.[24]

Corrupt electoral practices

Nova Scotia's political parties have long attempted to bend the province's electoral rules for partisan advantage. The notorious Electoral Franchise Act of 1931 provides a perfect illustration of this phenomenon. Designed to disenfranchise known supporters of the opposition, the act so mobilized the Liberals that it ultimately rebounded on its Conservative authors.[25] More successful was a recent Tory gerrymander that permitted them to defeat Liberal incumbent Bill Mac-Eachern 'who had been a thorn in their side' in Inverness South.[26] At the level of the individual candidate, corrupt practices have been largely confined to vote-buying, or 'treating' as it is euphemistically known throughout the region.

'Treating' may be on the decline elsewhere in the Maritimes.[27] Nevertheless, after the 1988 provincial election, two major vote-buying scandals erupted. The first involved long-time Liberal MLA Harold Huskilson of Shelburne. In April 1989, five of his party workers were convicted of bestowing either a bottle of liquor or up to twenty dollars in cash on prospective voters. Huskilson somehow managed to remain legally unscathed, although his funeral home had served as the workers' base of operations and he had earlier remarked that all parties 'bought votes with booze'.[28] Conservative delight over the affair soon abated, however, when a similar scandal ensnared lands and forests minister Chuck MacNeil. Again, party workers were convicted (on this occasion, for buying votes with driveway gravel) and, again, the candidate himself was not prosecuted (on this occasion, after the attorney general's office delayed referring the matter to a provincial county court judge until 9:45 of the evening the statute of limitations on election charges was to expire).[29] These transgressions may, of course, have been only two isolated events; alternatively, they may have been two particularly sloppy and ill-conceived instances of a significantly more pervasive phenomenon.

Releasing privileged information

In the modern era, most governments have vast data banks on many, if not all, of their citizens. This information may well have been gathered legitimately in the pursuit of a particular policy objective (such as the raising of tax revenue); it is widely regarded as improper, however, for the state to use this information for purposes other than for what it was designed. Unfortunately, Nova Scotia has been slow to recognize the ethical dangers inherent in such a situation. All other provinces (as well as the federal government) use statute law to ensure their employees do not disclose privileged information; only Nova Scotia relies simply on the wider common law obligation of confidentiality.[30]

This lax approach to privileged information was perfectly illustrated by two separate incidents in the final years of the Buchanan administration. In the first, Social Services Minister Edmund Morris, piqued by a critical editorial in a local newspaper, released information to reporters from the author's family benefits file (including details about an apparent discrepancy concerning the identity of her child's father). Morris was subsequently convicted of violating the provincial Freedom of Information Act, but not before his government-funded lawyer had argued in court that Morris had a 'duty' to release the information.[31] Convinced that this was merely a personal dispute between two individuals, Premier Buchanan did not ask an unrepentant Morris to tender his resignation.

The second occurrence of this type was even more controversial. At a June 1990 meeting of the Public Accounts Committee, former Government Services Deputy Minister Michael Zareski charged that Buchanan's administration was riddled with corruption. In response, Health Minister David Nantes released confidential information about a 1989 trip made by Zareski to a mental health clinic. Zareski, claimed Nantes, had left the clinic before his treatment was concluded.[32] The unstated implication was that Zareski's charges should not be regarded as credible because Zareski was not of sound mind. The courts, however, were unimpressed with these slurs; Nantes was convicted of violating both the province's Freedom of Information Act and the Health Services and Insurance Act.

Admittedly, it is not always those at the apex of the state who reveal confidential information. As the Zareski affair showed they can also be the 'victims'. Much has been written about the ethics of whistle-blowing by civil servants, and most of it is decidedly unsympathetic to the practice. F.F. Ridley declares that in the British parliamentary system, bureaucrats are 'non-persons as far as the law is concerned'.[33] Indeed, since the Crown is an abstraction embodied by ministers, 'no question of a higher loyalty to the state, a conflict of loyalties between state and government, need therefore arise'.[34] There can be no ethical justification for bureaucratic whistle-blowing, echoes secretary of the federal treasury board Ian Clark, because all obligations 'are discharged through the chain of accountability' up to the deputy minister and minister.[35] Nevertheless, even these analysts could probably concoct scenarios, however fanciful, that would justify whistle-blowing by a public servant. Kenneth Kernaghan and John W. Langford suggest four criteria, all of which must be met, before whistle-blowing could be deemed appropriate. There must be serious harm at stake, it must be supported by unequivocal evidence, it cannot be correctable through ordinary channels, and the whistle-blower must have reasonable grounds to assume that his or her disclosures will have some impact.[36] It should be noted that Zareski charged, among other things, that Premier Buchanan personally directed government contracts to his friends, improperly used government employees to work on his summer cottage, and received kickbacks from those doing business with the government. Would these extraordinary revelations satisfy the four conditions outlined above? Clearly, the stakes were high, Zareski's superiors were ostensibly implicated in the affair, and the matter ultimately played a critical role in the hounding from office of Premier Buchanan. Hence, leaving aside for the moment the fact that Zareski no longer was in the employ of the provincial government (a fact that admittedly does make some difference), one could only have reasonable doubts with respect to the second criteria, that of unequivocal evidence.

Fraud

From an ethical perspective, this is not a particularly interesting form of behaviour. Ultimately it reflects individual, rather than systemic, failings, although one might argue that these individual shortcomings are more likely to be made manifest in a pervasively corrupt context. Three members of John Buchanan's Conservative administration were found to have engaged in fraud; all three had cheated on their expense accounts. One, Malcolm MacKay, was defeated in the 1984 provincial election, when it was disclosed during the campaign that he had been receiving expenses as an out-of-town MLA although his residence lay within the 40-kilometre boundary used to distinguish between 'inside' and 'outside'

MLAs.[37] A second, Greg MacIsaac, was sentenced in 1988 to one year in jail for defrauding the province over a four-year period through his travel and accommodation claims;[38] John Buchanan's response to the matter was to take MacIsaac's chair out of the legislature and store it in the basement so that there would be no visible reminder of the transgression.[39]

The third miscreant did not disappear quietly into political oblivion. Culture Minister Billy Joe MacLean was also convicted (and fined $6,000) for cheating on his expense accounts. MacLean, however, resisted all suggestions that he should resign from the legislature (including those made by Premier Buchanan, a long-time friend and godfather to one of MacLean's children). When it became apparent that MacLean's dithering on the matter would enable him to use his MLA's stipend to pay his fine, Buchanan recalled the legislature, and in a one-day special session forced through *An Act Respecting Reasonable Limits for Membership in the House of Assembly*.[40] Under the terms of the act, anyone convicted of an indictable offence carrying a maximum punishment of greater than five years could not serve as an MLA until five years after the punishment was complete. Even this was not the end of the matter. MacLean succeeded in having the act overturned by the Supreme Court of Canada on the grounds that it unreasonably infringed on his democratic rights as a Canadian citizen, and successfully ran as an independent in the February 1987 by-election called to fill his vacant legislative seat. That a plurality of constituents in Inverness South would knowingly return to office an acknowledged forger may seem extraordinary; given the attention paid to the story by the national media, however, the by-election may well have been regarded by many of MacLean's Cape Breton constituents as an ideal opportunity to thumb their collective noses at both Halifax and Toronto. In the relative anonymity of the provincial election the following year, MacLean was defeated.

Influence-peddling

This is a complicated form of corruption since it normally requires the presence of three actors: someone outside the state who wishes a particular policy benefit, someone within the state who has the capacity to grant that benefit, and a third party who sells to the former his or her influence over the latter (although in some instances, the latter two parties may be one and the same). During the 1980s, there were three separate influence-peddling scandals, two of which were actually rooted in the previous decade.

The first of these revolved around the links between liquor companies, Liberal Party bagmen, and the provincial government of Gerry Regan. In order to ensure that the provincial liquor board would continue to list their products, brewers and distillers were advised to donate a share of their provincial sales to the coffers of the Liberal Party. For brewers, the amount was apparently two cents a case; for distillers, the corresponding fee was fifty cents.[41] Nor was this practice of 'tollgating' confined exclusively to the liquor industry. At both the 1983 and 1989 influence-peddling trials of Senator Irvine Barrow, the court was told of similar arrangements with respect to lawyers, contractors, and others providing services to the government.[42] Ultimately, two of Barrow's fundraising cohorts were found guilty of influence-peddling, but Barrow's earlier conviction was overturned on appeal.

The second such scandal actually spanned three decades. Roland Thornhill, who had run unsuccessfully for the Conservative leadership in 1971, amassed $140,000 in personal debts through the mid-1970s. When the Conservatives were victorious in the 1978 provincial election, Thornhill was named to the cabinet as minister of development, and a number of banks agreed in November 1979 to write off three-quarters of Thornhill's debt. Even before that time, there is evidence that at least one bank manager 'felt it was good to be nice to Mr Thornhill, as it would possibly help his position within the community as a banker to obtain business for the Royal Bank'.[43] Not surprisingly, the opposition parties objected to Thornhill's preferential treatment and claimed that 'a form of influence-peddling had taken place'.[44] Over the next decade, there were a number of byzantine developments in the case. The initial RCMP recommendation that a charge be laid against Thornhill was squelched by Attorney General Harry How and his deputy, Gordon Coles, but the matter resurfaced periodically until the January 1990 release of a royal commission report, which noted that Thornhill, among others, had benefited from the existence of a two-tiered system of justice in Nova Scotia.[45] Notwithstanding the evident cloud over his reputation, Thornhill entered the Tory leadership contest to succeed John Buchanan and narrowly lost in February 1991 to Donald Cameron, receiving 47 per cent of the votes on the third and final ballot.[46] Twelve days after the convention, Thornhill was finally charged by the RCMP over his banking activities of twelve years previously, but by the end of the year, the Crown had dropped all charges.

The final case of alleged influence-peddling was a by-product of the Zareski revelations of June 1990. In addition to implicating the premier in corrupt practices, Zareski noted that a number of the premier's friends, including Dartmouth lawyer Mark Cleary, had done remarkably little to merit the lucrative government contracts that they had received. Shortly thereafter, a masonry firm reported that Cleary had offered to use his close friendship with the premier to help them receive more government business, and, after a brief RCMP investigation, Cleary was charged with influence-peddling.[47]

Conflict of interest

Of all forms of corrupt behaviour, conflicts of interest have received by far the most analytical attention. An office holder is deemed to be in a conflict of interest situation if he or she has 'a personal or a private *pecuniary* interest sufficient to influence, or *appear to influence* the exercise of his (or her) public duties and responsibilities.'[48] Admittedly, some observers have attempted to expand this definition so that even such activities as influence-peddling fall under the conflict of interest rubric;[49] given that the former requires the involvement of two, or more commonly, three actors, while the latter needs only one, this conceptual elasticity should be resisted.[50]

What is striking about the Nova Scotia context is the relatively infrequency with which office holders have shaped the policies of the state so as directly to advance their own material interests. Other types of conflict of interest abound in Nova Scotia: a cabinet minister placing his girlfriend on the public payroll,[51] the premier ensuring that a fishing crony was able to sell to the province fifty thousand dollars worth of never-to-be-used, motorized toilet seat cover dispensers (a purchase subsequently described as a 'bum deal'),[52] the Speaker of the Legislature determining whether his brother had violated the rules of parliamentary procedure,[53] the minister of health having to approve the laying of charges against himself under the Health Services and Insurance Act.[54] Yet, aside from the unsubstantiated allegation of Michael Zareski that the premier himself was receiving kickbacks from certain government contracts, there is remarkably little evidence of Nova Scotia officials feathering their private nests through the performance of their public duties. Only with respect to the establishment of private trust funds for party leaders, a subject to which we will subsequently return, does a pressing concern over financial conflicts of interest seem warranted.

Clearly, the preceding pages have documented a depressing catalogue of recent public sector misconduct in Nova Scotia, a veritable cornucopia of corruption. Why should this be so? What are the characteristics of Nova Scotia that have permitted an unseemly quest for material advantage to imbue almost all aspects of political life? It is possible to extract two competing, but not completely unrelated, theories from the literature on Nova Scotia politics. The first emphasizes the nature of the provincial political culture. According to one analyst, people throughout the Maritimes possess 'the wrecker's mentality' in that they are 'patient and willing to wait for spoils'.[55] Others have observed that widespread electoral corruption in Nova Scotia is tolerated by 'the mores of the society'[56] and that even when confronted with evidence of improprieties, Nova Scotians have not been 'disposed to place blame upon individual politicians'.[57] Nova Scotia, it has frequently been emphasized, has a traditionalist political culture. A lax attitude towards public sector ethics, although gradually disappearing in other jurisdictions, has apparently continued to persist in Nova Scotia. Some may speak of the 'moral outrage' against the unethical conduct of both politicians and bureaucrats which was 'expressed world-wide by the public in the 1970s and 1980s',[58] but this moral outrage seemed to resonate only faintly in the Nova Scotia of Gerry Regan and John Buchanan.

One must be careful, of course, not to exaggerate the distinctive nature of Nova Scotia in this respect. In his classic study of rural Southern Italy, Edward Banfield traced the contours of a similar political culture, one he characterized as amoral familist. As in Nova Scotia, Banfield observed that his subjects tended to assume that public officials were corrupt, tended to use their franchise for short-term material gain, and tended to be indifferent to electoral appeals based on ideo-logy.[59] As in Nova Scotia, the pre-eminence of these orientations did little to heighten standards of public sector ethics. Admittedly, this is not the only type of political culture that can operate in this fashion; citizens of newly independent countries often have weak ties to the national community. Where the dominant corporate loyalties are to region, tribe, or family, the national state comes to be regarded in largely instrumental terms and concerns of public sector ethics are seen to be irrelevant.[60] There are echoes of this phenomenon in Nova Scotia, but they are relatively muted.

An alternative explanation for the apparently high incidence of public sector immorality in Nova Scotia is not cultural, but structural. Specifically, the under-developed nature of the private sector (at least by central Canadian standards) could tend disproportionately to push acquisitive behaviour into the realm of the provincial state. Hence, it has been observed that giving 'preferential treatment to political friends is often seen as a kind of social welfare that alleviates the effects of seasonal unemployment and uncertain economic prospects',[61] and that 'the temp-tation to reward party workers with civil service positions, particularly in depressed economic conditions [has been] too great to resist'.[62] Again, parallels can be found between Nova Scotia's circumstances and those that have elsewhere fostered public sector corruption. It is instructive, for example, that in developing countries the 'opportunities for the accumulation of wealth through private activity are limited' and that as a result, 'politics becomes the road to wealth, and those enterprising ambitions and talents which cannot find what they want in a business may yet do so in politics'.[63] And in nineteenth-century Britain, political corruption was much more prevalent among stagnant rather than prosperous communities.[64] In the modern era, where the state has the capacity to intervene (often in a discretionary fashion) in virtually all aspects of social life, some ethical problems are inevitable. These problems are likely to be compounded, however, in the absence of a dynamic private sector economy.

Still, one can only push this structural argument so far. As Table 2 makes clear, the proportion of the gross provincial product expended by the Nova Scotia state over the past five years is certainly not anomalous by Canadian standards. In fact, the state allocates a slightly smaller share of Nova Scotia's goods and services than is the provincial norm. Admittedly, the other Atlantic provinces that seem to be especially prone to instances of public misconduct are at the top end of the table. Nevertheless, there is no straightforward link between economic underdevelop-ment and a padded public sector.

Of course, the high level of public sector corruption in Nova Scotia might not be primarily rooted in some attribute of Nova Scotian society; given certain assumptions about the autonomy of the provincial state, it might well be wiser to look for shortcomings in either political leadership or in the regulatory regime that governs public sector behaviour in Nova Scotia. Certainly, many of the writings on the subject assume that changes within the state can lower the incidence of public sector corruption independently of any changes in society.

Putative ethical nostrums abound in the literature, from ethics agencies[65] to ethics commissioners[66] to greatly increased public sector salaries[67] (although exponents of this latter proposal might do well to consider the experience of such states as Gabon where legislators' zest for misconduct is unchecked by the fact that they earn more in a few months than a typical peasant does in a lifetime).[68] Relying on unwritten norms of ethical conduct has been manifestly unsuccessful in other jurisdictions;[69] much the same lesson can be extracted from the Nova Scotia experience. While the Criminal Code checks fraud, breach of trust, influence-peddling, and corrupt electoral practices, the law has, until recently, been essentially silent in the other areas of corrupt behaviour.

If changes within the Nova Scotia state can significantly reduce the level of public sector corruption, two things are required: stronger statutory regulation where the law can be effective, and cleaner political leadership where the law has clear limitations. Before 1987, for example, there were essentially no conflict of interest regulations for Nova Scotia MLAs. Although Premier Buchanan claimed in 1987 that such regulations were 'kind of hidden' throughout the House of Assembly Act, the only explicit conflict of interest rule in the statute was one that prohibited MLAs from simultaneously holding office and working for the government.[70] Eventually, the Buchanan government passed *An Act Respecting Conflict of Interest for Members of the House of Assembly and Members of the Executive Council.*[71] Under the terms of the act, all MLAs were required to file annually a statement of assets with a Nova Scotia Supreme Court trial division judge, who was responsible for investigating conflict of interest complaints and punishing any transgressors. Penalties under the act ranged from requesting an amendment in the MLA's statement of assets to declaring vacant the member's seat in the legislature. Opposition parties generally welcomed the legislation, but had two specific reservations.[72] First, they questioned whether judges, given the partisan nature of most judicial appointments in Nova Scotia, had the political independence necessary to police the act effectively. Second, they wondered why neither the MLAs' disclosure statements nor any disciplinary action taken under the act were to be made public. Instead, Nova Scotians were required to take the word of retired provincial Supreme Court Justice Thomas Coffin, who observed, after the legislation had been in force for a year, that he saw 'nothing suspicious' in any of the members' statement of assets.[73]

Justice Coffin may have imprudently assumed that all members had fully disclosed all assets. In 1991, it was revealed that Premier Buchanan had made a number of injudicious tax and real estate decisions and had been receiving monthly payments of $3,300 from a secret party trust fund to supplement his handsome salary as premier, payments that should have been included in his statement of assets.[74] Ultimately, it was ruled that, although Buchanan had clearly violated the intent of the legislation, he could not be disciplined since he was not a member of the legislature when the complaint was lodged against him.[75]

Given the foregoing, it is perhaps not surprising that Premier Buchanan never kept his oft-repeated pledge to introduce a code of political ethics. Admittedly, the efficacy of such codes is open to dispute;[76] nevertheless, Buchanan had declared in the 1988 campaign that the status quo was 'unacceptable' and that there was a pressing need for both an ethics code and an independent ethics council to investigate questionable conduct by public officials.[77] Neither had come into being by the time Buchanan left office.

In his first session as premier, however, Donald Cameron introduced a number of reforms in the realm of public sector ethics. Perhaps responding to the perception that expecting the Tories to 'clean up the justice system' was the equivalent of 'leaving the porch light on hoping that Jimmy Hoffa [would] make it home all right',[78] Cameron moved to have provincial judges selected by an independent body.[79] In addition, the 1991 session of the legislature enacted *An Act to Regulate Conduct in Order to Avoid Conflict of Interest in Government by Members and Government Employees Through Full and Open Disclosure*.[80] This statute had five major effects. First, MLAs (as well as their spouses and dependent children) were required to disclose in a *public* document all assets and sources of income. Second, MLAs and public servants were proscribed from participating in any decisions from which they might derive a personal benefit. Third, all political contributions over fifty dollars (including the identity of the donor) were to be made public. Fourth, MLAs and civil servants were prohibited from lobbying their former colleagues for a period of six months after leaving the public sector. Finally, authority for the prosecution of offences under the Elections Act was taken away from the partisan elections commission and given to a judge. This act

Table 2 Provincial Government expenditures as a percentage of Gross Provincial Product

Province	1986	1987	1988	1989	1990
Newfoundland	34.9	34.3	33.9	33.0	34.1
Prince Edward Island	31.3	32.4	31.9	31.8	31.4
Saskatchewan	26.8	26.3	27.4	26.8	27.4
New Brunswick	27.6	27.5	27.5	26.8	26.9
Manitoba	24.7	26.1	24.8	25.7	26.4
Quebec	26.4	24.4	23.9	24.1	25.0
Nova Scotia	24.7	24.4	24.5	24.4	24.3
Alberta	22.2	21.2	20.8	21.2	20.9
British Columbia	18.6	18.0	17.4	16.8	18.0
Ontario	18.8	18.8	18.8	15.4	16.3

Source: Statistics Canada, Provincial Economic Accounts, Catalogue 13-213, 1990.

Table 3 Assessment of their candidates' abilities by first ballot supporters
(Scale: 0-4)

Factor	Supporters' view of Callaghan	Supporters' view of Cameron	Supporters' view of McInnis	Supporters' view of Thornhill
Ability to win votes	1.76	3.24	3.35	3.36
Likeability	3.11	2.90	3.45	3.55
Good decision maker	2.95	3.57	3.11	3.36
Will help my area	2.22	2.74	3.23	3.27
A strong representative for this Province	2.66	3.68	3.31	3.40
Will appeal to women	2.51	2.90	3.10	2.78
Will appeal to youth	2.22	2.85	3.30	2.61
Will clean up politics	3.13	3.87	3.01	2.29

was further strengthened in the 1992 legislative session with amendments designed, first, to disclose the donors of all party trust funds (irrespective of when the donations were made), and second, to permit conflict of interest complaints to be made against former MLAs and bureaucrats for a period of up to two years after they have left the employ of the state.[81] The latter provision was designed to close what might be known as 'the Buchanan loophole'; the former, as we shall subsequently see, was designed to discomfort the Nova Scotia Liberal Party.

Yet not all matters of corrupt conduct are amenable to statutory regulation. In checking patronage and pork-barrelling, in particular, the reach of any law that is compatible with the basic principles of the British parliamentary system is likely to exceed its grasp. To control these abuses of power, clean political leadership is essential. This is not a strikingly original contention. Kernaghan has elsewhere stressed the virtues of relying 'on the ethical leadership provided by hierarchical superiors',[82] while Myrdal has acknowledged that 'it is quite hopeless to fight corruption if there is not a high degree of personal integrity at the top levels'.[83]

Does this leadership now exist in Nova Scotia? No unequivocal answer is possible. It is true that when Jeffrey Simpson, during the mid-1980s, was searching for two paragons of public sector virtue in Nova Scotia, he fastened upon Pat Hunt and Donald Cameron.[84] The former was a Conservative MLA who was elected in 1978, but who was denied his party's nomination in 1982 when he would not fire Liberal highway workers employed in his constituency. The latter was then an unknown Tory backbencher who had 'remained on the fringes of the Conservative caucus'[85] for his unwillingness to practise patronage politics in his constituency of Pictou East. Of course, that obscure backbencher is now premier with an opportunity to reform at least some of the province's political practices.

It is, moreover, suggestive that Cameron was able to win his party's top job without visibly compromising his views on corruption. Cameron initiated his leadership campaign with a commitment to clean up provincal politics, and repeatedly stressed that anyone who supported him in the hopes of receiving some sort of patronage plum was 'in for a rude shock'.[86] To emphasize the point, Cameron insisted that avowed Liberals were eligible to provide some of his campaign services,[87] and refused to dole out any free drinks at his hospitality suites.[88] Chastened by the fact that the party had fallen to a support level of 13 per cent in the polls before Premier Buchanan's escape to the relative safety of the Canadian Senate,[89] Conservative delegates responded positively to Cameron's apparent ethical probity. Since party activists have arguably the most to lose from a dramatic decline in the incidence of government patronage, their support for Cameron may seem somewhat surprising. Nevertheless, their enthusiasm for Cameron's anti-patronage campaign was confirmed by a post-convention survey partially undertaken by the author. As Table 3 reveals, Cameron's supporters gave him a 3.87 (out of 4) on his potential ability to 'clean up politics'; significantly, this is the highest score of any of the thirty-two entries in the table. Even those who voted for *other* candidates on the first ballot grudgingly gave Cameron a score of 2.93 on this dimension.

Admittedly, leadership has its limitations; Cameron could make little progress on this front if the overwhelming majority of Nova Scotians remained wedded to the virtues of patronage politics (although Cameron's ascension to the premiership would be even more improbable in such a context). Yet there is some evidence that Nova Scotians may be changing their orientation towards corrupt practices. Perhaps the most complete sounding of public opinion in the province was undertaken by the author in 1984.[90] When asked whether patronage was an acceptable part of the political process, Nova Scotians were ambivalent. While 44 per cent of the sample agreed that patronage was acceptable, 40 per cent disagreed with this position, with the final 16 per cent being unsure. Not all segments of Nova Scotia society held similar views on this question; those respondents who had at times lived outside Nova Scotia, or who had attended university, or whose self-designated social class was middle or upper were significantly less sympathetic to patronage than their less mobile, or less educated, or lower-class counterparts. Constructing two groups of polar opposites (that is, scrutinizing only those who have all three of the attributes associated with opposition to patronage and those who have none of them) should highlight this cleavage. Of the former group, 59 per cent were hostile to patronage practices; the corresponding figure for the latter was only 22 per cent. Intriguingly, only 4 per cent of the sample of privileged Nova Scotians, but fully 31 per cent of their less advantaged cohorts, were unable to judge the acceptability of patronage. This stark division, especially given the large numbers of undecided among the less privileged group, might be taken as evidence of a political culture in transition.

More recent survey results lend some credence to this speculation. Notwithstanding the opinions of the voters of Inverness South, a 1986 poll revealed that 88 per cent of Nova Scotians agreed with the decision to expel Billy Joe MacLean from the legislature.[91] And in 1991, 90 per cent of respondents to a newspaper survey described political patronage as a widespread problem in the province and 82 per cent declared that it had hurt Nova Scotians over the past fifty years.[92]

Finally, Vince MacLean's ill-fated tenure as leader of the provincial Liberal Party may suggest that there has been a change in the standard of ethical conduct expected of public officials. MacLean easily won the party leadership in 1986, and although the Liberals narrowly lost the 1988 provincial election, his stewardship seemed secure in the summer of 1990 with his party well ahead in public opinion polls and the Tories awash with charges of corruption. In October 1990, however, it was revealed that, like John Buchanan, MacLean's income as opposition leader was being supplemented (in this case, by almost $50,000 a year) from a secret party trust fund. MacLean's initial response to the disclosure was low-key; the additional salary was appropriate since he kept the fund's trustees at arm's length and since it went only to pay for the partisan component of his job.[93] Yet within a month, MacLean had backtracked; after initially indicating that he would continue to accept the income supplement, he then declared that he would only accept reimbursement for expenses.[94] For many Liberals, this concession was insufficient since much of the money contained in the trust funds had been raised through the nefarious toll-gating methods described earlier in the chapter, and since the funds, while designed 'to promote Liberalism', were not legally the property of the Liberal Party.[95] In short, the Liberal Party leader was being secretly financed with 'dirty money' controlled by outside sources.

Nevertheless, MacLean continued to defend the party's use of these trust funds throughout 1991. Only at the Liberals' February 1992 annual meeting did he call upon the party to sever all connections with the trust funds. 'The party must make a choice', he declared. 'We can continue to be seduced by trust funds that are outside the control of the party or we can aggressively pursue the more difficult road less travelled.'[96] The party concurred with MacLean's message, but then shot the messenger. They voted to take no additional monies from the trusts until an audit could determine how much of the funds were legitimately gathered, and then gave MacLean only 51 per cent support in a leadership review vote. Not surprisingly, MacLean resigned as leader shortly thereafter.

MacLean may have been too slow in responding to Nova Scotia's changing ethical standards. That a party as cash-strapped as the Nova Scotia Liberals ($3,000 dollars in debt with their bankers refusing to honour any cheques written by the party[97]) and facing an imminent provincial election, would willingly forego a four-million-dollar nest egg would, in previous years, have been inconceivable. Under new amendments proposed to the province's conflict of interest legislation, the names of the original 'contributors' to the trusts will have to be disclosed before payments from the funds can be made; if the Liberals are either unwilling or unable to comply with this stipulation, it may ironically come to pass that monies raised 'to promote Liberalism' will be forfeited to the Tory-controlled public treasury.

Any cleansing of Nova Scotia's public sector, however modest, would be cause for rejoicing. Admittedly, some analysts have claimed that corruption has a number of desirable side-effects; it can quicken economic development, overcome bureaucratic rigidities, strengthen mass-élite linkages, and so on.[98] Even so, these apparent gains are purchased at a real cost. It seems certain that public monies spent in order to secure some special advantage could be allocated more effectively in the public interest. It also seems certain that public sector corruption has a profoundly negative effect on levels of political trust. For a minimalist state involved in relatively few areas of social life, such trade-offs might be worthwhile. In the modern world of the interventionist state, however, where citizen cooperation and support are essential for the success of many public policies, and especially at a time when the reservoirs of regime legitimacy seem progressively to be evaporating, any reduction in levels of political corruption would have to generate a net benefit to society.

In the case of Nova Scotia, the extent of this reduction has yet to be revealed. Perhaps in twenty years, pork-barrelling may well have been lessened or even eliminated. Perhaps not. The effectiveness of particular remedies depends on the accuracy of the diagnosis. If widespread political corruption in Nova Scotia has been largely driven by cultural forces, then it is not unreasonable to surmise that a change in the nature of political leadership could erode those forces. The words and deeds of political élites, after all, can have an impact on political orientations throughout society. If structural forces have significantly been at work in the past, then there would be less cause for optimism. In other words, the realities of living with a perpetually depressed private-sector economy might continue to encourage public-sector corruption irrespective of any cues emanating from the apex of the state.

For such leadership to be taken seriously, of course, it must be accompanied by significant changes in the regulatory regime. As the preceding pages have made clear, the Cameron administration has introduced some reform legislation. Yet much remains to be done; the government, for example, should strengthen the influence and autonomy of the provincial Civil Service Commission, and formally recognize the confidentiality of privileged information. Such statutory reforms not only would have behavioural consequences in their own regard, but also would lend legitimacy to the premier's paeans to clean government.

Nevertheless, any change in the nature of public-sector conduct in Nova Scotia is obviously fragile. Entrenched behaviours are not changed overnight, and the well-publicized scandals of the 1980s represent only the proverbial tip of the public-sector corruption iceberg in Nova Scotia. Attorney General Joel Matheson may claim, notwithstanding his close identification with the previous regime, that there is 'no question in [his] mind that there has been a dramatic change under Donald Cameron', and that any tendering or hiring by the provincial government is now 'open and impartial.'[99] Perhaps surprisingly, Cameron himself is more cautious on this score. While expostulating that he finds the spoils system to be 'repulsive' and that hiring and firing on the basis of partisan affiliation is unacceptable in 'a so-called free country', Cameron nevertheless acknowledges that it may not have been eradicated at the local level in all parts of the province.[100] A fresh wave of scandals could wash away many recent advances. Shortly after the opening of the 1992 legislative session, it was revealed that Conservative fund raisers had been illegally compiling their mailing lists from confidential tax lists.[101] Premier Cameron tried to minimize the damage to his government by promptly calling in the Halifax City Police, by announcing that any funds raised by the appeal would be returned, and by accepting the resignation of a top party aide, the ostensible architect of the scheme.[102] Should the premier's personal reputation be tarnished by this scandal (he did, after all, sign the fundraising letter) or should longstanding rumours of the premier's involvement in patronage practices be confirmed,[103] or should he be implicated in any negligence in the Westray coal mine disaster,[104] then the vulnerability of any new standards of public-sector ethics might quickly be apparent.

In any case, the removal of corrupt conduct in the state is likely to be a Sisyphean labour. As old ethical issues are resolved, new ones are likely to emerge. The leader of the provincial New Democrats, Alexa McDonough, makes the point, for example, that the selling of government services and enterprises has an obvious ethical component.[105] Standards of behaviour are expected to be higher in the public than in the private sector. Any privatization initiatives, therefore, can be interpreted as permitting a lower standard of ethical conduct. The temptation to use public office for special advantage can never be entirely eradicated, especially in a province such as Nova Scotia, where party has traditionally played a strong role in organizing social behaviour. Even so, an end to the spoils system that has historically dominated Nova Scotia public life should be welcomed by all democrats.

Notes

1 Susan Hughes, 'Ethics dominated Nova Scotia politics in 1988', Halifax *Chronicle Herald*, 28 Dec. 1988: 1.

2 J. Murray Beck, 'Nova Scotia: Tradition and Conservatism', in Martin Robin, ed., *Canadian Provincial Politics*, 2nd ed. (Scarborough, Ont.: Prentice-Hall, 1978): 175.

3 Rand Dyck, *Provincial Politics in Canada*, 2nd ed. (Scarborough, Ont.: Prentice-Hall, 1991): 129.

4 Jeffrey Simpson, *Spoils of Power* (Toronto: HarperCollins, 1988): 182.

5 Peter Kavanagh, *John Buchanan: The Art of Political Survival* (Halifax: Formac, 1988): 19.

6 Kenneth M. Gibbons, 'The Study of Political Corruption', in Kenneth M. Gibbons and Donald C. Rowat, eds, *Political Corruption in Canada: Cases, Causes, and Cures*,

(Toronto: McClelland & Stewart in association with the Institute of Canadian Studies, Carleton University, 1976): 1-4.

7 Ian Greene, 'Conflict of Interest and the Canadian Constitution: An Analysis of Conflict of Interest Rules for Canadian Cabinet Ministers', *Canadian Journal of Political Science* 23 (1990): 241-2.

8 Jean-Pierre Kingsley, 'Conflict of Interest: A Modern Antidote', *Canadian Public Administration* 29 (1986): 592.

9 Robert S. Getz, 'Congressional Ethics and the Conflict of Interest Issue', in A. Heidenheimer, ed., *Political Corruption* (New York: Holt, Rinehart and Winston, 1978): 435.

10 James C. Scott, 'The Analysis of Corruption in Developing Nations', *Comparative Studies in Society and History* 11 (1969): 333.

11 Arnold Heidenheimer, 'Introduction', in Heidenheimer, ed., *Political Corruption*: 26-7.

12 John G. Peters and Susan Welch, 'Political Corruption in America,' *American Political Science Review* 72 (1978): 982.

13 See, for example, John Langford, 'Moonlighting and Mobility', *Canadian Public Administration* 34 (1991): 62-72; and Maureen H. Taylor and Alan E. Filmer, 'Moonlighting: The Practical Problems', *Canadian Public Administration* 29 (1986): 592-7.

14 David Bellamy, 'The Atlantic Provinces', in David J. Bellamy, Jon H. Pammett, and Donald C. Rowat, eds, *The Provincial Political Systems* (Toronto: Methuen, 1976): 11.

15 J.D. Love, 'The Merit Principle in the Provincial Governments of Atlantic Canada', *Canadian Public Administration* 31 (1988): 347.

16 Ibid.: 341-6.

17 Kavanagh, *John Buchanan*: 56-7, 130.

18 Pam Sword, 'Kerr denies patronage allegations', *Chronicle-Herald*, 27 June 1990: C1.

19 Alan Jeffers, 'Ombudsman will defuse debate!', *Chronicle-Herald*, 7 Feb. 1986: 1.

20 Alan Jeffers, 'Government Indulges in Flurry of Appointments', *Chronicle-Herald*, 11 August 1988: 1-2, and Judy Myrden and Brian Underhill, 'PC appointments "Desperate Acts"', *Chronicle Herald*, 12 August 1988: 3.

21 'Buchanan denies allegations of slush fund for N.S. Tories', *Chronicle-Herald*, 29 March 1985: A1.

22 Beck (above, n.2): 177.

23 Fortunately, no provincial electoral districts cross county boundaries.

24 Bruce Beaton, 'Potholes and Patronage: An Empirical Analysis', unpublished Honours thesis, Acadia University, 1992: 8.

25 Simpson, *Spoils of Power*: 179.

26 Agar Adamson, 'Nova Scotia: The Wisdom of Their Ancestors is Its Foundation', in Gary Levy and Graham White, eds, *Provincial and Territorial Legislatures* (Toronto: University of Toronto Press, 1989): 143.

27 See Ian Stewart, 'On Faith Alone: Petty Electoral Corruption on Prince Edward Island', Annual Meeting of the Atlantic Provinces Political Science Association, St John's, October, 1990.

28 'Five Liberal workers in Nova Scotia convicted of buying votes', *Globe and Mail*, 7 April 1989: A5.

29 See Brian Ward, '"Three-ring circus" earns Opposition's ire', *Chronicle-Herald*, 21 June 1990: A1-A2. See also Marilla Stephenson, 'AG to probe Commission', *Chronicle-Herald*, 22 June 1990: A3; and Wilkie Taylor and Brian Ward, 'MacNeil probe unlikely', *Chronicle-Herald*, 26 Oct. 1990: A1-A2.

30 Kenneth Kernaghan and John Langford, *The Responsible Public Servant* (Halifax: Institute for Research on Public Policy, 1990): 84-107.

31 Deborah Jones, 'Poor mothers' group tells N.S. Minister to quit', *Globe and Mail*, 6 June 1987: A6, and Eva Hoare, 'Morris found guilty', *Chronicle-Herald*, 16 Jan. 1988: 1-2.

32 Brian Ward, 'Opposition demands Nantes' resignation', *Chronicle-Herald*, 14 June 1990: A2.

33 F.F. Ridley, 'Responsibility and the Official: Forms and Ambiguities', *Government and Opposition* 10 (1973): 450.

34 Ibid.: 453.

35 Ian Clark, 'Ethics in Human Resource Management: Basic Bargains and Basic Values', *Canadian Public Administration* 34 (1991): 42.

36 Kernaghan and Langford, *Responsible Public Servant*: 95-8.

37 Michael Bird, 'Halifax County: PC hold appears strong', *Chronicle-Herald*, 29 Oct. 1984: A1.

38 Greg Guy, '500 march as Tories meet', *Chronicle-Herald*, 6 Feb. 1988: 1.

39 Kavanagh, *John Buchanan*: 5.

40 'Test of membership bill', *Chronicle-Herald*, 31 Oct. 1986: 10.

41 See Michael Harris, 'Two Liberal fund-raisers fined $25,000', *Globe and Mail*, 13 May 1983: 3; and 'Fund-raisers memos studied at N.S. trial', *Globe and Mail*, 17 Jan. 1989: A4.

42 See, for example, 'Executive tells trial of demands for funds', *Globe and Mail*, 22 April 1983: 5; and 'Ex-Senator innocent, trial told', *Globe and Mail*, 3 Feb. 1989: A3.

43 Kevin Cox, 'Former N.S. Deputy Premier sets discharge in fraud case', *Globe and Mail*, 16 Nov. 1991: A5.

44 Kavanagh, *John Buchanan*: 66.

45 'N.S. apologizes to Marshall, accepts inquiry's proposals', *Globe and Mail*, 8 Feb. 1990: A2.

46 There was much speculation at the convention over Thornhill's legal status. When questioned, Thornhill replied, with apparently unconscious irony, that he would deal with the matter in the future 'with conviction'. Interestingly, had Thornhill been charged immediately *before* the convention, it is likely that eventual third-place finisher Tom McInnis would have been elected leader, since he finished only thirteen voters behind Thornhill on the penultimate ballot and a post-convention survey by the author revealed that he was the consensus choice of delegates.

47 Mark Renouf, 'Buchanan clears first legal hurdle', *The Daily News*, 17 Sept. 1991: 4.

48 Privy Council Office, 'Members of Parliament and Conflict of Interest', in Gibbons and Rowat, eds, *Political Corruption in Canada*: 171.

49 See, for example, Kenneth Kernaghan and David Siegel, *Public Administration in Canada: A Text* (Toronto: Methuen, 1987): 454-7.

50 Gibbons makes a similar point. See Gibbons, in Gibbons and Rowat, eds, *Political Corruption in Canada*: 12.

51 'Buchanan dismisses patronage charge', *Globe and Mail*, 21 May 1986: A4.

52 Stevie Cameron, 'Toilet-seat covers called bum deal', *Globe and Mail*, 14 July 1990: A3.

53 Alan Jeffers, 'Premier behind Feagan letter', *Chronicle-Herald*, 15 April 1988: 2.

54 Kevin Cox, 'N.S. won't prosecute Minister', *Globe and Mail*, 18 July 1990: A4.

55 Bellamy (above, n.14): 14.

56 Beck (above, n.2): 178.

57 See Kenneth M. Gibbons, 'The Political Culture of Corruption in Canada', in Gibbons and Rowat, eds, *Political Corruption in Canada*: 241.

58 O.P. Dwivedi, 'Moral Dimensions of Statecraft: A Plea for Administrative Theology', *Canadian Journal of Political Science* 20 (1987): 701.

59 Edward Banfield, *The Moral Basis of a Backward Society*, in Heidenheimer, ed., *Political Corruption*: 129-37.

60 See, for example, W.F. Wertheim, 'Sociological Aspects of Corruption in Southeast Asia'; and Gunnar Myrdal, 'Corruption as a Hindrance to Modernization in South Asia', in Heidenheimer, ed., *Political Corruption*: 195-211 and 229-39.

61 Dyck, *Provincial Politics*: 38.

62 Jennifer Smith, 'Ruling Small Worlds', in Leslie Pal and David Taras, eds, *Prime Ministers and Premiers* (Scarborough, Ont.: Prentice-Hall, 1988): 180.

63 Samuel P. Huntington, *Political Order in Changing Societies* (New Haven: Yale University Press, 1968): 66.

64 See Arnold Heidenheimer, 'The Analysis of Electoral and Legislative Corruption', in Heidenheimer, ed., *Political Corruption*: 368. See also John P. King, 'Socioeconomic Development and the Incidence of English Corrupt Campaign Practices', in Heidenheimer, ed.: 390.

65 Warren R. Bailie and David Johnson, 'Governmental Ethics and Ethics Agencies', *Canadian Public Administration* 34 (1991): 158-64.

66 Ian Greene, 'Government Ethics Commissions: The Way of the Future', *Canadian Public Administration* 34 (1991): 165-70.

67 Gunnar Myrdal, 'Corruption: Its Causes and Effects', in Heidenheimer, ed., *Political Corruption*: 543.

68 Heidenheimer, 'The Analysis of Electoral and Legislative Corruption', in Heidenheimer, ed., *Political Corruption*: 369.

69 For a discussion of some of the dangers, see Michael M. Atkinson and Maureen Mancuso, 'Do We Need a Code of Conduct for Politicians? The Search for an Elite Political Culture of Corruption in Canada', *Canadian Journal of Political Science* 18 (1985): 459-80.

70 Alan Jeffers, 'Premier hedges on conflict guidelines', *Chronicle-Herald*, 6 March 1987: 2.

71 Statutes of Nova Scotia, 1987, ch. 4: 167-76.

72 See, for example, Gerry Arnold, 'Conflict bill introduced', *Chronicle-Herald*, 26 May 1987: 2.

73 Susan Hughes, 'Ethics dominated N.S. politics in 1988', *Chronicle-Herald*, 28 Dec. 1988: 2.

74 Cameron MacKeen, 'New committee will prevent secret payments—Premier', *Chronicle-Herald*, 16 April 1991: 1-2.

75 Kevin Cox, 'Judge rules out Buchanan inquiry', *Globe and Mail*, 10 Aug. 1991: A5.

76 See, for example, Kenneth Kernaghan, 'Codes of Ethics and Public Administration: Progress, Problems, and Prospects', *Public Administration* 59 (1980): 207-23. See also Kenneth Kernaghan, 'Codes of Ethics and Administrative Responsibility', *Canadian Public Administration* 17 (1974): 524-41.

77 Kevin Cox, 'N.S. pondering how to police behaviour of its politicians', *Globe and Mail*, 24 July 1990: A5.

78 Kevin Cox, 'Vote watch wears down N.S. Liberals', *Globe and Mail*, 25 June 1988: A5.

79 Roy Fendick, 'Cameron vows radical reform', *The Daily News*, 11 May 1991: 3.

80 Statutes of Nova Scotia, 1991, ch. 4: 25-45.
81 Bill 105, An Act to Amend Chapter 4 of the Acts of 1991, the Members and Public Employees Disclosure Act, had only completed first reading when this chapter went to press.
82 Kenneth Kernaghan, 'Managing Ethics: Complementary Approaches', *Canadian Public Administration* 34 (1991): 134.
83 Mydal, 'Corruption: Its Causes and Effects', in Heidenheimer, ed., *Political Corruption*: 544.
84 Simpson, *Spoils of Power*: 168-71.
85 Simpson, *Spoils of Power*: 171.
86 Kevin Cox, 'N.S. hopefuls seek clean image', *Globe and Mail*, 8 Nov. 1990: A3.
87 Donald Cameron, interview with the author, Halifax, 8 June 1992.
88 Even Cameron's supporters avoided his hospitality rooms at the convention, preferring to freeload in the suites of his major competitors.
89 'Tory popularity plummets', *Chronicle-Herald*, 14 June 1990: A3.
90 Of a randomly generated mail survey of 3500 Nova Scotians, just under 1500 questionnaires were returned (a response rate of 38 per cent).
91 Adamson (above, n.26): 151.
92 Stephen Kimber, 'Leaders not trusted, reader survey shows', *The Daily News*, 19 Feb. 1991: 5. It is, however, significant that this survey also discovered that 56 per cent of respondents believed that simply being in government eventually corrupts even good people.
93 'Liberals defend trust-fund salary', *Globe and Mail*, 12 October 1990: A4.
94 See Kevin Cox, 'Allegations haunt Nova Scotia Grits', *Globe and Mail*, 22 Oct. 1990: A4; and 'Party review sought', *Globe and Mail*, 14 Nov. 1990: A5.
95 Reg Fendick, 'Trust-fund illegality unproven, Grits now say', *The Daily News*, 6 Dec. 1991: 5.
96 Malcolm Dunlop, 'MacLean renounces ties with trust funds', *Chronicle-Herald*, 22 Feb. 1992: A1-A2.
97 Brian Underhill and Brian Ward, 'MacLean wins test; dissenters still vocal', *Chronicle Herald*, 2 March 1992: A1.
98 Arnold Heidenheimer, 'Corruption and Modernization', in Heidenheimer, ed., *Political Corruption*: 479-86.
99 Joel Matheson, interview with the author, Halifax, 8 June 1992.
100 Donald Cameron, interview with the author, Halifax, 8 June 1992.
101 Brian Ward, 'Legislature off to stormy start', *Chronicle-Herald*, 17 April 1992: A1-A2.
102 'Back to cleaning up politics', *Chronicle-Herald*, 23 April 1992: C1.
103 See, for example, 'Thornhill still dogged by loan probe', *The Daily News*, 8 Feb. 1991: 5; or 'N.S. Premier warns news media', *Globe and Mail*, 20 March 1991: A6.
104 See, for example, Brian Underhill, 'NDP fears files shredded', *Chronicle-Herald*, 21 May 1992: 1-2.
105 Alexa McDonough, interview with the author, Halifax, 8 June 1992.

The Canadian Federal Government

Patronage, unity, security, and purity

> Les régimes et les systèmes économiques et politiques
> ne meurent jamais de leurs scandales. Ils meurent de leurs
> contradictions. C'est tout autre chose.[1]

This was Jean Bouvier's conclusion about what he called the two scandals of the Panama Canal enterprise of the turn of the last century in France: that political regimes are not finished off by scandal and public moral outrage, but by deeper and more telling internal inconsistency. The first scandal, the financial failure of the Panama Canal company, was due, he said, to three factors: the objective conditions of the tropical climate and the terrible clay of the isthmus; French society; and human nature. The second aspect of the scandal was political. At least 26 and as many as 104 parliamentarians were discovered to have accepted bribes from the company, two prime ministers among their number. This massive failure of political ethics was a result of the entangled political, business, and newspaper structures of the Third Republic. The institutional fact that the individual members of parliamentary committees were free of party discipline, and could thereby vote as their conscience or pocketbook dictated, also played a part.

The puzzle presented by Bouvier is the apparent contradiction that even though the Panama scandal appeared to the public of the time to be a moral earthquake, no constitutional pillars fell. The scandal made money for newspapers, and cast into bankruptcy many notables, including the entrepreneur who had realized the Suez Canal project. It was apparently invested with a kind of tragic moral significance by the suicide of a ruined baron: this was interpreted as the old order unable to survive in a crass new world whose only value was money. But the political settlement in France was left untouched. The political and financial framework re-peopled its surfaces with figures of the same type as had brought about the Panama scandal, representing the very same interests, arranged in the same pattern of temptations in the stalemated institutions.

In fact, the scandals did not even provide enough energy or understanding for middling reforms. Those sharing power gingerly negotiated with one another only the most minor changes that history would see as woefully inadequate. Lasting public outrage and mounting frustration only drove the structures deeper into their contradictions. The longer term saw a tragic interplay between the public demand for change and the immobilism of the structures: a popular desire for a strong man as a solution to the ills of French democracy was strengthened, and the 'mendacious and merciless' French right opportunistically seized on elements of the scandal to try to ruin its eternal enemies, republicans and Jews.[2] Thus serious politics ultimately flowed from the Panama scandals, but in unexpected ways.

Does Bouvier's reflection about the lack of immediate importance of public standards of morality for the conduct of public affairs have value in the Canadian context? Canadian national politics has never seen anything so grave as the Panama Canal Company's deliberate corruption of a hundred members of the political élite—or at least not all at the same time. But Canada has never lacked imposing scandals. Nor has Canada ever suffered a scarcity of 'mendacious and merciless' publicists of scandal, of half-truths and of outright lies, hoping to profit in votes, power, or only revenge.

Some excellent Canadian scandals

Our first prime minister, Sir John A. Macdonald, financed his 1872 election with money begged from the railway entrepreneurs with whom he was working hand in glove. Trouble erupted when his telegram to one of them was brought to light:

> I must have another $10,000. Will be the last time of calling. Do not fail me. Answer today.[3]

The resulting Pacific Scandal did bring about the fall of the government and the accession to power of a somewhat reform-minded Liberal Party. But the Liberals of that time were a pale party, and thus the public was able to swallow any vestiges of its disgust lingering from the Pacific scandal to re-elect the Conservatives in 1878, that is, at the first opportunity. Nothing changed in fundraising. For a reminder of that, one need look no further than the Langevin Block across from the main buildings of Parliament. One of the most gracious buildings in Ottawa, the sandstone edifice that now houses both the prime minister's personal and political office and the Privy Council Office takes its name from Hector Langevin, Macdonald's minister of public works. Langevin would be forced to resign from cabinet in 1891 for having given contract favours over the years to a Quebec firm run by two brothers. In return, their firm sent back financial contributions to the Conservative Party. The comfortable arrangement came to an end when the brothers fell out with one another. The 'revelations'—that stunned no one in the political world but which angered everyone outside it—were then assiduously publicized by Joseph Israel Tarte, a one-time Liberal parliamentarian, in a newspaper he owned. Langevin came to the end of his life with his name a byword for corruption.[4]

The Canadian political framework was so torn and shamed that it could think of nothing better to do than to continue in this vein for the next hundred years. During the late 1980s, one of Langevin's successors in the dicey joint jobs of Quebec lieutenant for the ruling party and minister of public works, Roch LaSalle, was living through the process in which his own name was becoming his era's substitute for Langevin's. LaSalle was forced to resign from Brian Mulroney's cabinet in 1987, one of six 'resignations under a cloud' from Mulroney's enormous yet beleaguered first government of 1984 to 1988.[5]

But a resignation proves only that a minister has failed the prime minister's cost-benefit test. LaSalle himself was never tried or found guilty of anything. He was only forced to hang up his skates because of suspicion flowing in his direction due to the lack of adeptness of one of his associates. In his role as political organizer, LaSalle had delegated the Hull area, where the huge Museum of Civilization was under construction, to another Conservative politician, MP Michel Gravel. Gravel apparently did not have a light pastry hand, for he was charged in 1986 with ten counts of bribery or attempted bribery, thirty-two charges of defrauding the government, and eight charges of breach of trust. Opponents were not slow to suggest that the museum project, whose costs grossly exceeded all estimates, had become the party's tunnel into the Bank of Canada. With some luck and plenty of legal assistance, Gravel was able to delay his trial until after the 1988 election. The election won and his party safely back in power, in December 1988 Gravel nimbly changed his not guilty plea to a plea of guilty on fifteen charges that he had accepted or sought about $100,000 from contractors, architects, and others in connection with the museum. The changed plea made for a short trial and shielded most of Gravel's affairs from publication. He was sentenced to two years in jail, and fined $50,000.

But the Gravel case does not rest there. Revenue Canada has in the meantime assessed Gravel for $20,000 in tax, interest, and penalties on $35,000 he collected at a fundraising party in July of 1985. Gravel refused to pay and the matter went to the Tax Court of Canada. He presented himself as Roch LaSalle's fall guy who was now at the end of his tolerance and was drawing a line: 'I went to jail for Roch LaSalle. I was not going to pay his income tax.' A former aide to LaSalle testified that LaSalle had acknowledged the receipt of the money, but just before LaSalle could testify the court intervened with 'an unprecedented ban' on publication of the evidence.[6] In short, LaSalle will not say in public whether he took the money, either for himself or for the party. One can see the problem. In a separate but temporally parallel effort, a disappointed Conservative entrepreneur, Glen Kealey, finally succeeded by unbelievable persistence in launching another investigation of LaSalle. To get his day in court, Kealey had kept up a daily protest vigil on Parliament Hill in all weathers from November 1988 until he was given the hearing in July 1991 that led to the new investigation.[7] The Gravel-LaSalle-Kealey story fits well with the mounting conviction of the Canadian public that the Conservatives are even worse than . . . well, gentle reader, after all, worse than what?

When the leader of the previous Liberal government, Pierre Elliott Trudeau, resigned from the prime minister's job in 1984, he stepped down as head of a party that had formed the government for all but ten months of the past twenty-one years. He also ignited a smouldering public disapproval of his own government's general practices in rewarding its faithful. The appointments process took the brunt of the anger because it provided a focus. As part of his exit settlement, Trudeau identified during the month of June 1984 225 people to soak up all the currently vacant federal political appointments. Seventeen well-known Members of Parliament were chosen for full-time jobs, some of the jobs having been explicitly promised as inducement to run in the 1980 election. To the public it seemed a sudden and shameless demonstration of what political activism was all about. Trudeau's legacy to John Turner was a patronage cupboard bare except for the poisoned pill of putting these appointments into effect. Worse, in the election campaign that followed Trudeau's resignation, Turner made himself look weak and cynical when he made it clear that he would confirm the Trudeau appointments but would not defend them—although, as we shall see, there are some arguments in favour of political appointments. In the televised leadership debate with Mulroney, Turner was quite easily backed into saying that he had 'no option'. Mulroney hit the perfect note in his reply, 'You had an option, Sir. You could have done better.' We threw the rascals out.[8]

Once in the prime minister's job, Mulroney demonstrated what his own free choice would mean. It would indeed mean doing better . . . well, sort of. Mulroney did business as usual, including the traditional designation of patronage ministers for the provinces and regions, with some results we have already noted. The improvement was that the new Conservative prime minister headed in 1984 a party that had embraced technology. In anointing the winners of appointments, Mulroney was able to work with an efficiency that would have been envied by Macdonald, Langevin, and Laurier. Joe Clark had done quite a bit of the groundwork: in his earnest minority government of 1979 Clark had begun work to improve management of the federal political appointments made by Governor-in-Council. Pertinent features of political appointments and their enabling authorities were drawn together and classified into clusters in ways that made better sense to the politicians whose interest at that point was clearly focused on how to cut bait for the inevitably-near election. According to Jeffrey Simpson, when the Clark government precociously lost a vote of confidence after only months in office, and then lost the 1980 election, the party continued its project on better identification and management of political appointments in Opposition. It now had the insider knowledge to do so, and it was motivated by its conviction that the Clark breakthrough had at the least shown that the Liberals could be decisively beaten. By 1984 the party had a computer file at its headquarters that listed 3,500 Governor-in-Council jobs against vacancy dates and other basic facts. There is some disagreement about what happened after the 1984 election returned the Conservatives to power. Simpson's book suggests that party insiders simply put a computer disk into a front jacket pocket behind a blue silk puff and strolled from Conservative Party headquarters into the sanctum of the Langevin Block, where they installed their programs and files in the computers in the prime minister's office.[9] Another story holds that Privy Council Office had independently continued the Clark appointments project after the election of the Liberals in 1980, and by the last days of the Trudeau government had built up its own machine-readable computer files of Governor-in-Council positions. There is more pleasure in the second version. It allows us to believe that without Clark's homework, the departing Trudeau would never have had a neat listing of the full range of vacant appointments, a listing that could help to engage the full range of his generosity to his supporters—and incidentally to doom Turner.

So this is our Canada, and it is entertaining to write about it. It could be almost as entertaining as writing about France if one had a century of distance on it, plus the knowledge that it had stayed in business. So doubts do build up. First there is what we can call the Bouvier doubt: is there a relation between public outrage at the way politics is conducted and the deeper problems of federal Canada? If so, what is required to address the public's concerns: adjustments to the political appointments process and the numbers of such appointments, or nothing short of a complete transcendence of politics as we know it? Second is self-doubt. Do my own prejudices decide what I can see? Third, there is doubt of others, of their sketchy facts and lack of fairness. For the simple fact is that there exists no full and true history of political corruption as such, but only histories of corruption revealed (scandal).[10] Sometimes these stories are only cobbled together and clumsily forced upon losers and scapegoats. True or false, all become media product. The direct coverage of the criminal law is painfully narrow and cautious, as it should be, and very slow, which it probably should not be.

To complicate matters still further, the very most basic ethical positions of the producers and consumers of scandal go unrecognized. As moralists, most of us are like Monsieur Jourdain of Molière's *Le bourgeois gentilhomme*, who spoke in prose without knowing it. We speak our ethics in ignorance of what we say. We rarely come to terms with the way our most basic convictions shape and colour the stories we live and tell one another. For surely, if I believe that I must justify each of my actions against principles that are universally defensible, I have a very different habit of mind than if I believe that the context and effects of an action as well as the intent behind it can justify or excuse it. This is true whether I am a politician, a civil servant, a journalist, or only an observer. When I think I must work from principles, I am at least equally impressively severe with myself and with others. When I try to appreciate contexts and understand persons, I will find it easier to excuse myself than other people. This is because I conveniently have all the exonerating information about myself, whereas I generally know little about others, to whom I in blissful ignorance feel free to impute all sorts of awful motives.[11]

Problems of political morality, in short, speak to our deepest and yet most confused beliefs about who we are as individuals and what we can condone as permissible action in public life.

The next part of this paper begins by suggesting the typical 'families' of difficulties that afflict modern liberal democracies like our own. A simple typology is offered for classifying kinds of ethical failure by public office holders. The paper then describes what appear to be distinctive and important kinds of ethical failure that take place in national public life.

The government in Ottawa is faced with different challenges than the provincial governments because the national government has particular duties: perhaps most notably, it is responsible for maintaining state security from both external and internal threats; and it is responsible for national unity. The paper thus concentrates upon the use of the politics of rewards (patronage) in the eternal Canadian struggle for national unity, and on the politics of manipulation, coercion, and suppression of facts in the national security function. The politics and ethics of the 'purity war', in which parties whip up public moral anger, are also discussed.

While much that the paper has to say is relevant to conflict of interest as an ethical dereliction, the paper does not lay out the major historical developments in either that debate or the federal institutional framework for handling potential conflicts of interest of office holders. The federal debate is well documented and interesting,[12] but it is at a crossroads. The Senate-House of Commons joint committee that studied Bill C-43 through the spring of 1992 put those provisions to one side and recommended a different framework. No new legislation had been tabled at the time of writing.[13] As for the ethical dimensions of conflict of interest *per se*, they have been set out in Allan Tupper's chapter in this volume.

The bargain in liberal democratic society: respecting public office

A liberal democratic society is one in which there is broad agreement to confine the struggle over what substantial directions public life will take—what should be done, by whom, and who will enjoy what benefits—to party combat in electoral politics. Argument and reason are supposed to reign in the electoral contest, and the result is supposed to put to bed for the life of a government the question of who will have executive authority and will thus be obeyed. The norm of 'turn-taking elections' is perhaps the most essential foundation of modern democratic government. A second feature of liberal democratic society is a widespread agreement to, as Mr Trudeau once memorably said, 'keep the state out of the bedrooms of the nation.' The political agenda is deliberately limited, ideally to items that can be addressed by fact and argument. The sphere of what is culturally 'private' (religion, consensual sexual choices, whether one will found a family, intellectual conviction . . .) is respected and even enlarged to the extent possible. Political parties are supposed to construct their platforms on issues that are clearly *public* matters, social, economic, and political projects and tasks of management that are—arguably, at least—within the capacity of limited government to promote or prevent.

The election over, what liberal democratic society wants from the public official in the ordinary run of things is reasonably clear. The basic duty of public officials (in the performance of the tasks to which they have been elected or appointed) is to act correctly within the confines and procedures of the law and the rules (the job description) of their office. Thus the personnel of the winning party are expected to actively seek partisan and ideological goals, but to do so according to the system rules and the narrower rules governing their own offices that together define fair play. In this way it is hoped to maintain a level playing field between the political interests that contest for power—and as well to maintain popular patience for the democratic norm of turn-taking elections.

The idea of public office is a Roman legacy, while the first clear expressions of liberal constitutionalism date from the European monarchies. The idea of public office as a clearly-defined set of duties and powers made the extension of state power possible and acceptable to the public, because it delivers a more rationalist, predictable, and thus accountable mode of government than any other arrangement. In a definition by Gianfranco Poggi, the idea of office consists of 'honourable but also onerous prerogatives and responsibilities which remained invariant as a succession of people assumed them'.[14]

The problem is, of course, that an emphasis on majoritarianism and process as a way of choosing between a number of quite different alternatives depends on a general social tolerance for what amounts to political-ethical relativism. Majoritarian ethics say, 'if this is what the voting majority wants, then we will abide by it'. But the problem is that the content of one's desired goals has greater inspirational value than just a fair method of making decisions, although we mostly want both. That one has had a fair trial by one's peers is no great source of satisfaction if one is hanged at the end of it. To be exonerated by a dubious process is likewise an imperfect outcome, albeit one that would be preferred by most people.

It is not surprising, therefore, that it will occur to both politicians and officials that office itself is a resource that can help them in a covert or strategic pursuit of policy outcomes. Power can be used to extract the wealth they need to build clienteles, or help allies to hold on to political power, or even to manipulate outcomes. A great deal can be accomplished towards making certain outcomes inevitable, all without being publicly recognized or without risking the votes of the groups whose interests are being undermined.

Thus we see the first of the two basic motives behind all process failures by public officials: the office holder's desire to get a result, to achieve an outcome that will benefit a greater cause: a principle, party advantage (including holding on to power), social peace, or the *patrie*.

The other motive is that of personal gain. It is useful to remember that the personal gain of the office holder may not cause direct loss to the public. For example, postal workers or police could take a fee or gifts for providing small services to housebound or frail people. But they would nonetheless be acting beyond their formal scope of office and therefore improperly. For although side benefits can easily be taken from many public offices, and it is thus even argued that corruption can be functional (and in this sense 'good') for a political and social system, side benefits are still properly understood as wrong in the legal and moral senses.

The means by which the public official illicitly seeks a particular substantial outcome likewise fall into two broad categories. These are, broadly, (1) methods of enticement, and (2) methods of coercion or coercive manipulation. This last should be understood as including the invention of facts and the manipulation and suppression of fact and argument. The citizen whose opinions have been formed by propaganda, or who has been turned away from an historically accurate understanding and analysis of an event by deliberate suppression and distortion of the record has been manipulated.

Corruption takes place in secrecy: if it is not secret, wrong action is only simple error or abuse that can be observed and fairly readily corrected. Corrupt officials quietly use the pockets of illogic (loopholes) in official structures, acting under the cover provided by their official role, using their knowledge of the institution. Thus the corrupt official is strategic in the way he or she 'farms' the office, the institution, and even the constitution.

In principle therefore all cases of objective and perceived wrong action by office holders will fall into one of four catagories: (1) for personal gain, carried out by coercion or coercive manipulation; (2) for personal gain, by the use of entice-ments; (3) for the benefit of a principle or collectivity and carried out by coercion or coercive manipulation; (4) for a principle or collectivity and carried out by rewards. The victim might be the public interest in general; the person(s) cor-rupted and later exposed; or only the person(s) coerced.

One can readily list a few everyday examples: pork-barrelling, or delivering public works and projects to the politician's constituents; influence-peddling, or selling access to decision makers; bribery; graft, the most general term for illicit benefits; patronage, or favour; and conflict of interest as self-administered patron-age. The puzzling term 'honest graft' occurs in American work on machine politics, to point to the optimal corruption that leaves the insider better off without directly taking away from someone else. Money and power are usually what is wanted, but not always. Favours in great variety can be exchanged willingly, or extorted, including sexual favours. To complicate matters, delayed gratification is very much a feature of the scene: debts are incurred and webs of obligation are spun in pursuit of long-term goals.

As for the use of coercive means, one can mention the suppression or intimida-tion of witnesses; tampering with the files and thereby with what can later be known as historical truth; and bullying of every kind from physical threat through to intimidation and mere name-dropping. Another kind of coercion is the deliberate orchestration of public disapproval, helpfully amplified by the media. Still another is when those temporarily in the majority seize their oppor-tunity to change the rules to ensure their desired outcome. One could call this the manipulation of justification. Examples in a parliamentary system are the abusive use of closure, and switches from consensual rules to majoritarian rules through the sudden imposition of a majority decision to rewrite the rules. State secrecy is certainly sometimes a kind of coercive manipulation.

Patronage in Canada: buying our separation

Patronage is known as a grey area, partly because it is usually successfully calculated to evade the narrow provisions of the Criminal Code. But another reason is that observers are divided about whether patronage is simply and always ethically wrong, only wrong in a practical sense because it is wasteful and essentially ineffective, or ethically wrong yet still an absolute necessity in political life.

The origins of Canada itself, according to an influential book by Gordon Stewart, are to be found in patronage: nineteenth-century Canadian politics were largely a fight about who was to control patronage.[15] Patronage, as defined by Reg Whitaker, is:

> . . . transactions in which inducements derived from control of the state (jobs, contracts, favours) are given or promised by a political party or its representatives in exchange for political support by a client.

Whitaker explains that patronage is in direct contrast to bureaucratic redistribution, where the policy outputs of the state are even-handedly directed to universally defined categories of citizens.[16]

Political appointments and patronage appointments

Appointments are only a small part of overall patronage, although a visible part to be sure. Some writers distinguish between political appointments in the sense of positions that are used strategically to help a government achieve policy control, and patronage appointments, as positions used to reward past partisan service or to provide an active party worker with a stipend.[17] But the federal government itself operates with one grand category, appointments awarded by Order-in-Council (OIC), for which the prime minister has the last say if he wants to exercise it.

One can think about OIC jobs in terms of their numbers, their timing, and their location in the overall framework of government. In federal Canada, each OIC job runs on its own timetable: we as yet have no tradition that the officials whose appointments are owed to political preference will have the ends of their term of office tied to the electoral fate of the politicians who appointed them. The normal rhythm is that about a thousand OIC appointments (also sometimes designated GIC for Governor-in-Council) are made in the course of any given year within the senior personnel system administered jointly by the prime minister's office and the Privy Council Office.[18] In terms of numbers, after the February 1992 budget cut of more than forty small agencies and their various councils and boards, the global number of full- and part-time OIC jobs is thought to be in the neighbour-hood of 3,500.

In regard to where political appointments are placed in the governmental structure, it is clear that in Canada the most important jobs in the area of making and administering policy are deputy ministers (34 in 1992), associate deputy ministers (12), and heads of important agencies (94). These positions are awarded by the government because their clear purpose is to help the government to maintain control of the public service sector and to feel comfortable about the degree of that control. If a prime minister does not like the way a department or agency is being run, he can change the top appointee, placing an individual whom he knows to be sympathetic to the aims of the party for the public policy to be implemented in that area. So far in Canada, prime ministers have almost invari-ably chosen at least departmental deputy heads from among the group of expert functionaries who have already proved in their careers under the terms of the Public Service Employment Act that they would be capable of doing the complex job of guiding and controlling a major institution. (While the prime minister is free to recruit outside the federal public service, no recent federal government has found it easy to recruit from outside people who will accept the conditions of work, remuneration, and risk, and who are clearly meritorious for the difficult top jobs.)

Other full-time federal OIC appointments include about 800 full-time judicial appointments, as well as an undetermined number of attractive ambassadorial positions. (Senate seats and lieutenant-governor jobs are in a class by themselves.) The rationale for the liberty of the prime minister in judicial and ambassadorial appointments is much less clear. For example, how can the Federal Court be expected to function really effectively with lightweights on the bench? What does it cost the taxpayer when their quixotic and poorly-reasoned decisions are appealed to the Supreme Court and overwhelmingly overturned? And how is it that a bankrupt nation can afford to pay for the rest and recuperation of tired partisans in the foreign countries that enjoy nice climates and exciting and livable capital cities? Many commentators thus think that true patronage begins here.

The lion's share of OIC appointments consists of the remaining groups of part-time positions on boards and agencies such as those judging claims for parole or refugee status, and the places on the boards of close to 400 Crown corporations and agencies. Most of these positions are remunerated by per diem allowance and expenses. No published information is available about total sums of money paid out in any given year. There are also about 400 part-time judicial appointments in the OIC group.

Another and separate political appointments system is administered at the Treasury Board Secretariat for ministerial-exempt staff, the estimated three to five hundred people who run the prime minister's office and other ministers' offices. These positions are made and terminated by the minister concerned, and the Public Service Employment Act contains provisions for overseeing the access of 'exempt' appointees to permanent jobs in the merit system. Still another form of patronage is 'the list' of lawyers of the right political colour named as standing agents of the Crown, who thus receive professional patronage in the form of work. The list is administered by the Justice Department.

No one except the various insiders can know the costs of the various elements of the political appointments systems—OIC, exempt, and Department of Justice —or how incomes compare to the salaries paid to merit civil servants at similar levels of skill, nor indeed the kinds of difficulties caused by the variable perform- ances of the various beneficiaries. More than judges enjoy the complete indepen- dence and invulnerability of a judge, at least for the duration of their term of office. (Yet it can be said that a number of political appointees perform their duties so carefully that career bureaucrats will work hard to convince a new government to keep them on, as in the case of a handful of Citizenship Court judges and some board members.)

Because it is easy to be impressed by the numbers and outraged by the lack of accountability, it is useful to provide a comparison. Each time the American presidency changes partisan hands, the president-elect finds himself in charge of a massive head-hunting operation. Martin Walker, writing for the *Guardian*, has provided a chronicle of the personnel responsibilities of incoming President William Clinton.[19] Clinton had to pick his cabinet, whose members are the heads for the fourteen executive departments of the American government, and their deputies, much like a Canadian prime minister. But he also had to think about another 1,150 senior presidential appointments, which require confirma- tion by the US Senate. Then he had another 550 or so senior appointments that do not need Senate approval, plus a complement of about 1,800 lower-level patronage jobs, many in the White House itself. These jobs filled, he could then think about putting his new government's stamp on policy implementation by the 'bureaucracy': of the 8,800 jobs in the Senior Executive Service, he would be allowed to fill up to 10 per cent with patronage appointees. Nor was his work then really over. He could start to think about extending his partisan influence into the total of 4,300 Senior Executive jobs in the civil service that can be filled by the president drawing from a list of career civil servants—*or* from a list of political appointees. From this account we can discern the timing, numbers, and placement of American patronage. The American system tries to award its patronage all at once, although in practice there are considerable delays in getting people in place, and they will wander away at their own rhythm. In absolute numbers, Clinton seems to have around 9,000 positions at his disposal, a little more than double the number of awards made in Canada, a country with about a tenth the US population and less than a tenth of its wealth. Its location or placement is of course an even stronger contrast. American political appointees take over the 'commanding heights' of each of the only loosely connected baronies of the executive departments, whose independence is then strongly checked by Congress. Canadian political appointees more nearly represent some- thing like the 'collecting depths' of the non-departmental segment of public sector employment, placed as they are on the boards of companies and in agencies that are apparently outside the control of ministers and thus somewhat outside the scope of responsible government.[20]

A more controlled comparison can be made between our system and that upon which our machinery is modelled. The British prime minister appoints the same top departmental officials, and senior judges and diplomats. He or she also names life peers to the House of Lords, clearly an honour but by no means so well rewarded financially as appointees to our Senate. Because Britain has an established church, the British prime minister also chooses bishops. But lacking from the British prime minister's repertoire are the great numbers of relatively well-remunerated positions as heads and board members of public companies and independent agencies. In Britain, departmental ministers and their officials are allowed to hold on to funds to provide moderate rewards for numerous part-time positions.[21] A more striking contrast is that in Britain all ministers' offices, including the prime minister's, are run by civil servants as a regular part of the training of high-flyers. Ministers may have one or exceptionally two policy advisers who are partisan appointments paid by state funds (the prime minister having less than ten), but they are otherwise served by officials. This means that amateurish skirmishes by the political staff trying to win turf from career officials are less frequent and serious. Thus Canadian federal political appointments to this point in our history roughly mirror the British style of government in generally allowing the civil service to function as an expert, career civil service. Yet the Canadian appetite for patronage reward reflects that of the American partisan system, and perhaps even proportionally exceeds it, as seen by our large number of appointments in the non-departmental area of the federal government's architecture. Historically, then, a two-faceted approach has operated in Canadian federal government, one that could be characterized as 'my spouse is not my lover'. This has allowed Canadian parties to reward and encourage and make merry with their partisans (lovers) and at the same time to govern the household and much of the estate alongside and through the career civil service (the spouse), and to allow the spouse's merit system to operate relatively undisturbed.

Appointments are the most visible part of patronage because they involve the bestowing of social and professional honour and status in addition to financial rewards: they often confer the right to 'act like somebody' in important places. Appointments thus touch a civic nerve that is not wholly rational (centred on efficiency worries) because we sense that the quality of the incumbents of establishment positions defines our own worth as subjects. One is led to this speculation because in financial terms appointments most likely represent only a minor portion of the total patronage bill. Consider the other forms of patronage. Government contracts are awarded to clients of politicians in consideration for a kickback to the party (or even to the individual); business donates money to party influence-peddlers in return for preference; relatives, acquaintances, and ministerial assistants may be pushed into the bureaucratic or 'merit' hiring system by a variety of stratagems, on occasion scaling in a matter of months the appointment levels that a career bureaucrat would take years and even decades to climb. This kind of patronage is essentially unmeasurable, and becomes known to the broad public only by accident, as a result of rumour, and occasional criminal charges.[22]

In what sense is the total of patronage thought to be the locomotive force of Canadian politics? At some risk of caricature, one can note the main aspects of a current argument in a few sentences. When Canada was ruled from Britain, it was natural that the modest number of government jobs and contracts would be completely centralized in the British colonial office. Much of the energy for the fight for independence came from the desire of local politicians to control these jobs and contracting authorities—and of course, honours—in order to build their own political bases from the wealth being extracted from the country.

With self-government came control over the patronage resource, still very highly centralized. The national government then began paying out money and jobs to the two linguistic communities, the French and the English, to build support in each. With the growth of government in the present century and the steady elaboration of the Crown sector, the state supported more and more positions that could be used to build the parties at the same time the country was being built. Over time, two parallel élites were solidly embedded, controlling and organizing their followers, maintaining social and political peace in their separate fiefdoms. In S.J.R. Noel's words, 'Patronage flowed down, votes flowed up, and the result was political stability.'[23] Yet the party in government would find that it had become the hostage of the increasingly onerous patronage requirements of not one but two communities. Therefore increasing amounts of wealth—jobs, contracts, favours—had to be conjured from the material fabric of the state and paid out in patronage. And this only to maintain the standard of life that had come to be expected, and thus political stability. The parties had become like the small boy in D.H. Lawrence's story about the 'rocking-horse winner'. He was able to predict the winners of horse races for his high-living parents only by rocking himself to exhaustion on his wooden rocking horse.

Necessary evil or just evil?

But is this Canadian dependence on patronage 'functionally' good or bad? In the good old bad old days patronage was said to be functional for Canadian politics—at least so long as the francophone elite had enough wealth to cement its unity—because payments averted direct conflict over resources between the two linguistic groups. In fact, in some circles the fight for Quebec sovereignty is rather dismissively interpreted as a repeat of the earlier struggle with Britain over the local right to award all patronage. The argument that patronage is functional (and thus good in that sense) essentially says that, in contributing to political party cohesion, patronage served the cause of liberal democracy—or at least a rock-bottom definition of it. Since the first development of mass political parties in Canada, parties have been the mechanism for achieving an alternation in the personnel of leadership, and have also provided the energy and general direction of the executive. Thus because patronage has funded the development of our party democracy, thereby allowing for the peaceful alternation of leadership, it is often suggested that we ought to see it as good for Canadian democracy.[24]

This argument—that patronage is good because it creates a spirit of compromise in political life—is familiar from Americans' analysis of their politics. The Tolchins, for example, accept the fact that the power to dispense public wealth in an informal way will encourage some officials to skim the public interest for private gain, that is, to steal a percentage for themselves. They nonetheless view patronage as an effective and honourable way of extending 'government by the people' into rule-ridden bureaucracy.[25]

Lippmann sees patronage systems as inevitable 'natural governments' which bind people together in a complex of favours and coercions, and which continue to operate below the constitutional government that has been superimposed. Lippmann does not think natural governments are naturally *good*: 'In many countries it is only too plain that the constitutional system is a mere façade behind which the real exercise of power depends on the barter of privileges and the use of violence.'[26] Even an advanced industrial democracy can see its constitution challenged: witness the demonstration of power by the Mafia in Italy in the summer of 1992 when it showed that it could reach at will through the most elaborate state security to kill judges.

James Q. Wilson sees patronage as a way of overcoming systemic rigidity. He traces a theory on the pervasiveness of favours and pay-offs in the US system to 1904, as then stated by Henry Jones Ford. The analysis says that what the founders of American democracy put asunder in the separation-of-powers system, the politicians must join together if any business is to get done. The boss, the machine, the party, the bagman, all must try to coordinate through the exchange of favours the activity of the independent branches of American federal government.[27] Patronage will by the nature of the separation-of-powers system be spread broadly, because even opposition partisans will receive favours from the president in return for support on individual votes and policies.

It has also been suggested that a 'good' patronage machine can be built on merit. S.J.R. Noel has drawn out the implicit rules of the political machine that Ontario's premier Oliver Mowat built during his years in power, 1872 to 1896, and which lived on in victory until 1905. These rules are (1) do not offend the disappointed, (2) give rewards only to those who deserve them and are seen to deserve them, and (3) do not waste patronage. The argument is essentially that the meta-rules that guided the Mowat machine wisely created honorific rewards that extended the value of even modest material rewards, within a party base that shared a culture. A governing party following these rules could even afford to show restraint in the amount of patronage that it took out of the economy. The Mowat machine of Noel's description comes through as something like a kindly and wise monarch, one whose actions served the broad interests of the body politic. But there is something missing—public disclosure, public standards, and accountability: the patron is judge in his own cause, and the public purse and the service the public will receive are hostage to his or her arbitrary preferences.

Noel's rules for the modern patronage prince include two strategic or instrumental injunctions to recognize media power. The first is that the patron must not offend the media, presumably because they influence public opinion. The second is not to mix patronage with pork-barrelling: if the whole project or program is 'political', openly calculated to buy constituency support, do not draw attention to a weak base in logic by giving the top job to a known party supporter with no obvious related talents. Thus our prime minister can cause a federal prison to be built in his own riding without too much public outrage, but will refrain from appointing the head of his riding association to the warden's job. Patronage and merit are intertwined, so that critical momentum is slowed. In a later article, Noel adds a supplementary rule for good patronage. In his view the kind of patronage that was truly useful in the building of party foundations was above all made to measure for the values and power structures of the local communities.[28]

Reg Whitaker's assessment is less comfortable. In his view the net effects of Canadian patronage are overwhelmingly negative. He says that our politicians have failed us:

> Patronage was distributed from the centre in such a way as to integrate local élites into the national network of the party, but the means did not transcend the differences of local community, province, language or religion by substituting common national symbols of loyalty: rather, they only reinforced the degrees of localism and provincialism already in existence. Neither a national ruling class (as in Britain) nor a national ideology (as in America) emerged in Canada. The result was a unique mixture of executive dominance and persistent localism.[29]

Thus in Whitaker's view patronage served party, but party did not in turn serve the country's longer-term requirement to develop a shared project for society. Patronage, in his view, is obstructive and wasteful when it is extensive and rich enough to provide the whole reason to draw citizens to undertake public service —it stunts the development of other reasons to become active in public life, and in so doing stifles the best ideals of citizenship. Whitaker's work leads one to reflect that the beneficiaries of the patronage pot who are smiling all the way to the bank are probably not meditating on the selfless satisfaction of civic pride—or at least not unless they are total humbugs. The two Canadian language groups in fact needed to consider deeply how their interests might be concerted and their differences transcended in imaginative common projects to put a new stamp on half a continent. Instead, the first riches of the country were raided for simple payment to maintain separation. Our two communities were deliberately insulated from one another with our own money.

One might add another feature of the two patronage solitudes. It is a truism of Canadian politics that the huge Quebec voting base, for a long time one-third and now a quarter of the national vote, is usually delivered *en bloc* to one or another lucky leader, and it is often enough to deliver the election. This deliverability of Quebec (at least to date) has many repercussions. The first is that our prime minister is very likely to be a Quebecker—certainly more than a third or only a quarter of the time. The second is that Quebeckers are disproportionately likely to be put in charge of the departments that are the richest sources of patronage, such as Public Works, for the simple reason that the party in power must satisfy Quebec for its own electoral survival. In consequence, anglophone élites, who dispense a good share of patronage but whose votes do not flow back up to them with the same regularity, can feel that they are held to ransom by the very success of the Quebec élite, including the prime minister himself, in delivering the Quebec vote. Thus at the same time as Quebec's 'deliverability' is exploited by the political parties for all it is worth, anglophone prejudices and frustration are fed. And the francophone community is driven to greater and greater efforts to maintain its vote as a bloc in order to protect Quebec's role in the federation and to protect the role of the federalist part of Quebec's élite in Canadian public life.

New-style patronage: to those that have, or, much gets more

Another negative feature that Whitaker notices is the modern transformation of federal patronage from rewarding the participation and votes of working-class people to an élitist system of well-paid middle and upper-middle class jobs and rewards. In effect, federal patronage has evolved into a system in which wealth is extracted from the economic base and paid out to relatively wealthy people who are already fully committed to the system and benefiting nicely from existing political and social structures.

Besides the relatively modest number of salaried full-time government jobs, new-style patronage is paid in the form of advertising, public relations, and polling contracts; in pervasive and very highly paid management-consulting contracts to private-sector consulting firms, who in 1992 were routinely billing a thousand dollars a day for senior consultants from blue-ribbon firms; and in consulting fees to academics. The lead-up to the October 1992 referendum on the Charlottetown Accord provides a case study of how the new patronage circulates, and of its scale. Journalists picking the referendum carcass reported that the Conservative Party's polling firm Decima Research received $937,000 in work before the campaign. A registered lobbyist worked closely with Senator Lowell Murray, an infringement of conflict of interest guidelines, and Murray's office further paid out $300,000 in two months to a firm in which the lobbyist's husband is a principal. The other principals of the firm included the co-chair of the 'Yes' campaign in the referendum, as well as a former press aide to the prime minister.[30] The scope of the new patronage in more normal times can be appreciated through departmental budgets for 'personal services' contracts. And enormous amounts are paid in professional fees to lawyers on 'the list' for Justice Department contracts for the government's legal work. It is less often noticed that the fastest-growing group in government (apart from tax collectors) is auditors and other workers of the 'counter bureaucracy' who are taking over, putting a rationalist 'spin' on, and vastly expanding the kinds of surveillance of bureaucracy that politicians used to take a rough stab at in the House of Commons. The control industry is straight overhead expense for the bureaucracy that provides services to people, lowering its productivity with every dollar of its own growth. Unlike many parts of the American control apparatus, which it can be noted must provide surveillance of an important 'transient' element in government, the Canadian industry has been reluctant to justify its own fees against the savings that it can identify. Other prizes include the top jobs in 'privatized' agencies that continue to enjoy secure sources of government work without the necessity for either fiscal disclosure or civil service routine, and in the companies providing temporary personnel to the government departments who have been forced to dismiss their own personnel to meet their quotas for cuts. Temporary personnel agencies can skim as much as a quarter of a secretary's wage of less than twenty dollars an hour. Often the agencies do not even find the employee, but merely provide a modality to allow the department to hire someone it has already identified, who indeed may be a person who was released from permanent employment.

Professor Noel has suggested a new framework for understanding the systemic purposes of the new patronage:

> . . . since the early 1970s it has become increasingly evident that the emerging modern functions of political patronage are, symbolically, the promotion of multiculturalism and, organizationally, the building of personal entourages.[31]

The symbolism of affirmative action and 'integrative' appointments is presumably intended to garner as-yet-uncommitted voters and activists from among the gender-challenged and new Canadians. The need for patronage to build entourages for politicians is related to the changing role of parties. Parties, says Noel, have been tamed by state financing given in recognition of the 'essential systemic function they play in maintaining the framework and setting the ground rules for the pursuit of political power'. The real heat is found in the competition inside parties for the leadership achieved or respectably failed. The candidate depends upon his or her groomers and handlers and speech-writers, and plenty of them. They work at low salaries for two or three years in hopes that their challenger will take the prime ministership or a cabinet post. At that point a much better life begins. They serve for a few years in the ministerial office at a salary equivalent to that earned by a twenty-five-year civil servant. Four years later, they will again be paid off in consulting assignments, and, should they choose to join a lobbyists' firm, rich fees. A certain number will compete for jobs in the regular public service, where the value of experience in a minister's office is by no means seen as a disadvantage. Noel's work nicely supplements Whitaker's observation about the new class-bias of patronage in Canada.

One can add to Noel's basic picture of entourage politics the additional costs that Canadians incur because of the volatility of our electorate's preferences. Each election sees large numbers of completely new incumbents in ministerial offices.

John Courtney estimated that after the election of 1984 fully 60 per cent of the Conservative caucus had not been members of the previous parliament.[32] He notes that these figures are 'staggering' when compared to turnover and replacement in Great Britain and the United States.

Conflicts of interest as patronage you give yourself

Conflict of interest, it has been said, is only self-administered patronage. Even though there are many kinds of ambiguities connected with defining conflict, the core idea is that it is a wholly selfish betrayal of the trust of public office. There is no social generosity in it, no public cause. Vincent Lemieux recently enumerated the federal patronage cases that most ignited the interest of the French-language Canadian press during 1989 and 1990. The big cases in the eyes of the print media were the following: that of André Bissonnette, who was alleged to have profited from insider knowledge leading to a land flip while a minister; Michel Côté, also a minister, who had accepted a loan from an individual who could have been a client of his department; and that of Senator Michel Cogger, who had received a fee in five figures from a client who was allegedly seeking a government contract through Cogger's interventions. In other words, all involved accusations of selfish advantage-seeking.[33]

Yet possibly the most interesting case involving a perceived ministerial conflict of interest in the Mulroney period is that of Sinclair Stevens, a Toronto businessman whom Mulroney had appointed to the portfolio of Regional Industrial Expansion. A special judicial inquiry under Judge William Parker reported in 1987 that Stevens had violated, not the criminal law, but Prime Minister Brian Mulroney's more encompassing 1985 conflict of interest guidelines for ministers on fourteen occasions.[34]

Stevens was apparently afflicted with a kind of polymorphic entrepreneurialism. One of his schemes was to convince the Vatican to endorse an issue of gold 'Christ coins' to mark a Papal visit to Canada, in return for part of the profit on sales of this tasteful artefact to the faithful. On occasion his business seemed to become almost inextricably intermingled with the Crown's, if only because the same contacts were useful to move along both government work and his own projects. Stevens himself just did not see what others thought the ethical problem was in his search for cash to keep his companies afloat, or the subsequent award of government contracts that were in his control to some of the same people and firms that had helped him out. He apparently sincerely believed that his wife, a lawyer, was a suitable choice to be the director for his blind trust, inspiring many complicated jokes about how blind one's trust should be.[35] He was done in because there was a Boswell to his Johnson: his personal assistant had taken prolific notes on her own and Stevens's dealings, and she had kept the notebooks. In retrospect, the prime minister's choice of Stevens for the particular portfolio that became his downfall appears inexplicable. The case does amply show, however, that conflict of interest is quite lacking the 'tragic' dimension that haunts the party-building aspects of some patronage.

The politics of coercion: bourgeois realism and dirty hands

Patronage politics is arguably a politics of plenty. Politics becomes more harsh where bribery and cronyism are either unavailable or inappropriate. In the section that follows, we talk first about the use of coercion in politics, before moving to lying and manipulation as more subtle ways of limiting the freedom of the person being influenced.

Machiavelli posed the problem of coercion and manipulation in politics as one of 'dirty hands'. He argued that no holds can be barred in seeking national security and national purposes. In fact, his position is that what the French call *raison d'état* is reason enough. In Stuart Hampshire's words:

> Machiavelli implied that morality in politics must be a consequentialist morality, and the 'must' here marks a moral injunction. A fastidiousness about the means employed, appropriate in personal relations, is a moral dereliction in a politician, and the relevant moral criterion for a great national enterprise is a lasting success; and success is measured by a historian's yardstick: continuing power, prosperity, high national spirit, a long-lasting dominance of the particular state or nation in the affairs of men. So Machiavelli argued.[36]

F.G. Bailey, a sociologist and anthropologist, is a modern Machiavelli. He argues that leadership involves dealing with the real world, which is continually throwing up challenges. Because new elements by definition have not yet been assessed in moral terms, the leader is necessarily always outside and above common morality.[37]

The leader handles his (or, more rarely, her) personal entourage by art, cutting deals and using the helpers' personal weaknesses as necessary. The mass, however, is almost scientifically manipulated at a distance through polling, which creates an image of what the public wants, wholly without reference to the kind of public policy that is feasible in the circumstances. The leader's 'metaculture' is thus a set of rules about what works—rules that are more empirical and practical than moral, and which are continually subjected to revision and objective tests of efficiency.[38] The rules range from those about how to win without cheating to how to cheat without being caught and punished.[39]

Leaders are only inhibited from the most absolute kinds of villainy by three factors: by the normative standards they preach for their opponents; by rivalry and competition for the prizes and thus the threat of exposure as *bonne guerre*; and by what Bailey calls the reserve of unbelievers, citizens with a well-developed and mellow sense of cynicism about politics coupled with a dedication to active good citizenship. The saving grace of Bailey's political universe, a veritable marketplace of lies and stratagems, is competition: wherever a leader manages to quell competition, terrible repression is the sure result.

David Shugarman, among other ethicists, has attacked this whole consequentialist or *raison d'état* habit of mind as 'bourgeois realism'.[40] Divested of its romantic notion of the heroic loneliness of the statesman decision maker, its propositions are, he says, wholly deceptive, and further encourage the deliberate admittance of wicked means.

'Transcendent purpose' mentality

Regimes that try Machiavellian methods to combat internal opposition find themselves prey to special forms of corruption. Among these is the corruption of the sense of justice of followers in the name of a cause or of society as a whole. The amoral follower is the person who has become completely immured in a mentality that will more or less unconditionally accept the line of action suggested by leaders. Such followers are the foot-soldiers of political disasters of every possible scale, from the Holocaust to Richard Nixon's 'fixers'. In Edwin Yoder's words, the amoral follower believes that 'transcendent political or bureaucratic purpose' can justify any method, including the exemplary punishment of innocents, so long as it maintains the desired social order'.[41] The paradigm case is that of the French officer Dreyfus, whose superior officers framed him in 1894 to shield one of their number because, being Jewish, Dreyfus seemed better suited to be cast as a traitor. In this way the army could maintain class solidarity and even heal itself, while presenting the treason to society in the guise of a morality play on the danger of allowing ambitious Jews to become integrated into important social institutions. The discovery of evidence exonerating Dreyfus two years later provoked the adversaries of a review of his case (nationalists, monarchists, clerics —and anti-Semites) into wild excesses, on the grounds that the army and the state must be protected against the asocial celebration of individual rights, such as those of poor Dreyfus.[42]

But the 'realist' mentality is seldom a program for clear thinking. Ruthlessness combined with selfish fear leads as often to disaster and farce as to saved honour. American politicians, driven by the cold war mentality, undertook actions that are now frankly disowned as intemperate, emotion-driven blunders—even by insiders and allies. For example, George Ball, US under secretary of state from 1961 to 1966, recently sketched a short list of Central Intelligence Agency actions, in addition to actions against Cuba, that he saw as blunders: deposing leaders in Guatemala and Iran; financing a military coup in Chile in 1974 that murdered President Allende; overthrowing Somoza's dictatorship in Nicaragua in 1979; and then trying to overthrow the successor Sandinistas for the next ten years with all the concomitant offences against the American constitution.[43] The year 1993 may even see the CIA and other agencies in the American bureaucracy investigated for building up the Iraqi military machine in the period leading up to the Gulf War of 1991.

In the United States, the mentality of 'transcendent purpose' connected with the cold war had a long run in the McCarthy period, roughly from the start of the Alger Hiss case in 1948[44] to the eventual censure of Senator McCarthy in 1955. Witnesses before the House Un-American Activities Committee were actually given money to fabricate their testimony. Even so, the false witnesses could not hear any moral alarm bells, possibly because their lies seemed to them to be fully justified on national security grounds, the cash seen as mere compensation for the bother of giving testimony.

Canada's external politics were decided by Great Britain until the twentieth century, after which we became by and large a client of the United States. Therefore, for most of our history, others have decided for us what our main moral risks as a state would be. All the same, Canada did buy into the cold war with more than a client's dedication, and had its own anti-Communist crusade, low profile in the Canadian way. Citizens were secretly listed by the RCMP as suspected persons only to learn of it when they lost their jobs, or were turned back at the American border, taken off trains, or removed from airplanes. Pierre Trudeau beat the ban on entry to the US by getting himself elected prime minister: this was not a tactic open to everyone. Other people whom we admired then and still admire now, including the poet Irving Layton and the violinist Steven Staryk, not to forget the writer Farley Mowat, were pulled up in the RCMP net.[45]

Any six middle-aged Canadians could provide over dinner a list of other major and morally questionable political episodes in our history, particularly if one would include the coercive manipulation of justification. To do so pulls in, for example, the following kinds of disputed issues: the trial and hanging of Louis Riel; the abrogation of the rights of minorities in the Second World War[46]; the displacement during the 1950s of Inuit from their traditional territories to the most northern extremes to help make a case for Canadian sovereignty in the High Arctic[47]; the delayed recognition of land claims of Native peoples; aspects of the October Crisis in 1970 when hundreds of people were imprisoned without due process; and even the packing (under the 'constitutional loophole' mentality) of the Canadian Senate with eight emergency senators in order to pass expeditiously the Goods and Services Tax.

Nor are we without recent examples of a 'transcendent purpose' mentality in the federal bureaucracy. In 1991 the most senior officers in the federal Privy Council Office devised with ministers an elaborate strategy to help the government avoid giving an explanation to the House of Commons for the accelerated entry to Canada, as an immigrant, of the former ambassador from Iraq to the United States, Mohamed Al-Mashat. As our country had just been at war with Iraq, the public and the opposition in the House of Commons felt entitled to an explanation for the diplomat's entry in the retired class. The political damage-control plan involved publicly naming a senior public servant as guilty of the failure to inform a minister, even though a memorandum had in fact gone forward to the minister and had been waylaid by accident by the minister's Chief of Staff, before it could reach the minister. A public servant and a senior aide were thus to be found guilty of the inexistence of something that did exist. The Clerk of the Privy Council actively implemented the political strategy that flew in the face of reality, legitimating—if only accidentally—a kind of kangaroo trial of officials by a government majority in a House of Commons standing committee.[48]

Canada's RCMP scandals

Of the riches offered, we will explore in somewhat more detail the RCMP scandals following upon the October Crisis of 1970. The purpose of the offending officers was to bolster the status quo. The scandals also illustrate the mechanism of affective blindness. Anglo-Canadian admiration for and loyalty to 'the Force', as we often call it, impedes our comprehension of the sense of outrage among Quebeckers that the Mounties went too far.[49]

Reg Whitaker has again provided a rich analysis of the events. The scandals are to be understood against the backdrop of the October 1970 crisis. The federal government sent troops to maintain order in Quebec in apprehension of a widespread insurrection, signalled, they thought, by two political kidnappings. At some point after 1970, whether by direct instruction is unknown, it became understood by some officers in the RCMP that they could break the law in the service of counter-terrorism.

The Mounties' infractions remained more or less secret only until the late 1970s, when there was a series of revelations of RCMP illegality, violence (including planting bombs and a prophylactic fire to burn a barn rather than let it be used for political meetings), provocations by agents who had infiltrated separatist movements, the disruption of political parties and groups, and unauthorized access to confidential data on citizens. When the Quebec government (under the Parti Québécois) set up the Keable Commission to look into the actions of the Mounties in Quebec, the federal government followed with the McDonald Commission. The RCMP were found to be responsible for fourteen illegal actions. One of these was, amazingly enough, planting a bug on their own minister, the solicitor general, who the Mounties felt was too far on the left of the political spectrum to deserve to be their leader. And so indeed, they believed, was a good proportion of the electorate: in the late 1970s the Mounties held security files on 800,000 individuals, or about two good-sized cities' worth of Canadians, which suggests a certain inability to discriminate. The Mounties confirmed to the McDonald Commission that they had secret sources inside the Quebec government in the 1970s, and that they had been collecting information on members of completely legal groups.

In Parliament, the politicians were unable to come to grips with the problem of how the Mounties' illegal activities could be controlled, in the light of their own electoral aspirations. The Tories, Whitaker notes, adopted a line designed to please their own voters: the RCMP was blameless and the fault lay solely with the Liberal government who had misused or misdirected the police. New Democratic Party politicians, who had been the first to condemn the suspension of civil liberties through the 1970 crisis, were in turn silenced by the tactic of lumping them in with the communists.[50]

The upshot of the political havering was that all the sections of the McDonald report that would have justified criminal charges against individual officers were removed from the report at the direction of the government. Finally in 1983, the government tried to address the causes of the events through a reorganization of the national security machinery. This reorganization is referred to as the 'civilian-ization' of our security and intelligence service, accomplished by moving the function out of the uniformed services to an independent agency with a modest element of supervision by a committee chosen from members of the Privy Council. The main improvement, Whitaker judges, is that the kind of intelli-gence work that most frequently leads to over-zealousness has been removed from the mythic legitimating aura that surrounds the men in red tunics.

Nor do the security revelations end with the McDonald Commission findings. In April of 1992, as both old and new rumours about the extent of RCMP activity in Quebec circulated, the Quebec minister of justice stated that he might still prosecute some of the actions on Quebec territory and asked the federal govern-ment for the suppressed sections of the McDonald report along with background papers.

A month later, in May, Claude Morin astonished at least the rank and file of the Parti Québécois and the independence movement by publicly confirming his identity as 'Q1', the Mounties' best-placed Quebec informer. Morin, for years a respected civil servant before becoming a senior strategist for the Parti Québécois and a cabinet minister in the PQ government in 1976, was paid by the RCMP for three years on his own admission, and for longer according to other sources. In an apologia published in *Le Devoir*, he claimed that the Mounties had been investigat-ing the possible infiltration of Quebec by foreign governments, and *not* the PQ, and that he had directed the fees he had received to good works and PQ finances. His motive for sustaining the RCMP contact had been the welfare of the PQ and the higher interests of Quebec, comforted by a certain intellectual interest in the security game itself, plus a soupçon of arrogance about his own capacity to manage his own handlers.[51] Not the least interesting feature was the timing of the pressure that forced Morin to speak only in the period closely preceding the 1992 referendum on Canadian unity: the man who once calculatedly decided to go along with the Mounties had himself become a pawn in a game serving someone else's purpose.

The purity duel and the partisan lie

The purity duel in partisan politics consists of strategic exaggeration, fact selec-tion, and outright lying, with the goal of manipulating voters into rejecting one's opponent. Bayless Manning has explained the duel in the American context, or at least the context that lasted up to the more polarized politics of the Bush-Clinton contest of 1992. The precondition in the United States, according to Manning, is the 'extraordinary Two-party non-System', that is, a massive majority committed to an ideological centre, with two purely 'brokerage' parties contesting office. In the absence of ideas, politicians must find a way to distinguish the various candidates from one another. This they have classically done by concentrating on purely moral grounds of dispute. The electoral contest then takes place between a few bad guys and a few other bad guys who work frantically to put each others' histories and capacities in the worst of all possible lights. The voter chooses the individual he or she judges to be the lesser of the two evils.

The purity attack is conducted in one of two ways. The first is the conspiratorial method, in which isolated instances of impropriety are selected or invented, and a rationale is then spun to connect them in a pattern of meaning. The idea is to make the 'facts' appear to be illustrations of massive hidden corruption, or key covert actions in what was an intricate plot to bring about an existing problematic situation. The second or general method, where souls or situations are discovered to be irremediably tainted, is to escalate standards to such an impossible extent that virtually any finding or observation will seem to illustrate the claimed flaw.[52]

As Manning further notes, purity duel systems are unstable and tend to escalate. This in turn creates sharp ironies, for example, that the public's sensitivity to perceived financial corruption in both administration and political life rises steadily even as the amount of actual corruption decreases. Part of the reason for the decrease in financial corruption can be credited to the fact that the purity duel has raised standards. But mostly, improved honesty is a result of modern methods of financial audit and better management control.

Sometimes distortion can be so programmatic that it takes on an ideological function, even though the attack itself is personalized. The French term for this mode of political discourse is *langue de bois*. In an article about the independence debate in Quebec, journalist and communications specialist Richard Vigneault recently summarized its rhetorical tactics:

> . . . the systematic use of abuse; the discrediting of any opponent, who will be conceived as the enemy; any disagreement assimilated to treason; the spoken word used as a weapon; ideas recast as a protective shield; suffocating of all debate by assimilating it into the strategic combat; the rejection of any ethical restraints; the denial of any moral question; the negation of any solution that is not cast within the black and white framework . . . seeking to get rid of all contradiction . . . to the point of suppressing the messenger.[53] [Free translation]

John Diefenbaker in the late 1950s and early 1960s was an ardent purity duellist. One interesting Diefenbaker electoral tactic was to use prevalent cold-war fears and suspicions to suggest that the opposition Liberal Party was tainted with a fatal communist stain, thus feeding off the momentum generated in the American system. He made the link by first demonizing a few civil servants who sought elected office under the colours of the Liberal Party. Any intellectual civil servant who believed that government had a role to play in society was by definition a socialist. And a socialist was only a communist in sheep's clothing. Such people would naturally be eager to infiltrate the highest government apparatus. Thus the Liberal Party had been tainted by its own expedient of recruiting civil service mandarins to run for public office, and was consequently morally unfit to govern a free Canada. Diefenbaker concentrated his fire on Walter Gordon, Mitchell Sharp, Tom Kent, and Maurice Lamontagne, trying to cast the Liberal Party as a victim of these sinister forces. Lester Pearson he dismissively identified as an 'ineffective dupe of the Kremlin', probably because the amiable

Elmer Fudd image that Pearson often projected was difficult material even for Diefenbaker, to say the least.[54]

Peter Newman has described Diefenbaker's campaign in the 1962 election, a campaign that Diefenbaker thought of as a great trial of the vaguely-described bureaucratic villains:

> In 1962, he attempted to distract attention from the nation's problems by setting up an enemy for the voters to hate. By personal attacks, which grew in intensity to become the main theme of the campaign, he tried to portray in the public mind an image of the Liberal Party as 'the same old bunch'—a group of unrepentant, unsavoury characters dedicated to fooling the population under the guise of socialistic promises that would ruin the country. During the campaign, Diefenbaker's cabinet ministers echoed their leader's message by referring to leading Liberals as 'apes', 'stinkers', 'criminals', 'skunks', and, most often, 'oddballs'.[55]

Diefenbaker was outraged when Lester Pearson was able to form a minority government after the second-shoe 1963 election, his own minority government of 1962 having been quite unable to maintain its cohesion. Diefenbaker and Eric Nielsen then formed a vengeful team. Together they took three Quebec ministers out of Pearson's minority government. In fact, it was an easy success, requiring only a willingness to put aside any residual sense of fairness. A minority government by its nature cannot call a vote of confidence. This simple fact, combined with the fact that Members of Parliament can say whatever they please, as often as they please, protected by parliamentary privilege, gave Diefenbaker and Nielsen their hunting licence. They were able to shake the government by orchestrating 'revelations' day after day to weave a tapestry of accusations. They skilfully identified every available parliamentary forum to repeat their accusations to fix them in the public mind and to maintain momentum. They worked the tone of their allegations to drive an ethnic wedge through the minority government, tapping the worst of the House's Anglo-Saxon prejudices against French-Canadians. While one would not want to say that the ministers under attack were innocent of all misjudgement, the parliamentary campaign to destroy them was the *langue de bois* of Canadian politics at its worst: a fanatical sense of superiority aimed at the other ethnic group, with no sense of measure or consequences.[56] The classic irrefutable smear was used with telling effect against the minister of justice, Guy Favreau: Favreau had the power to do what he was accused of, Diefenbaker could read corrupt motives back into Favreau's actions, there were bits of evidence that could be fitted into a big theory, thus Favreau certainly must be guilty.[57] This time it was a flawless trial—except that there was no defence. Two of the three politicians who were ruined in this strategic game died shortly after leaving Parliament. The whole story of this period and the way the fates of these three politicians were manipulated for partisan gain is part of Canadian federal history that is missing and apt to remain so: it is unlikely to be written by anglophones or federalists, because the subject matter is politically embarrassing and painful, or by francophone nationalists, because humiliated federalists are no longer of great interest or utility.

As for Pierre Trudeau, he was not only a francophone intellectual, but one who had extensively toured what was then called Red China. Literature readily available in western Canada before the 1968 election, which was indeed repeatedly pressed on this writer, claimed that Trudeau embodied the two great faults of foreign intellectuals: he was a homosexual and a communist. When Trudeau became minister of justice and then prime minister, the Conservatives hammered at him in the House of Commons day after day as an undisguised communist. The grand theory of Trudeau's moral turpitude was generous enough to accommodate both his apparent communism along with his vulnerability to corruption by occult forces such as the Liberal Party in its gift of a swimming pool for the official residence.[58]

But winning the election would turn the moral tables on the Conservatives. After 1984, the Liberals, now in opposition, borrowed the tactic of steady moral denunciation of the Conservative government. The Liberals and New Democratic Party worked well together to corner the government in Question Period, orchestrating volleys of speakers to reinforce one short and neat accusation, putting the burden on the prime minister for explanation. The themes were self-servingness, corruption, cronyism, and 'imperial' high living: everything that had been used against the Liberals while in power that could offend the moral sense of the citizen on a salary, and some of the details were excellent. A complicated series of revelations then tarred more than a half-dozen ministers, about fifteen ordinary backbench Conservatives, and two or three senators. At one point the RCMP even had a special unit, since disbanded, solely to investigate politicians. The tactic of moving to furious moral escalation at every occasion enabled the two opposition parties to take a series of ministers out of the largest majority government that Canada had ever seen: Fraser, Coates, Bissonnette, Stevens, LaSalle, and Côté. One reason the opposition could do this was that early in the first Conservative government it had sympathizers among the Tory backbenchers who had been in Parliament through the Trudeau years: they had bought their own moralism. Backbench disapproval of its own cabinet's behaviour was one of the factors underlying Mulroney's decisions early in his first government to seek quick resignations rather than to even consider riding out parliamentary storms.

In parentheses, and somewhat ironically, the chain of ministerial resignations helped to confirm the belief of the Canadian media that ministerial resignation is the only true manifestation of responsible government—the 'shooting gallery' doctrine of ministerial responsibility. This mindset would provide the context for the refusal of the relevant minister to perform the constitutional duty of providing answerability (an explanation) in the House of Commons in the Al-Mashat case, to which we referred earlier. The new doctrine appeared to be that if the minister even appeared to know about an event, then he must be held politically liable, which would mean that he was responsible to volatilize on the spot.

As the government's mandate wore on, Mulroney and his party turned out to be even more vulnerable than the previous regime to charges of high living: the public was first irritated and then almost fixated upon the cost of decorating the prime ministerial residence, especially when the bankrupt decorator fled the country and Mrs Mulroney's firm instructions to change carpets and then change them back again; was then impressed by the number of pairs of Gucci loafers in the prime ministerial closet (85); and gasped at the size of the prime minister's entourage (35) on an Asian tour, and at the two plane-loads of gear.[59]

By 1991, polling had convinced the Conservative government that the dramatic decrease in public approval of their seriousness and of Parliament in general was attributable to the detective capacity of the rag-tag Liberals and the daily wild accusations levied and parried in Question Period, and to the lack of effective self-regulation by the House of its own members' behaviour. The government House Leader, himself one of the most rough-and-tumble of politicians, suddenly became a statesman to ask the House for a higher standard of civility and self-control.[60] Even more interesting, the House of Commons Board of Internal Economy passed in 1991 some controversial amendments to the Parliament of Canada Act, with the aim of recovering and perhaps strengthening the House of Commons tradition of self-regulation. The amendments provide that the Board has 'exclusive authority' to determine the propriety of any use of Commons funds. The provision became a kind of trump card for a time: MPs whose use of Commons funds was in question could ask the Board for a ruling, and so long as the Board absent-mindedly omitted to determine it, the judicial system could apparently be held at bay. But in January of 1992 a Quebec Court justice ruled in one MP's case that House privileges do not include criminal immunity, and in December another judge in the general division of the Ontario court system refused to let the Board further extend an eighteen-month delay in the prosecutions of another two MPs.[61]

Conclusion

I have tried to create an expectation about the typical kinds of defects that go along with the advantages of procedural democracy, or at least the defects of too much faith in bare procedure at the expense of substance and the fostering of a sense of political community. This chapter has provided a discussion of the corruption of government from its best purposes through the indiscriminate use of patronage, the mentality of Machiavellian politics or 'bourgeois realism', and has discussed the 'purity war' tactics that debase political debate, and prevent the public education that might help us to transcend ourselves. The ruthless mentality of bourgeois realism as it has shown itself in federal politics, as well as our various purity wars, are both capable of worsening the divisions in this country that patronage cannot heal.

In the chapter's opening remarks, an exemplary old scandal was used to pose a worry to be kept in mind through the discussion. Are the morality problems of federal Canada serious enough to qualify as a 'contradiction'—a machine of destruction at the heart of our country? Over the longer term, are we doomed to watch a collision between the demands of the Canadian public for a politics cleansed of patronage, and a deaf immobilism in political practices—simply because patronage is the only form of partisan reward and political glue that the governing party has at its disposition to unite French and English speakers behind the federal project? Will the longer term in Canada see a 'tragic interplay' between a public demand for a politics of civic virtue and effective performance, and the incapacity of politicians to provide even so much as an honourable 'watch' on our ship of state, let alone to deliver on their promises?

The factors weighing against us are serious. The indulgence of élites in patronage and conflict of interest in federal Canada is probably next to impossible to change, because there are several mutually reinforcing causes of its prevalence. First, patronage has been in our structures and in our blood since even before we became independent as a country. It has always seemed a perfectly normal motive for public service to many if not most of us. Second, all our provinces have become progressively more addicted to 'profitable federalism' as a rationale of national unity. This means that allegiance has unceasingly to be bought, and opportunistic dissent is the new status quo. During the constitutional discussions that led up to the Charlottetown Accord of August 1992, provincial politicians were openly brokering their support for what was unanimously described as our national future against items like highways. No road, no country. Worse, as fiscal pressures on the state mount, senior politicians increasingly fall back on the old techniques of patronage and raids on the assets of the public sector within a context of policy immobilism. They feel they must do so to cement their own leadership and keep their seats. Take one issue: the deconcentration of civil service jobs from the National Capital Region to ministers' ridings. The problem with badly planned asset raiding, such as the processing of citizenship files in Nova Scotia (Liberals) or of immigration files in central Alberta (Conservatives), is that the state is rendered ever less productive and predictable, and less controllable through concerted public action.[62]

Third, the potential for clumsy conflict of interest increases in direct proportion to the Canadian version of political amateurism, which currently combines two trends. The first is the Canadian tendency towards electoral volatility, sending wave after wave of new members to the House of Commons, so that a long-term political career is a rarity, and our most important ministers can be utter novices to public life and to reflection on public life. As in all things, this is a question of proportion. A second interesting feature is the party shift towards disproportionately choosing the amateurs who will govern us from among the business occupations. Until quite recently, to take the argument by one of several possible ends, lawyers have been the modal occupational group in the House of Commons, and dominated cabinet. An early section of this chapter showed lawyers have historically been the single most favoured occupational group in the awarding of federal patronage jobs. The professional patronage system of the

Justice Department has traditionally groomed and fed lawyers so that they could make themselves graciously available for the burden of public office. Through the Trudeau period of roughly 1968-84, lawyers held about half of all Cabinet seats. But with the 1984 election, lawyers slipped below twenty per cent of the House of Commons membership for the first time in Canadian history. In the Mulroney governments, business figures outnumbered lawyers by about three to one.[63]

Now, one can recognize that lawyers have certain qualities for public life that business figures do not possess to the same extent without claiming that lawyers are always good representatives, or even that one wants lawyers *en bloc* in public life. The advantage of lawyers, even as rank amateurs in political life, and only over most other rank amateurs, is that because of their training lawyers are disproportionately likely to understand and observe the standards of public office. They understand the reasons for the provisions of the Criminal Code that deal with breach of trust and corruption of elected and appointed officials. As a condition of entry to law schools they acquire a broad liberal education that includes history, the foundations of democratic theory, and education in how our representative institutions work, and some public policy. In addition, lawyers charge fees for professional services, a contained and consensual transaction. Business figures, on the other hand, are proportionately less likely to have received such a concentrated training in civics (although many are capable of impressive learning in the House of Commons). They put together deals that can involve several players and layers of transactions over time, and are therefore much more likely both to become public knowledge and to be interpreted in a hostile way. The business community does not meet in solemn conclave to expel sinners from its midst when they are caught in wrongdoing. Thus lawyers were perhaps stuffy, but the new business élite can make even that failing look like an advantage. And besides the burden of opportunistic amateurism, it might also be noted parenthetically that federal Canada supports a large number of politicians and political assistants for the size of our population and the task at hand, especially given that many important government responsibilities are acquitted at the provincial level. We have almost as many politicians at the federal level as now govern the United States, which has ten times our population.

One can sum up to this point. It seems safe to predict that patronage in Canada will surely endure, that conflicts and offences will increasingly occur and will be exposed, and that the public will feel angry and frustrated at the lack of responsiveness to its disapproval. These are the reasons suggested so far: first, our history in trading favours within élites; second, our divisiveness; and third, the fact that there have been measurable and even dramatic changes in the personnel of our politics, landing us with a political personnel that is overall too numerous, under-occupied, under-prepared for thinking imaginatively about feasible policy in an increasingly demanding world environment, and which is even under-socialized in the requirements of political probity.

But describing our situation is not necessarily the same thing as understanding it. It is a healthy instinct to look beyond our own difficulties, and to try to understand what parts of our dilemma are peculiar to Canada, and which are the widely-shared difficulties of liberal democracies. According to Gianfranco Poggi, in all the developed liberal democracies political parties have been narrowing the range of issues that they will contest. He points out that since the Second World War, politics in all western democracies has become narrowly technocratic. The political process 'has come to revolve chiefly around economic issues—primarily, *which* state policies can best promote industrial growth'. Poggi sees this radical narrowing of the political agenda as 'a kind of economic sublimation of politics'. It embodies an uncritical mindset that all worthwhile social and cultural needs can and will be addressed by the private sphere if there is economic growth, and further believes that growth can be assured by the correct application of available and specific technical knowledge.[64] Growth becomes the sole end, with almost no attention to the social purposes that growth was originally worshipped as serving.

In narrowing the range of issues on which they will contend, Poggi says, parties have come to resemble one another almost more closely than can be supported by constitutional theory of liberal democracy. The idea of turn-taking elections is trivialized when the agenda is never altered or broadened or made more imaginative, and the same interests are always served. Politics is reduced to questions of who is most likely to be able to do the unique thing that must be done—if only we could know what it was. Competition over occupancy of government is thereby almost everywhere undertaken as a value in itself. Those who contest for office are becoming haphazard groupings of people, whose cohesion and power as a team has been neither built over time nor tested. Their companionship, such as it is, is that they are prepared to argue that they jointly possess the correct technical tools and a formula to master the economy.

Reliance on the pure self-interest of comparatively small numbers of partisan activists increasingly means that parties no longer cultivate and work with the kinds of people who could relay to them popular demands for new and interesting policy. An active and involved mass party membership can ideally constitute a party's sensory apparatus in society, looking outward into daily life for information about what factors create difficulty and how people understand their lives. When the active membership is small and concentrated at the commanding heights of the party, and looks upward for rewards instead of outward for information, parties cannot recognize and respond to spontaneous social forces. An example of the consequences of isolation is that none of the pro-European politicians seriously anticipated a 'No' vote by either Denmark or France in the 1992 referendums on closer political unity among the Common Market countries. In the event, Denmark did vote no and France provided only a cripplingly weak yes. In the case of Canada, we see that the mainstream Canadian parties have simply failed to recognize that their own practices help to confirm the two solitudes in their isolation. For another example, we see today that the environmental movement has had to develop an organizational apparatus completely outside the traditional party structures. At the same time, a separate trend of mounting structural deficits has established itself. State penury means that there is little money available for program innovation, or even enough to support the popular health care and education programs. This confirms the narrowness of the electoral agenda, and the conviction of politicians that growth, or alternatively, cuts, are the most worthy items for discussion.

A second problem is the apparent tendency of the purity war to escalate. The purity war in the modern commercial media context feeds off the requirement that politicians find a way to distinguish themselves from their competitors. It is perfect for the profit-making dynamic of the media, and its appetite for sensationalist, easy-to-assimilate news product that can be packaged as compelling and money-making 'infotainment'.[65] But inflation devalues the entertainment value of accusations that used to shock, thus ever wilder 'facts' and rhetoric are necessary to get the attention of the mass public. In the US election campaign of 1992, the incumbent Republican Party used the apparatus of the state to try to collect personal information that could be used against the chances of the challenger, Bill Clinton. President George Bush even signed God with the Republicans for the great battle.[66] The name-calling mentality is also technically compatible with the 'sound-bite' packaging that dominated political advertising (as well as news) at least until the 1992 American election campaign: political jousting on television was made affordable to the parties by reducing debate to bursts of words nine to thirty seconds long that were used in 'mood' commercials. For some time it was thought that Canadians would not buy into negative campaigning to the same extent as Americans, but that smug belief was put to rest by the last two elections, according to research conducted for the Royal Commission on Electoral Reform. We also saw Canadian examples of negative campaigning in television commercials for the October 1992 referendum campaign.[67]

All these forces do seem to reduce the tolerance of the public for the political class and for what politics has become. People learn a general contempt for the whole political system at the same time as they form their strongest candidate revulsion. Between two-thirds and three-quarters of Canadians are moderately to seriously disaffected with the political process.[68]

So it may be that all or most liberal democracies are experiencing something close to 'contradiction' in Bouvier's terms: political incapacity coupled with rhetorical ruthlessness leading to an equally aggressive disaffection of the target public—politics with attitude. Yet for Canadians to take comfort from the general misery could be a mistake. Political incapacity and disaffected publics may be the pneumonia that finishes us off in the final stages of our unity problems.

But of course it could also happen that political agendas will be reflated to include ideals of community and *projets de société* without special measures—as a consequence, even, of the end of the neo-conservative parties' turn at forming governments. Having had the experience of first winning and then alienating whole electorates over solid periods of time, adherents of minimalist government may even realize spontaneously that the business stability agenda is simply not enough to provide what is now, for some solemn reason, called 'governance' for society. The lords of industry and of the press may become less adamant about what sorts of public goods can and cannot be provided. As well, there are likely any number of sensible measures that could be taken to address isolated elements of the larger problems (such as the perceived feeding frenzy of entourages).[69]

Again in the direction of optimism, the American election campaign of 1992 had its high as well as its low points, and perhaps signalled some changes in the role of the media in political campaigning and political education. In the US, the explosion of new cable television channels has already reduced the market share of the big networks in the prime time audience to about 60 per cent. And because of their need to fill air time, the new channels made it possible for the first time for the candidates to reach signficant numbers of people as live candidate programming rather than almost exclusively filtered through the interpretation and analysis of media personalities, or presented in the coloured aspic of commercials. Ross Perot proved that as many as twenty million people would stay tuned for a thirty-minute talking-head lecture—on economics and the deficit, no less.[70] Thus it may prove that, from being a driving force leading to destabilization of American politics, the purity war might dwindle to an incidental accompaniment to an increasingly substantial politics.

Further, if one can be forgiven for somewhat recklessly mongering hope, states could even directly address through public policy what amounts to the problem of getting citizens to consent to be governed, and to participate in building agendas for the kind of government they want and can respect. One of the things that seems to be needed is a public space for citizens. Perhaps political discourse has become narrow and hostile because modern citizens have not recognized a modern way—an effective and fitting medium—to communicate with one another, in order to learn efficiently about public issues and to add to a substantial agenda for democratic politics. But all the communication devices invented after radio and television individualize communication. Computer modems and facsimile devices, for example, offer connection only as a one-on-one event, or an event that can be extended with meticulous care one by one to other individuals who have had the foresight and wealth to provide themselves with the right equipment and learn the rituals that make it work.

What is needed, on the other hand, is an effective and simple way to communicate casually and cordially with and among groups of ordinary people. Poggi has suggested that this necessary medium has got to be television, reconceived and imaginatively and determinedly used as a public good. Television is capable of creating and in fact does create a whole culture. Thus if anything is a 'public good', like water and air and civility, it is television. The liberal democracies, Poggi argues, must be convinced to provide for an important amount of individual and group access by citizens—as both producers and consumers—to non-profit television. High-quality information and debate ought to be provided as a public *entitlement*, the basic right of citizenship, and without constant mean-minded partisan cutting, harping about profit, and bullying about content.[71] It is simply no excuse to say that freedom will die if the state regulates so much as one or two channels to provide open and balanced access to those who want to engage in explanation and debate. As Charles Lindblom, a long-time investigator of politics and markets, points out in a major restatement of his beliefs about pluralism, freedom dies just as surely when price determines all access to and content of the media as it does when markets determine nothing.[72]

In short, we might try to define a meaningful right of assembly for modern life, where technology has made communication at a distance seem like a natural preliminary to face-to-face contact. The role of the new cable channels in the 1992 American election may be an indication that Poggi's vision of how to build an enduring and civilized conversation in public life is truly feasible. If there is a better idea than his—building a public space by use of a medium that already exists, is suited to regulatory techniques, and whose use can be readily monitored —I am most definitely among the great many who will be glad to hear of it.

Notes

I am grateful to my editors, Allan Tupper and John Langford, and to my fellow contributors Ian Stewart, Kenneth Kernaghan, Stéphane Dion, and Tom Pocklington. I would also like to thank colleagues Susan Sherwin, Peter Aucoin, and Vince Wilson, and my sister, Katherine Sutherland. I owe David Braybrooke a special thanks and recognition. He provided whole lists of exciting and crucial references, and by his long-time intellectual and personal example prepared me to internalize, through the course of preparing the paper, the importance of the ideal of civility.

1 One can suggest as a rough translation, 'Political and economic systems never die from their scandals. They die from their internal contradictions, which is entirely something else.' Jean Bouvier, *Les Deux Scandales de Panama* (Paris: René Julliard, 1964): 204.

2 Philip M. Williams, *Wars, Plots and Scandals in Post-War France* (Cambridge: Cambridge University Press, 1970): 16.

3 Macdonald to Allan, *Report of the Royal Commissioners* (Ottawa: 1873): 118, quoted in David Cruise and Alison Griffiths, *Lords of the Line: The Men who Built the CPR* (Markham, Ont.: Viking, 1988): 69. The authors suggest that the railway magnates built up very careful documentation as insurance.

4 Jeffrey Simpson, *Spoils of Power: The Politics of Patronage* (Toronto: HarperCollins, 1988): 91.

5 For detail on ministerial resignations see S.L. Sutherland, 'Responsible Government and Ministerial Responsibility: Every Reform Is Its Own Problem', *Canadian Journal of Political Science* 24, 1 (March 1991): 91-120. Marcel Masse was to come back after clearing up a difficulty over his election expenses.

6 See Patricia Poirier, 'Lasalle got cash, court told', *Globe and Mail*, 18 Sept. 1991: A3, and Patricia Poirier, 'Tax Court places ban on publication of Gravel evidence', *Globe and Mail*, 27 Sept. 1991: A3.

7 In July 1991, an Ottawa Justice of the Peace allowed charges to proceed against thirteen Conservatives and three senior RCMP officers, based on seventeen days of

hearings into Mr Kealey's allegations. Two months later, the Crown dropped all charges except some involving LaSalle. (These were dropped in the fall of 1992, although the police investigation remained active.) See Mark Kennedy, 'Kealey divulges details of "corruption" testimony', *The Ottawa Citizen*, 12 Dec. 1991: A2. Kealey's personal story is told in another piece by Mark Kennedy, 'Determined to be Different', *The Ottawa Citizen*, 7 September 1991: B1.

8 Simpson, *Spoils of Power*: 23; 25-6; 352.

9 Simpson, *Spoils of Power*: 26.

10 Walter Lippmann, 'A Theory About Corruption', in A.J. Heidenheimer, ed., *Political Corruption: Readings in Comparative Analysis* (New Brunswick, NJ: Transaction Books, 1970): 294.

11 This prevalent habit is documented in the body of psychological work loosely described as attribution theory.

12 See for example the special issue on ethics in government and business of *Canadian Public Administration* 34, 1 (Spring 1991); Michael M. Atkinson and Maureen Mancuso, 'Do We Need a Code of Conduct for Politicians? The Search for an Elite Political Culture of Corruption in Canada', *Canadian Journal of Political Science* 18, 3 (Sept. 1985): 459-81; Kenneth Gibbons and Donald Rowat, eds, *Political Corruption in Canada* (Toronto: McClelland and Stewart, 1976); Kenneth Kernaghan, 'Codes of Ethics and Public Administration: Progress, Problems and Prospects', *Public Administration* 59 (1980); Kenneth Kernaghan, *Ethical Conduct: Guidelines for Government Employees* (Toronto: Institute of Public Administration of Canada, 1975); Kenneth Kernaghan and John W. Langford, *The Responsible Public Servant* (Halifax: Institute for Research on Public Policy, 1990); John W. Langford, 'Conflict of Interest: What the Hell Is It?', *Optimum* 22, 1 (1991/92): 28-34; and Jean-Pierre Kingsley, 'Conflict of Interest: A Modern Antidote', *Canadian Public Administration* 29, 4 (Winter 1986): 585-92. For a discussion of the two extremes of machinery to police ethical behaviour, see Michael M. Atkinson and Maureen Mancuso, 'Conflict of Interest in Britain and the United States: An Institutional Argument', *Legislative Studies Quarterly* 16, 4 (Nov. 1991): 471-93. For a useful discussion of typical control mechanisms in Canadian legislatures, see Carolyn Thomson, 'Conflict of Interest: A Comparative View', in Robert J. Fleming, ed., *Canadian Legislatures 1987/88* (Ottawa: Ampersand Communications Services Inc., 1988): 47-69. For a wider range of backbencher offences, including sexism, laziness, general greed, and opportunism, see Robert Fife and John Warren, *A Capital Scandal: Politics, Patronage and Payoffs—Why Parliament Must be Reformed* (Toronto: Key Porter Books, 1991). Their conclusion is that the only way to cure backbenchers of rampant immorality is to give them more power in the conduct of government.

13 Government of Canada, Special Joint Committee of the Senate and House of Commons, *Report to the Senate and the House of Commons on Subject-Matter of Bill C-43, Conflict of Interest for Parliamentarians*, June 1992. The report recommends the establishment of an office called a 'jurisconsult' to advise and oversee a limited disclosure provision for ministers, parliamentary secretaries, and MPs, similar to and replacing the service now provided to political office holders (ministers and senior officials) by the Office of the Assistant Deputy Registrar General of Canada. The report's central principle that there is nothing wrong with *having* a conflict of interest as such (that is, in having an interest that could be assisted through government channels), and that the important thing is how the conflict is resolved. It proposes the following definition:

for an office holder to be in the wrong, an objective interest should be present, and the member should reasonably have known of it.

14 Gianfranco Poggi, *The State: Its Nature, Development and Prospects* (Oxford: Polity Press, 1990).

15 Gordon T. Stewart, *The Origins of Canadian Politics: A Comparative Approach* (Vancouver: University of British Columbia Press, 1986): 31.

16 Reg Whitaker, 'Between Patronage and Bureaucracy: Democratic Politics in Transition', *Journal of Canadian Studies* 22, 2 (Summer, 1987): 56.

17 Randy Colwell and Paul Thomas, 'Parliament and the Patronage Issue', *Journal of Canadian Studies* 22, 2 (Summer, 1987); and S.L. Sutherland and G.B. Doern, *Bureaucracy in Canada: Control and Reform* (Toronto: University of Toronto Press, 1985): 65.

18 In the Order in Council personnel system, the Prime Minister's Office takes the initiative in identifying, reference checking, and recruiting candidates for any job in the government that is awarded through an OIC, while the Privy Council Office provides advice to help the PMO meet the criteria and legal requirements set out in the legislation or order describing that position. If asked, the PCO will make its own recommendations.

19 Martin Walker, 'Bush's bird in the hand', *Manchester Guardian Weekly*, 6 Dec. 1992: 20.

20 The net effect of the different placement of political appointees is of course impossible to discuss sensibly without going into a lengthy discussion of the different institutional frameworks, and their internal mechanisms for controlling and influencing the contribution of non-elected officials to policy making and governing.

21 Jack Stilborn, 'Political Patronage: A Newly Troubled Tradition', *Backgrounder* (Research Branch, Library of Parliament, 1989): 21; James P. Pfiffner, 'Political Appointees and Career Executives', *Public Administration Review* 47, 1 (Jan./Feb. 1987): 58; Samuel E. Finer, 'Patronage and the Public Service in Britain and America', in A.J. Heidenheimer, ed., *Political Corruption: A Handbook* (New Brunswick, NJ: Transaction Books, 1989): 102-4; and Anne Davies, 'Patronage and Quasi-Government', in Anthony Barker, ed., *Quangos in Britain* (London: The Macmillan Press, 1982): 170.

22 Jeffrey Simpson's *Spoils of Power* is a thorough documentation of episodes in which patronage has become public knowledge.

23 S.J.R. Noel, 'From Parties to Symbols and Entourages: The Changing Use of Political Patronage in Canada', in Alain-G. Gagnon and A. Brian Tanguay, eds, *Democracy with Justice: Essays in Honour of Khayyam Zev Paltiel* (Ottawa: Carleton University Press, 1992).

24 Ian Stewart worries about the 'extremely slippery' nature of the argument on behalf of patronage here, protesting that I do not expose its weakness at this juncture: "Even if one accepts the highly dubious assumption that parties are essential to democracy, it does not follow that strict party unity is [necessary] or that all methods which advance that goal [unity] are, or that goal is equally important in all institutional arrangements." (Personal communication, 2 Nov. 1992.) I share Stewart's view that the argument on behalf of patronage is slippery and even wrong, but I leave it to Whitaker (below) to rebut the patronage argument, which I think he decisively accomplishes.

25 Martin Tolchin and Susan Tolchin, *To the Victor: Political Patronage from the Clubhouse to the White House* (New York: Random House, 1971): 3-26.

26 Lippmann (above, n.10): 296.

27 James Q. Wilson, 'Corruption: The Shame of the States', in Heidenheimer, ed., *Political Corruption*: 298.

28 Noel (above, n.23): 198-9.

29 Whitaker (above, n.16): 59.

30 Mark Kennedy and Chris Cobb, 'Conflict guidelines didn't stop lobbyist from working for minister', *The Ottawa Citizen*, 2 Dec. 1992: 1.

31 Noel (above, n.23): 202.

32 John Courtney, 'Reinventing the Brokerage Wheel: The Tory Success in 1984', in Howard Penniman, *Canada at the Polls* (Durham, NC: Duke University Press, 1988): 201.

33 Vincent Lemieux, 'Les nouvelles formes du patronage', in Gagnon and Tanguay, eds, *Democracy with Justice*: 211-13.

34 See W.D. Parker, *Commission of Inquiry into the Facts of Allegations of Conflict of Interest Concerning the Honourable Sinclair M. Stevens* (Ottawa: Minister of Supply and Services Canada, 1987). Relevant clauses from the legislation covering Parliament, the sequence of codes that have governed the conflict regime over the years in the federal government, and the provisions of the Criminal Code are all in appendices.

35 See Rod McQueen, *Blind Trust* (Toronto: Macmillan, 1992). Part of the Conservative caucus remained quite sympathetic to Stevens, and believed that he had been sacrificed to a public opinion driven by the Liberals. Their view is not far from that examined by Steven Chibnall and Peter Saunders in 'Worlds Apart: Notes on the Social Reality of Corruption', *British Journal of Sociology* 28, 2 (June 1977): 138-54. A definition of 'sin' was forced on the businessmen offenders/losers in a British scandal that has some interesting parallels to the Stevens case.

36 Stuart Hampshire, 'Public and Private Morality', in Stuart Hampshire, ed., *Public and Private Morality* (Cambridge: Cambridge University Press, 1978): 50.

37 F.G. Bailey, *Humbuggery and Manipulation: The Art of Leadership* (Ithaca: Cornell University Press, 1988): 7.

38 Ibid.: 167.

39 F.G. Bailey, *Stratagems and Spoils: A Social Anthropology of Politics* (Oxford: Basil Blackwell, 1977): 19.

40 David P. Shugarman, 'Ethics and Politics: The Use and Abuse of Politics', in Don MacNiven, ed., *Moral Expertise: Studies in Practical and Professional Ethics* (London and New York: Routledge, 1990): 208.

41 Edwin M. Yoder, 'A scholar's fight against the demagogues', *Manchester Guardian Weekly*, 10 May 1992: 19.

42 Zola published his 'J'accuse' in 1899. Dreyfus was pardoned a year later, but was only reluctantly reintegrated in 1906.

43 George Ball, 'JFK's Big Moment', *New York Review of Books*, 13 Feb. 1992: 16-20.

44 The Hiss case was brought to the forefront again with the opening of the KGB files at the end of 1992. A Russian historian, Dmitri Volkogonov, said on the basis of a search of Soviet military intelligence archives that Hiss, 87 years old in 1992, had never collaborated with the Soviet Union's intelligence services nor been a member of the Soviet Communist Party. Alger Hiss was a State Department lawyer when he was accused in 1948 by Whitaker Chambers before the House Un-American Activities Committee of having passed secret documents to Chambers, whom Hiss said he knew under a different name as a journalist, and a fellow member of the American

Communist Party. Hiss was convicted in 1950 on two counts of perjury—lying about the documents and lying about his relationship to Chambers—and imprisoned for four years. In essence he was imprisoned for protesting his innocence. The prosecution lawyer whose political career began with the conviction of Hiss was Richard Nixon. See Jeffrey A. Frank, 'General offers latest twist in Hiss case', *Manchester Guardian Weekly*, 8 Nov. 1992: 18.

45 Len Scher, *The Un-Canadians: True Stories of the Blacklist Era* (Toronto: Lester Publishing, 1992).

46 For the treatment of the Japanese, see a recent book by Ken Adachi, *The Enemy that Never Was* (Toronto: McClelland and Stewart, 1991).

47 See Andrew J. Orkin, 'Using the Inuit as human flagpoles', *Globe and Mail*, 4 Dec. 1992: 19.

48 See S.L. Sutherland, 'The Al-Mashat Affair: Administrative Accountability in Parliamentary Institutions', *Canadian Public Administration* 34, 4 (Winter 1991): 573-603. The event clarified yet one more time the realization that Canadians are capable of every sort of abuse requested: we have however been lucky in a relative lack of daring in those requesting.

49 Reg Whitaker, 'Canada: The RCMP Scandals', in Markovits and Silverstein, *The Politics of Scandal* (New York: Holmes & Meier, 1988): 38-61. See also Robert Dion, *Crimes of the Secret Police* (Toronto: Black Rose Books, 1982), where Dion claims that some 200 agents were involved in a wide range of activities.

50 Ibid.: 80.

51 See 'Moi, Claude Morin, informateur de la GRC: L'ancien ministre péquiste raconte comment il a collaboré avec les services secrets canadiens de 1975 à 1977', *Le Devoir*, 8 mai 1992: B8; Gilles Lesage, 'Qui joue avec le feu s'y brule', *Le Devoir*, 9 mai 1992: A10; and Graham Fraser, 'Ottawa abuzz over Morin', *Globe and Mail*, 9 May 1992: 1.

52 Bayless Manning, 'The Purity Potlach: Conflict of Interests and Moral Escalation', in Heidenheimer, *Political Corruption*: 307. Oliver Stone's 1991 film *JFK* on the assassination of J.F. Kennedy is a contemporary example of conspiracy theorizing.

53 Richard Vigneault, 'La langue de bois des ténors nationalistes', *Le Devoir*, 18 août 1992: 13. Vigneault was quoting from Jean-François Kahn's analysis in *La guerre civile* (Paris: Seuil, 1982).

54 Peter Newman, *Renegade in Power* (Toronto: McClelland and Stewart, 1963): 325.

55 Ibid.: 324.

56 S.L. Sutherland, 'Inexperienced Ministers 1949-1990: "The Easy Way" and Electoral Volatility', in Herman Bakvis, ed., *Representation, Integration and Political Parties in Canada* (Toronto: Dundurn Press, 1991), Vol. 14 in the Research Studies of the Royal Commission on Electoral Reform.

57 See David Brion Davis, ed., *The Fear of Conspiracy: Images of Un-American Subversion from the Revolution to the Present* (Ithaca: Cornell University Press, 1971): 201. It is a classic strategy of conspiracy theory that evidence of power along with the possibility of self-interested motives is enough to 'prove' a hidden control over seemingly fortuitous events.

58 Simpson's *Spoils of Power*: 331-54 discusses major events during the Trudeau period.

59 See Brian Tobin's remarks in the *Commons Debates*, 12 June 1986: 14284.

60 See Matthew Hart, 'The gripes of wrath: of wild anger, frenzied rage', *Globe and Mail*, 18 May 1991: D1.

61 See Stephen Bindman, 'Court refuses to wait for Board', *The Hill Times*, 3 Dec. 1992: 1.

In the same issue, a fourth Conservative MP was reportedly being tried in Ontario Provincial Court for fraudulent contracting in the order of two hundred thousand dollars. Part of the money was allegedly used to treat members of the MP's riding association to a trip to Mexico. See Ingrid Phaneuf's story on p. 5.

62 Ken MacQueen, 'Vegreville looked after, so why not put P.E.I. causeway in Yellowhead?', *The Ottawa Citizen*, 29 Nov. 1992: B1.

63 See John Courtney (above, n.32) and Denis Olsen, *The State Elite* (Toronto: McClelland and Stewart, 1980), especially ch. Two, 'The Political Elite'.

64 Poggi, *The State* (above, n.14): 139-40. This does not deny that there can still be 'ideological' or value-driven disagreement on how to achieve economic growth, although economics does seem most often to be presented as though it constitutes a body of scientific knowledge. The problem is that it becomes difficult to 'factor in' political discussion of non-economic questions without being accused of some form of cultural fundamentalism.

65 See Carl Bernstein, 'Journalism and the growth of the idiot culture', *Manchester Guardian Weekly*, 14 June 1992: 21. The media need for 'product' was important in the career of David Duke in Louisiana, and the media would not let Duke's celebrity status ebb despite his repeated failures to gain office: see Julia Reed, 'His Brilliant Career', *New York Review of Books*, 9 April 1992: 20-4. Ross Perot's novelty status also helped him gain and keep exposure at the start of the 1992 US presidential campaign.

66 The Republican God is one tough Khantian cookie: the platform meant that 'a women who has had an abortion, even after being raped, and her doctor, would both end up in the electric chair for murder'. See Martin Walker, 'Bush claims God as a Republican', *Manchester Guardian Weekly*, 30 Aug. 1992: 8. American church leaders got together to declare that writing God's name into the party membership list is blasphemous. See 'God not a Republican, churches warn Bush', *The Ottawa Citizen*, 31 Aug. 1992: A6.

67 Photographs of the 'No' politicians Lucien Bouchard and Jacques Parizeau—Bouchard with a Mafia-style five-o'clock shadow and Parizeau lighted in pale green to bring out the deposits of cigarette tars between his teeth—were used with a voice-over explaining that their smiles were because they believed that the destruction of Canada was near. Chris Cobb, 'Parizeau, Bouchard targets of Yes side ad', *The Ottawa Citizen*, 22 Oct. 1992: A3.

68 Walter Romanow, Walter C. Soderlund, and Richard G. Price, 'Negative Political Advertising: An Analysis of Research Findings in Light of Canadian Practice', in Jane Hiebert, ed., *Political Ethics: A Canadian Perspective* (Toronto: Dundurn Press, 1992): 165-90, Vol. 12 in the Research Studies of the Royal Commission on Electoral Reform and Party Financing.

69 An obvious move, for example, would be for the state to provide or regulate the amount of money that can be spent by candidates for party leadership.

70 On the media and the campaign, see Martin Walker, 'Plane tales of Clinton's time-zone travellers', *Manchester Guardian Weekly*, 8 Nov. 1992: 8.

71 Poggi, *The State* (above, n.14): 194-7.

72 Charles E. Lindblom, *Inquiry and Change: The Troubled Attempt to Understand and Shape Society* (New Haven: Yale University Press, 1990). Lindblom makes a number of suggestions about open-ended inquiry and communication in ch. 16, 'Reducing Impairment'.

7

Alberta: The search for an ethical balance

The study of government ethics in modern Alberta raises interesting issues. The province enjoys a reputation as a scandal-free democracy whose leaders have seldom confronted serious charges of financial conflicts of interest. During more than two decades of uninterrupted Progressive Conservative government after 1971, the honesty of important Alberta politicians has seldom been an issue. No major scandal, replete with accusations of serious high-level wrongdoing, deception, or other abuses of democratic process, has occurred. Two significant events in Alberta's recent political history, the collapse of the Principal financial empire and the huge financial losses of NovAtel, a government-owned firm, raised vexing questions of political judgement but scarcely a rumour of political or bureaucratic corruption. In a lighter vein, evidence of Alberta's ethical health is found in the provincial Liberals' 1989 list of ethical shortcomings in the Conservative government, which notes that a minister may have channelled public funds to a chess tournament organized by his brother!

An absence of major scandal and the apparently limited abuse of public office for personal financial gain have not removed ethical questions from Alberta's political agenda. The province's politics are dominated by concerns about the conduct of its public officials. Like other Canadian jurisdictions, Alberta is confronting assertions about the declining integrity of its politicians, about its eroding standards of political morality, and about its need for more rigorous regulation of official conduct.

Why is it that Alberta's government, which seems honest, is widely thought to be unfair and even corrupt? My answer lies in the governing Progressive Conservatives' style, *modus operandi*, and basis of support. Under Peter Lougheed's dominant leadership between 1971 and 1985, the Conservatives, backed by allies in Alberta's legal, commercial, and corporate élites, saw themselves as talented governors who were performing a public service by running the province instead of pursuing business careers, and for whom public office became a possession, not a trust. Ethical debate bored them, and both

Lougheed and his successor, Donald Getty, refused to acknowledge errors of judgement or to engage their critics in serious argument about standards of conduct. Under this rather regal view of governance, a minimalist view of ethics emerged. An ethical public official was one who acted legally and avoided narrow conflicts of interest. But such views never rested easily among all Albertans. A particular problem is the Conservatives' refusal to see as problematic patronage or the close links between past and present Conservative politicians, corporate élites, and senior officials forged during two decades of one-party dominance. A reluctance to engage in ethical discourse and an excessive tolerance of cronyism have created deep concerns about the fairness, impartiality, and effectiveness of the provincial government.

As Theodore Lowi observes, the study of government ethics allows us to catch societies 'being themselves'.[1] This observation rings true for modern Alberta, where the ethics agenda reflects the insecurities, conflicts, and frustrations of a changing society. The evolution of conflict of interest rules, from the guidelines issued by Premier Lougheed to ministers in 1973, to the 1991 Conflicts of Interest Act, reveals contradictory forces. The study of political ethics in Alberta provides a laboratory for students interested in the assertion that the statutory regulation of official conduct is a necessary, if not sufficient, condition for the attainment of responsible behaviour. It also forcefully raises a classic question—can democratic government easily be effective and ethical?

My starting point is Peter Lougheed's approach to ethical questions throughout his premiership from 1971 to 1985.[2] I try to put his views in context with a changing Alberta society and to show how present discontents are linked to his response to ethical problems. I then turn to Donald Getty's premiership from 1986 to 1992 and argue that his approach to ethics followed Lougheed's, but that this perspective was increasingly at odds with a changing society. I examine the 1991 Conflicts of Interest Act, a major change in Alberta's approach to conflict of interest, in this context. By examining the controversy surrounding the private lives of two recent solicitors general, I then probe changing attitudes to the personal lives of politicians. I conclude with two questions. Is a 'scandal machine' emerging in Alberta?[3] Is the ethics agenda of the last two decades receding as new social forces emerge and as the Conservatives' electoral hegemony weakens?

Ethics in the new Alberta

The story of Peter Lougheed's 1971 electoral victory and his dominance of Alberta politics until 1985 are well known. Hence only a few important characteristics of the underlying politics are examined here. The first point is that the Conservatives claimed to represent the emerging values of a modern, urban Alberta. The austere Social Credit regime that had governed uninterrupted since 1935 had lost touch and had been replaced by 'modern' politicians who would

make Alberta a force in Canadian and North American affairs. Second, the Lougheed governments were interventionist. In concert with local and foreign capital, the provincial government was committed to diversifying Alberta's resource-based economy. If, as it is widely asserted, an active state with close links with business is susceptible to corruption, the 'new Alberta' would certainly face its share of ethical controversies. Third, Premier Lougheed and his advisers saw themselves as men of action. Their world comprised two camps—the 'doers and the knockers'. The public agenda was too full for quiet reflection as the new Alberta beckoned. Unlike the nation-building drive of René Lévesque's governments in Quebec as described in Chapter 4, Lougheed's province-building embraced no pretensions of moral leadership. The agenda was economic— Alberta was to be made richer and more powerful. Alberta can readily be described, as the United States has been in these matters, as a society where action is prized over introspection.[4]

Two other forces merit attention. The 1971-82 period, the glory days of Tory electoral dominance, were years of unprecedented economic growth. The oil boom filled provincial coffers, fuelled spectacular growth in Edmonton and Calgary, and brought immigrants to the 'new West'. The society was acquisitive, ambitious, and self-confident, or as Lewis Thomas described it, 'vulgarly rich'.[5] And as the boom proceeded, the Conservatives' electoral hegemony was established. As testimony to Lougheed's shrewdness, the elections of 1975, 1979, and 1982 produced legislative oppositions of six, five, and four members respectively.

The government adopted a hard line about the need for a powerful cabinet unfettered by legislative oversight. Secrecy was elevated to a virtue by Lougheed, who expected loyalty from his followers and who viewed dissent as a personal affront. Without sarcasm, one might ask why this combination of circumstances —a booming economy, an interventionist state run by ambitious politicians, and a weak opposition—produced so little corruption.

Until the passage of the Conflicts of Interest Act in 1991, the conduct of Alberta ministers was governed by guidelines issued by Premier Lougheed in 1973.[6] Lougheed declared that no wrongdoing had prompted the guidelines, which he had personally devised. Rather, he was acting to assure the public that information was available about ministerial business holdings, to prevent ministers from inadvertently entering into conflicts of interest, and to give evidence of his government's concern with standards of ministerial conduct. Ministers were obliged to file a public statement with the Clerk of the Legislative Assembly that disclosed the legal description, but not value, of their personal and familial land holdings in the province, the names of private companies doing business in Alberta in which they had a financial interest, and a description of all proprietorships and businesses in Alberta in which they or their family had an interest. Ministers were prohibited from owning shares in public companies whose decisions might be affected by government policy, but they were allowed to establish blind trusts into which shares in public companies could be placed. Members of the legislature were also subject to the Legislative Assembly Act, which prevents them from contracting with the government and requires them to make public disclosure of persons associated with them, including spouses and some private companies and partnerships. MLAs must not vote on matters in which they have 'a direct pecuniary interest'.

In 1975, the ministerial guidelines were extended to senior civil servants, at which time Lougheed worried about their possible impact on his capacity to recruit senior managers. Senior officials were also subject to the Code of Conduct and Ethics for the Public Service of Alberta, forged in 1978. This code, which has no basis in law, outlined policy on such issues as outside employment, political activities, and the receipt of gifts by provincial civil servants.

In a 1973 editorial the *Edmonton Journal*, which later became a harsh critic of Conservative ethics, lauded the guidelines.[7] Lougheed was praised for acting progressively and for wedding the competing principles of public disclosure and ministers' privacy. In 1973, Lougheed's guidelines, which are permissive and *laissez-faire* by today's standards, seemed progressive.

Government ethics in practice

By the mid-1970s, controversies about conflict of interest and ethics were entrenched parts of Alberta politics. No major scandals had occurred, but many episodes and allegations of wrongdoing surfaced. Let us look at three illustrative examples.

A telling debate unfolded in December 1979, when it was revealed that Premier Lougheed and his wife had, on an unspecified number of occasions, accepted free airline tickets from Air Canada and CP Air for personal vacations.[8] In the ensuing debate, Lougheed and his associates revealed their thinking about the links between public duties, private interests, and the appearance of conflict of interest. On no occasion did the premier admit that his acceptance of such gifts was wrong in principle. His first defence was that the public would see nothing wrong in his free travel—a well-rested premier was necessary for good government. Next was the argument that the free travel was acceptable because the premier, as instructed by a former aide, believed that such travel was 'a national policy' extended by the airlines to the first ministers. Was there a conflict of interest or an appearance of one? Lougheed scoffed at this suggestion by asserting that the airlines in question were federally regulated and hence beyond his influence. No response was tendered to his critics' concern that CP Air was a rival to Pacific Western Airlines, an airline then owned by the government of Alberta, and that CP Air's parent firm was a major resource conglomerate with extensive interests in the oil boom. Did the episode suggest that Alberta needed a code of conduct for elected officials that prohibited the acceptance of such gifts? Lougheed responded ambivalently and added the remarkable idea that if he could not receive free trips for personal vacations, the government would have to reconsider existing policy for free travel by MLAs in the conduct of their public duties. In a revealing statement, the deputy premier, Hugh Horner, argued that Lougheed could make much more money in the private sector and that 'if we want to get chintzy about this type of thing, we won't get anyone leading anything'.[9]

The opposition condemned Lougheed's free travel and called for a statutory code of conduct. Lougheed was assailed for employing a double standard, insofar as the code of conduct for provincial employees prohibited the acceptance of substantial gifts. Editorial writers worried that the premier seemed incapable of grasping an elementary ethical issue and unwilling to engage in a serious debate. The failure to give account was as serious as the offending behaviour itself.

In the second incident, in July 1981, Premier Lougheed appointed Mr Justice Brennan of the Court of Queen's Bench as a one-person commission into alleged wrongdoings by present and former Alberta politicians in complex land transactions surrounding the expansion of the city of Edmonton's boundaries. The inquiry was required because of allegations that important Conservatives had used confidential information to benefit themselves and corporations, and that former ministers, acting as lobbyists for development companies, had acted improperly in influencing present ministers.

Brennan's report, which is a fascinating study of corporate-political relations in a major land play during a resource boom, details the lobbying activities of former ministers and their links with businessmen.[10] Among other things, Brennan learned that a former executive assistant to an Alberta cabinet minister had urged realtors to work with a company with which he was now associated because his firm 'had the politicians and knew where to buy'.[11] In light of such testimony, Mr Justice Brennan worried about the 'ugly cloud of suspicion of impropriety' that hung over the public officials who were involved in real estate speculation.[12] In the event, he found no evidence that past or present politicians had used confidential information to benefit themselves or those they represented. But to the premier's chagrin, the commissioner went beyond this question and probed the ethical conduct of several individuals and the propriety of the system of influence he observed. One minister had been 'careless' to the point of negligence in voting on the annexation proposal even though he owned land in the affected area. A former attorney general, Jim Foster, had acted 'most improperly' when conversing with present ministers about the annexation. Foster had personal financial interests at stake and was a lobbyist for developers. He and Don Getty, an influential minister in the 1971 and 1975 Lougheed cabinets and Alberta's premier from 1986 to 1992, were lobbyists for development companies and were 'quite prepared to take advantage of the fact that they are former Cabinet Ministers and friends of current members of Cabinet.'[13] Brennan concluded: 'The evidence in the Inquiry made it abundantly clear that former Cabinet Ministers have a very distinct and definite advantage over other lobbyists or persons who wish to present their views on a particular matter to members of Cabinet.'[14]

Was such a system of influence fair to those who lacked 'the wisdom and the wherewithal' to employ former ministers? Did it impair the judgement of legislators? Premier Lougheed answered such questions by rejecting calls for clearer and tougher rules, by highlighting Brennan's conclusion that no one had acted illegally, and by dismissing his arguments about a *pattern* of ethical problems in the Conservative government.

The third important, by some measures incredible, ethical controversy concerns the activities of the Alberta Energy Company (AEC). Created by provincial statute in 1973, AEC was a major player in Alberta's booming resource economy and an instrument of Lougheed's development strategy. It is a mixed-ownership company, with shares being held by the provincial government and private investors. In explaining the operation of the AEC, Lougheed and Don Getty argued that the corporation was run by an independent board and that it was not an instrument of provincial policy. This explanation became untenable in the face of evidence that the company had a privileged relationship with the government, that Lougheed was committed to its financial success, and that the cabinet had at its disposal a range of instruments that were used to favour the AEC.

In 1975, the AEC became an ethical question when the government amended the company's statute to permit MLAs and ministers, despite their capacity to influence the firm, to hold AEC shares outside blind trusts and with an exemption from conflict of interest rules. In defending the legislation, Getty accused his detractors of harbouring negative feelings about an important provincial initiative and sidestepped the thorny question of conflict of interest.[15] He defended the legislation on the sole ground that the AEC was like any other firm in the province. Why should MLAs and ministers be denied a business opportunity? By 1979, eighteen ministers held varying numbers of AEC shares, which by then had tripled in value. Eight ministers held shares in a blind trust. In refusing to change the legislation, the provincial treasurer, Lou Hyndman, argued that ministers had seldom bought or sold shares since 1975. Had there been market transactions before and after government decisions, he might be more concerned. In a stern editorial in 1979, the *Edmonton Journal* demanded that the offending section of the AEC's statute be repealed. 'Such an obvious conflict-of-interest would not be tolerated in most jurisdictions. But Alberta's ethical standards are its own.'[16] The Conservative government had added a new dimension—the state-sanctioned conflict of interest—to an already overloaded concept.

Another feature of Alberta's ethics agenda in the Lougheed years was the frequent introduction by the tiny opposition of conflict of interest legislation. The opposition focused on the need to restrict the lobbying and employment activities of former ministers and officials. After the Brennan Inquiry, a Social Credit bill proposed a five-year 'cooling-off' period, a time that probably still constitutes the Canadian record for its length. Interestingly, the New Democrats, the opposition party that saw itself as Alberta's social conscience, never pursued conflict of interest questions vigorously. During the 1960s, under the aggressive leadership of Neil Reimer, the party indulged in the risky strategy of attacking the Social Credit premier, Ernest Manning, on questions of personal integrity.[17] The crafty Manning deflected such attacks with disastrous results for the New Democrats, many of whom were deeply uneasy with Reimer's strategy. As a witness to and participant in these dramatic events, the party's subsequent leader, the late

Grant Notley, was fearful of politics that focused on the personal integrity of popular leaders or even hinted at 'scandalmongering'. Notley was cautious about conflict of interest and often subdued in his criticisms of the government's conduct. The Alberta experience shows that an opposition party will not necessarily seize upon ethical controversy as a means of distinguishing it from its rivals. The NDP's approach to ethical controversy, as shaped by its history, was timid in the 1970s. Such timidity disappeared in the mid-1980s when the NDP seized upon government ethics as an element of its electoral strategy.

In defence of the realm

Three themes emerge from our brief tour of ethical controversy during the Lougheed years. First, most of the controversy fell in the grey areas of conduct where offending behaviour was legal but wrong by some standards. The acceptance of gifts, ownership of shares in government companies, and lobbying of present politicians by former politicians were prominent problems. Second, most of the questionable conduct was related to Lougheed's strategy of economic development or to circumstances related to the oil boom. The third theme is that the wrongdoings described here, when placed along a continuum of severity, fell between the extremes of minor transgression and serious scandal. All of them generated substantial, although generally short-lived, public debates. None of them, by itself, was remotely threatening to the government's survival. But the accumulation of these sins contributed to a sense that the government was unfair.

As Jeffrey Simpson argues, Lougheed liberally used patronage.[18] Alberta's 'thoroughly modern' leader practised some very traditional politics, which in the early years of his government may perhaps have been justified on 'functional' grounds—notably as a tool to mould his nascent Conservative Party into an electoral dynasty. But the Brennan Inquiry and many other examples suggested that the patronage was extensive and, in the face of electoral hegemony, not easily justified as an essential element of a party-building strategy. Lougheed's patronage was more like the dispensations of a king to well-placed persons who were already members of his court. Patronage established a pattern of influence through the network of regulatory agencies, boards, and quasi-public firms that were prominent forces in Lougheed's economic development strategy. A sense of systemic wrongdoing was reinforced through the inevitable blurring of party and government in a one-party-dominant system.

In 1979, Robert Clark, the leader of the Alberta Social Credit Party argued, 'the most shameful act of the government's recent history with regard to ethics is the way they flaunt the question.'[19] Clark's criticism highlights Lougheed's refusal, as a dominant leader, to engage his critics in ethical debate. Lougheed's unyielding defence of the status quo of rules and regulations, his refusal to discuss even modest improvements in the face of changing conditions and growing public concern, and his failure to acknowledge personal and governmental errors of judgement contributed to a malaise about government ethics.

What explains this failure to examine alternatives and to respond to criticism? Lougheed obviously saw his critics' standards as irrelevant and he was prone to imperious behaviour. But his views about ethics must be related to his general views about democratic politics, views that were endorsed by his influential associates.[20] Prominent here is the idea that massive electoral majorities are evidence of public support for all governmental activities. Not accidentally, Lougheed argued that his impressive electoral victory in 1979 vindicated his position on the free airline tickets. He claimed that his landslide majority reflected public support for his policies and his ethics.[21] To his mind, what was right by his standards was self-evidently right in the minds of a majority of Alberta voters. Otherwise, why was he reelected with huge majorities? It must be understood that Lougheed was not advancing the controversial, but interesting, proposition that a person's major achievements in important areas (in his case superior management of the provincial economy) trumped or neutralized occasional ethical slips. He was genuinely puzzled by his critics' concern about the appearance of wrongdoing. For a man of action, such an abstract notion was irrelevant as a guide to conduct. On this subject, Lougheed's response to the Brennan report is instructive.[22] In rejecting a judge's arguments about the problems caused by the lobbying of former ministers, Lougheed reduced a complex matter to two simple empirical questions—was the lobbying successful, and were the practices described by Brennan widespread? His 'extensive checking' revealed that Brennan was wrong in fact, and that therefore there was no problem. Such lobbying was infrequent and, more importantly, unsuccessful. Therefore only a confused person would see a problem.

Lougheed's opposition to tighter conflict of interest rules also highlights his views about a good political career. To his mind, Alberta politics was enriched by the flow of people from business into politics and back into business. The need to recruit the best minds from the private sector was more important than the need to avoid the appearance of bias. Government effectiveness was the overriding objective. Restrictions on the employment opportunities of former public officials were wrong and impractical.

Peter Lougheed, an intelligent and powerful leader, was uninterested in ethical debate. He felt no obligation to seriously consider alternative definitions of ethical problems. His failure to justify controversial positions, to give some credence to alternatives, and to recognize competing values had serious long-term consequences. In Lougheed and Getty's Alberta, effective government was one produced through an alliance of élites united through a web of patronage, friendships, and personal loyalties. Other important values like fairness, impartiality, and the avoidance of conflict of interest were downplayed. Moreover, evidence suggests that the conflict of interest rules were laxly administered and that clear procedures for dealing with ministerial misconduct had not been developed even in the mid-1980s.[23] As late as 1985, Lougheed referred to calls for a code of conduct for politicians as nonsense, a comment that reflects an indifference to inadequate procedures.

Ethics in the Getty years

The Old Order in disarray

Walter Lippmann argued that the United States confronted political corruption in 'fits and starts'. From time to time, a reformist zeal emerges as 'the civic conscience begins to boil'.[24] His views ring true for modern Alberta where, in the mid-1980s, coincident with the premiership of Donald Getty, questions of political ethics became more controversial. Getty presided over wrenching economic adjustments in the middle and late 1980s after the oil boom turned to a traumatic bust.[25] Alberta has a substantial public debt and unemployment is much higher than in most of the Lougheed years. The Tories now face a substantial legislative opposition, led by the New Democrats but bolstered by an aggressive contingent of Liberals. Lougheed's strategy of waging political war against Ottawa and eastern Canadian business is less urgent as questions about taxes and public expenditures are enjoying unprecedented attention. The Alberta mass media are now aggressively concerned about the conduct of public officials. And perhaps most importantly, the Conservatives' cardinal claim—that their style of politics produces superior government—is in tatters. The collapse of the Principal Group and the enormous losses at NovAtel reveal a government that in important economic matters looks amateurish and by some critics' standards, incompetent. Questionable ethics can no longer be seen as incidental by-products of effective government.

While much had changed in Alberta, Premier Getty followed Lougheed's approach to political ethics until 1991, when his government passed the Conflicts of Interest Act. Getty's acceptance of Lougheed's standards and his *laissez-faire* approach to the regulation of official conduct are not surprising. He was a senior minister in Lougheed's governments between 1971 and 1979. He brought the controversial amendments to the Alberta Energy Company Act before the legislature in 1975. And his activities as a lobbyist, after leaving public office in 1979, were discussed in the Brennan report. But while espousing Lougheed's views, Getty did not defend them as forcefully as his predecessor. He lacked Lougheed's presence. In responding to questions about his personal conduct and that of his associates, Getty was vulnerable. And in one important area, his publicly expressed views differed from Lougheed's, but to his detriment. Like Lougheed, Getty argued that good public officials were business people who planned to return to the private sector after a stint in public service. But Getty elaborated by lamenting the personal sacrifices endured by politicians. For Getty, proposals such as cooling-off periods were unfair additions to an already unpleasant job. His view, that a political career was a source of financial loss and personal sacrifice, exposed him to criticism and even ridicule.

Alberta's more aggressive ethics agenda in the late 1980s and Lougheed's legacy of neglect soon weighed heavily on Getty. The opposition alleged many wrongdoings. The problem of the Alberta Energy Company reappeared, as forestry development became a key element in Alberta's development strategy and as the

AEC became a player.[26] The minister of forestry, lands and wildlife, Leroy Fjord-botten, an important decision maker in Alberta's forestry boom, owned $100,000 worth of shares in AEC. He acknowledged no conflict, even though the government authorized a $96 million loan guarantee to the company as part of the financing for a mill. Getty himself was the object of an opposition effort to create a scandal in 1988 over his acceptance of a flight from California to Edmonton on a private jet owned by NOVA Corporation, a Calgary-based resource conglomerate. In defending his travel arrangements, a sometimes angry premier asserted that the flight was accepted so that he could return to Alberta to cope with a domestic emergency when commercial flights were not available. The Liberals and New Democrats argued that Getty's acceptance of the flight reflected poor judgement and highlighted the need for stricter rules about the acceptance of gifts by politicians.

Amidst controversy about conflict of interest, Getty announced in July 1989 that an independent review of the rules was required. He appointed a Conflicts of Interest Review Panel chaired by Mr Justice Wachowich, Chief Justice of the Provincial Court of Alberta. The tribunal was instructed to review the rules, to recommend changes if necessary, and to examine the AEC legislation. The committee was obliged to consider the impact of conflict of interest rules on the quality of people who might enter public life.

The committee dutifully reviewed the literature, examined the experiences of other jurisdictions (Ontario's approach particularly impressed it), and reported in February 1990.[27] The report's conclusions are important, as they established the framework for the 1991 Conflicts of Interest Act. The panel concluded that there was not a conflict of interest crisis in Alberta. Public officials had maintained high standards of conduct. But the panel offered the opinion that the times were changing. Citizens distrusted politicians and stricter regulation of official conduct was required if public faith was to be maintained in government. A modern, comprehensive conflict of interest regime was required. Public officials must avoid conflicts of interest and conduct their duties with integrity. The panel rejected electoral results as an effective arbiter of ethical conduct. In proposing a statute, it undercut Getty's defence of Lougheed's apparently obsolete rules.

The Wachowich committee proposed a comprehensive conflicts of interest statute for ministers and MLAs, with a separate statute for senior civil servants. The key figure in the proposed regime for politicians was an ethics commissioner, an officer of the legislature, who would have broad administrative, investigative, and educational duties. The commissioner would oversee a system of 'filtered' public disclosure of politicians' personal and familial financial interests. Politicians would be obliged to divulge their interests to the commissioner, who would then decide which of these interests would be made public. Ministers were subject to other strictures, including the need to eschew employment likely to cause conflicts with their public duties, and prohibitions against holding shares in public companies except as approved by the commissioner. A central proposal, and one long championed in principle by the opposition, was a one year cooling-off period for ministers whose employment and lobbying activities would thereby be curtailed. Despite its rejection of the status quo, the Wachowich report was virtually ignored by the media and Alberta's opposition parties.

While strangely quiet about the principles espoused in the Wachowich report, Alberta's media and opposition parties found ample improper conduct to report on. The *Globe and Mail* ran a series of major stories on Mr Getty's personal finances and his views about public life. The subsequent controversy yields lessons about how ethical questions are conceived and debated in Alberta and, I think, in other parts of the country in the early 1990s.

The *Globe*'s detailed stories represent the first major use of investigative journalism against a major political figure in modern Alberta.[28] The main allegation was that, as premier, Getty speculated in oil and gas investments in the province. He was part-owner of several producing wells and had expanded his interests while serving as premier. His assets were apparently not in a blind trust and the implication was that he had personally made investments. Such investments, even if legal, were seen as unwise because the provincial government wielded extensive control over Alberta's oil and gas industries. Royalty reductions, for example, would increase investors' profits—the premier was a rule-maker, a referee, and a player. To this proposition Mr. Getty responded, 'So what? What can I do as premier that would somehow benefit me?'[29] A second aspect of the exposés was their revelation that a development company owned by prominent Conservatives had, before Getty's return to public life in 1985, extended him a mortgage at market rates on his Edmonton house. The firm seldom mortgaged residential properties. The stories observed many links between prominent Alberta politicians, businesspeople, and professionals. Finally, the *Globe* provided further detail into the premier's ideas about how his return to public life had caused him personal financial hardship.

The *Globe* stories touched off a furor, which even featured a feud among journalists, some of whom objected to an eastern newspaper imposing its brand of political morality on Alberta.[30] Such sideshows not withstanding, the stories yielded only a few new insights into government ethics in modern Alberta. They provided further evidence that Alberta's conflict of interest guidelines for ministers were loose and did not prohibit certain types of questionable conduct. Getty's holdings were not in a blind trust, but apparently a trust whose contents were known to a politician but beyond his direct control was permissible under Lougheed's 1973 guidelines. The stories again established that Alberta's rules were permissive compared to those prevailing in several provinces, those proposed by the Wachowich report, and those favoured by the opposition parties. The stories provided details about the close relations between Conservative politicians and Alberta business people. Getty's defence again revealed that he opposed the emerging consensus about the need for a conflict of interest statute. Tough rules, he argued, would deter capable people from undertaking public service. The notion of apparent conflict of interest perplexed and annoyed him as it had Peter Lougheed. He again expressed views that now seem old-fashioned.

Beyond these limited conclusions, the *Globe* stories produced facts that were interpreted differently by reasonable people. As a result, their impact on Alberta politics and ethical discourse is unclear. For example, the stories can be read as inspired by a distaste for Getty's upper middle-class lifestyle, hence their obsession with details about his houses and the journalistic ridicule of his comments about financial sacrifice. The further exposure of links between business, legal, and political élites let the opposition argue 'We told you so!' and probably reinforced the perceptions of Conservative cronyism. Finally, the controversy about conflict of interest provided critics with a convenient pad from which to pursue their own agendas. For example, the *Edmonton Journal* employed hyperbole in an editorial when it declared that unless Getty sold his oil interests he would 'lose whatever credibility he has left in Alberta. . . . His inadequate response suggests he is unsuited to his job.'[31]

Getty's extensive use of patronage, especially in the form of well-paid civil service positions, reinforced his government's image as one built on cronyism. The works of S.J.R. Noel, Reg Whitaker, and Jeffrey Simpson highlight the suspicion and distaste with which patronage is now viewed by many citizens as Canadian democracy changes and as citizens relate to public institutions in new ways.[32] They show how patronage is assuming new forms and how its use requires considerable political skill.

Getty enthusiastically employed patronage in a sceptical political climate. But his problems with patronage grew deeper and more complex. Recent events have given rise to the suspicion that Tory patronage is producing government that is not merely unfair but also corrupt and administratively ineffective.[33]

A widely publicized episode that linked patronage with unethical behaviour was the case of Joe Dutton. A former aide to Premier Lougheed, Dutton was appointed director of Alberta's office in Hong Kong. A series of major stories in the *Calgary Herald*, remarkably similar in tone and style to the *Globe*'s investigations of Getty, noted that Dutton, after leaving public employment, established himself as an immigration consultant.[34] His business was profitable and relied on his reputation as a politically connected person. He started an investment program for Hong Kong immigrants that promised to invest their monies in shopping centres in western Canada. The funds apparently ended up in a Saskatchewan gold mine that is not yet profitable. Angry investors felt duped by a man who in their eyes was a public official. Opposition politicians implied it was influence-peddling and argued that such activity besmirched Alberta's reputation abroad.

As reported, the Dutton affair raised many questions. His most questionable activity, the unapproved transfer of investors' funds from one project to another, raises questions of business ethics, law, and, I suppose, character. The conclusion that his period of public employment was spent in the pursuit of personal business activities, while obvious to the critics, is unproved and probably cannot be satisfactorily determined four years after the fact. For Getty's and Lougheed's critics, however, the issues were crystal clear. In the words of Ray Martin, the leader of the New Democrats, 'political hacks' were using 'public connections for private gain'.[35] Cronyism had gone 'rotten' after years of rampant patronage. Such views were shared by the media. Marc Lisac, the *Edmonton Journal's* political columnist, concluded that 'Dutton and the way he earns a living is part of their [Conservative] culture.'[36] Can we generalize about the ethical conduct of patronage recipients from Dutton's case? For Lisac, the answer was easily answered in the affirmative. The Dutton story was not 'an aberration in the chronicle of Alberta under the Conservatives. It is one more illumination.'[37]

Controversy about political patronage assumed a new dimension in 1992 as part of the public debate about NovAtel Communications Ltd, an Alberta-based company that engaged in cellular telephone production. The NovAtel saga is complex. The firm was established in 1982 as a joint venture between Nova, the major Calgary-based resource conglomerate, and Alberta Government Telephones (AGT), a provincial Crown corporation. In 1988, Nova sold its interest to AGT, citing disappointment with the firm's performance. In 1992, Alberta finally followed suit and sold its stake. But by then the province had absorbed staggering financial losses of at least $566 million.

Under intense pressure to explain its role, the government commissioned the provincial auditor general to examine the NovAtel affair. The ensuing public debate raised issues that are at the heart of Alberta politics, notably industrial strategy, the feasibility of economic diversification in a resource-dominated economy, and the government's role in these matters. But Alberta's ethics agenda assumed centre stage when the auditor general argued that effective corporate performance presumed committed, expert, and independent boards of directors. NovAtel's boards, appointed by the government, did not pass muster. The auditor general's report never mentioned patronage. But his first recommendation made his views clear. 'The Province should consider using the expertise of the Public Service Commissioner to short-list suitably qualified candidates for appointments to the boards of all Provincial agencies and Crown-controlled organizations. I recommend that the primary criterion of selection be proven relevant expertise.'[38] No reasonable person could conclude that weak boards of directors or patronage are entirely responsible for NovAtel's losses. On the other hand, the auditor general, an independent critic, publicly linked inexpert appointees with governmental ineffectiveness and thereby highlighted a powerful, perennial idea against patronage.

The discussion of political patronage has an interesting trajectory in Alberta politics. Lougheed's patronage surprised many observers who were mystified by his reliance on a old-fashioned device. From initial expressions of surprise and disappointment, the debate shifted to one in which patronage was seen to be cronyism, the rewarding of already well-heeled friends without reference to contribution or expertise, which made government look biased and unfair. Recent allegations and public debate, especially the Dutton affair, linked patronage with corruption. Finally, the auditor general activated public concern by advancing a 'good government' case against patronage.

Elsewhere in this book, Kenneth Kernaghan, John Langford, and Sharon Sutherland raise important concerns about the relationships between elected and appointed officials. Curiously, given the Alberta Conservatives' extensive and long-standing use of patronage, the political-bureaucratic relationship is seldom explicitly or systematically assessed. Is there now in Alberta a superficially American style of government, where between ministers and the permanent, 'merit' civil service there exist numerous important officials who are the appointees, friends, and ideological soul-mates of the government? Do civil servants exhibit, or feel pressured to display, the eager-beaver mentality of British Columbia officials that Langford observes in his chapter? In a patronage-driven, one-party-dominant system with an excess of official secrecy and strong norms of team solidarity, are civil servants likely to challenge ethically suspect political actions or orders?

The Conflicts of Interest Act, 1991

In the wake of the Wachowich report and in the face of continuing controversy, the Conservative government confounded its critics, reversed its long-standing philosophy, and introduced a conflicts of interest statute for MLAs and ministers in April 1991. The law generally met the demands of opposition parties and Alberta journalists, who had demanded such legislation in the face of official misconduct and what seemed, to their minds, an antiquated approach to conflict of interest. The critics' views reflected a faith in the capacity of laws to produce the standards of public conduct that were thought lacking. The province is now moving into a new era for the regulation of official conduct.

The Conflicts of Interest Act closely follows the recommendations of the Wachowich report. It applies to both ministers and MLAs, although the conduct of ministers is more rigorously regulated. A separate statute for senior civil servants was announced in the 1992 Speech from the Throne. A new officer of the legislature, an ethics commissioner, is to be appointed for a five-year term through recommendation of the Legislative Assembly. The commissioner is charged with interpreting and administering the law, and with undertaking investigations and educational activities. The law demands disclosure to the commissioner of MLAs' financial interests and those of their spouses and dependents; the commissioner will decide which materials will be made public. It limits elected officials' capacity to receive and retain gifts and it demands that ministers either divest themselves of publicly traded securities or place them in a blind trust whose structure must be approved by the commissioner. Perhaps most significantly, the act restricts ministers 'post-political lives'. For six months after leaving office, ministers are prohibited from seeking or receiving contracts from government agencies with which they have had 'significant official dealings' during their last year of service, and from working or lobbying for organizations with which they were involved during their last year in office. The commissioner's sanctions against sitting members range from reprimand to expulsion. But he or she may only recommend sanctions to the legislature, which must ultimately decide. The act confers substantial discretion on the commissioner who can relax virtually any condition and obligation on the grounds that a rigorous application of the law might be unfair or impractical in particular cases.

True to form, Conservatives did not root the law in a clear philosophical framework, nor did they argue why alternative approaches were rejected. They again revealed their inability to see their critics' concerns. On second reading, the attorney general merely indicated that the bill was driven by a need to assure the public that politicians understood their ethical duties and that public and private interests must not conflict.[39] The opposition parties, who had long demanded such legislation but who had never developed a compelling rationale for it, were forced to complain about details.

The Liberals, the New Democrats, and the province's editors assailed the six-month cooling-off period as inadequate. This concern reflected their anxiety that two decades of Tory rule had resulted in an unfair, possibly corrupt, cronyism. The weakening of this system was an important concern for the critics. A six-month cooling-off period was no obstacle to the perpetuation of a rotten system.

Another opposition theme was the act's too-restrictive definition of conflict of interest. On this issue the government gave no quarter and rejected the ideas of apparent or potential conflict as 'airy-fairy' notions. The rambling debate on this point is interesting as a reflection of contemporary politicians' ideas about the meaning of conflict of interest and the deeper notion of public office as a public trust. Several opposition members advanced elastic definitions of conflict of interest, ones that embraced the expenditure of public funds to promote a party's electoral prospects.

The Conflicts of Interest Act moves Alberta into uncharted seas and my analysis is thus speculative. One interesting aspect of the debate is how quickly the reformers lost faith in a statutory code of conduct. Ironically, given the media's calls for such legislation, the act was given short shrift by the columnists. Writing in the *Edmonton Journal*, Marc Lisac argued that the government was unclear about the law's rationale. An important reform had indeed been achieved, but somehow the government's heart was not behind it and hence the act was deficient.[40] Don Braid, the *Calgary Herald*'s political columnist, was scathing.[41] The act was a 'public relations' exercise whose seemingly demanding provisions would, by unspecified means, be sidestepped by Tory opportunists.

The law's longer term beneficial impact on Alberta government is easily missed. For the statute establishes, through force of law, a new minimum set of standards in certain areas of public conduct. For example, it prohibits certain post-employment activities of ministers and, regardless of the length of such prohibitions, defines as unacceptable certain longstanding practices. It breaks the vicious circle that is created when conduct is regulated either by informal rules like Lougheed's ministerial guidelines or by the élite political culture, the 'rules of the game', which themselves justify conduct others see as wrong. Under these circumstances, a law establishes boundaries which if overstepped can result in punishments recommended by an independent officer of the legislature. Elites are no longer completely self-regulating, and governments' ethics can to a degree be reordered by external intervention.[42]

The Conflicts of Interest Act will further embed ethical debate in Alberta politics. The ethics commissioner must entertain complaints about wrongdoing and will provide a focal point for the aggrieved.[43] Moreover, an impartial arbiter with considerable discretion is now a force and the commissioner's annual report, pronouncements, and reports on specific cases will provide many opportunities for debate. Speculation and hence media stories will abound about ongoing and possible investigations. The legislature's authority to overrule the commissioner's recommendations, if used, will generate intense debate. Politics will remain important, but debates will occur in different milieus and under different procedures and rules.

An example of these tendencies is found in the government's refusal to proclaim the act or to give good reasons for its slowness even though the first commissioner, Robert Clark, the leader of the Social Credit Party during the Lougheed years, was appointed in 1992. In Alberta's ethically aware environment, critics assert that the government fears the act, especially its public disclosure provisions, and will delay proclamation until after an election.[44] In this argument we see the first instance of a Canadian government accused of conflict of interest by political manipulation of an act designed to promote ethics!

Private lives of public persons
Alberta politics is increasingly concerned with the private lives of politicians.[45] Those who see this concern as a good thing stress the need to understand the character of public figures. They presume that a person's private conduct illuminates their actual or probable public conduct. Moreover, politicians must lead by example. Improper personal conduct can undercut the integrity of government and the quality of democracy can suffer. Such concerns outweigh the competing value of personal privacy. Those who worry about an obsession with character, and an attendant fascination with private conduct, fear that able people will eschew public careers simply because they value personal and familial privacy. Another concern is that a relentless pursuit of character can deflect interest from policy concerns. If we must choose, do we want to be governed by saints or by hardworking, honest people who may have personal shortcomings but who are committed to good government? A rigid morality may prevail, with the result that we believe that good government only results when we are led by the angelic few who meet extraordinary standards of personal probity.

The debate about character, and its concern with private conduct, is complex. It raises philosophical questions, arguments about the differences between character and personality, and ethical concerns about how one learns about and judges another's private conduct. The character debate is also intertwined with the question of conflict of interest. British government, which eschews written codes of conduct, assumes that legal regulation is unnecessary when persons of good character embrace public life. And as Bruce Payne argues, conflict of interest regimes can only prevent or limit certain forms of misconduct.[46] A focus on character allegedly allows us to understand the motivations of public officials.

In November 1983, an Edmonton constable, in the course of looking for stolen vehicles, found Alberta Solicitor General Graham Harle sitting in a car with a prostitute. The story was covered by the media and Harle submitted his resignation to Premier Lougheed, who accepted it without explanation. For his part, Harle claimed that, as an insomnia sufferer, he was undertaking research into the controversial problem of prostitution.

Two aspects of this case stand out, especially when contrasted with recent examples. First, the debate was remarkably brief and by today's standards quite civilized. The newspapers ran several hard news stories, the columnists wrote brief commentaries, and the dailies produced a single editorial. No probing investigations of Harle's background were undertaken. There was no commentary or speculation about other aspects of his personal life other than to mention that he was married. The opposition refused to comment—the matter was a private one. Interestingly, the commentary was generally supportive of Harle and critical of Lougheed. In its editorial, the *Edmonton Journal* defined the matter as one of personal morality and argued, 'There was no profound transgression.'[47] Moreover, the media must carefully consider its duties before moralizing about or investigating the private conduct of public figures. Other commentators lamented the loss of an effective minister over a trivial episode. How could the prudish Lougheed dismiss Harle after he had refused to act against ministers whose conduct had been rebuked by Mr Justice Brennan in his 1982 inquiry? One cabinet minister and a columnist argued that the incident impaired Harle's capacity to conduct his portfolio.

The contrast between the treatment of Harle in 1983 and that of Alberta Solicitor General Steve West in 1992 is profound. It reflects deep changes in Alberta society and politics, changes that have occurred in less than a decade. The cases are not identical. But at their root are the issues of character and individuals' suitability for high public office as manifest by their private conduct.

In February 1992, Premier Getty promoted Steve West, then minister of parks and recreation, to the portfolio of solicitor general even though West is not a lawyer. Some notoriety already surrounded West. In a 1991 interview, he mentioned that he was a 'roughneck', that before entering the legislature in 1986 he had challenged alleged drug dealers in his home town and that he had been briefly jailed for alcohol-related offences, once in Ontario when he was nineteen and once more recently in Alberta before he had been elected.[48] These admissions caused no commotion at the time. But a storm erupted in 1992 when West's former wife, arguing that she felt compelled to raise questions about West's character in public given his new portfolio, maintained that the couple's 1969 divorce had involved physical abuse, not simply adultery as stated in the legal records. West had not always voluntarily made maintenance payments.

At the outset of the controversy, which dominated Alberta politics for a month, the issues seemed clear. In a balanced editorial, the *Edmonton Journal* noted that some facts were in dispute but that the allegations put a 'cloud' over the solicitor general's head.[49] Could a man whose private life called into question his respect for the law and the presumption of innocence be the solicitor general? Could a man accused of spousal abuse and non-payment of maintenance credibly address the problem of family violence? What message was the government sending to Albertans? Premier Getty defended West principally on the ground that he was an effective man whose contribution to public life should be judged by his performance, not on allegations of personal misconduct. In a dramatic announcement to the legislature after a month of controversy, West argued for the need to separate the private and public conduct of politicians and stated that, since alcohol abuse was a thread in the accusations, he would not drink as long as he held public office.[50]

In contrast to the Harle case, the media and the opposition parties aggressively pursued West who, unlike Harle, held his ground, refused to resign, and challenged his critics. Evidence about an unhappy marriage that had ended in 1969 assumed centre stage. The media then presented much more evidence about West's private life and by implication about his character. Such evidence, which included details about disputes with a neighbour and alleged verbal abuse of patrons in bars, revealed that West was nicknamed 'Genghis Khan' by his colleagues, that his present marriage was 'strong', and that the solicitor general was 'as strong as a horse'. In the face of allegations about drunken misconduct, immediate neighbours mentioned to reporters that they did not know that the solicitor general drank—the Wests were 'excellent neighbours'. And in employing bizarre logic, the *Edmonton Journal* asked addiction counsellors, none of whom knew or had counselled West, to analyse his public statement about abstinence from alcohol.[51]

The West case raised many questions but yielded few answers. First, the debate generated no consensus about West's suitability for high public office. The editors, political analysts, and opposition parties condemned the appointment, while letters to the editor and man-on-the-street' interviews revealed support for West, indifference, and acceptance of the media-Opposition consensus. Second, media coverage of the West story, when seen in context with the exposés about Getty and Joe Dutton, reveals a sea change in its attitude to the private lives of Alberta politicians. For three gruelling weeks, we daily heard details about a minister's personal life. But did these details, some of which were the merest gossip, teach us about the issues at stake, or help us to pass judgement, or did they merely move us closer towards a *People* magazine view of democratic politics? Third, important aspects of the character question were ignored even though they were important in the debate. For example, implicit in West's defence was the notion of character development. He had learned from past errors, had publicly admitted those errors, and in a way, had asked for forgiveness. To his mind, he was now a better person. Are these ideas merely pathetic rationalizations, or can adults in public life learn and grow in stature and integrity?

Conclusion

Our analysis of government ethics in modern Alberta reveals a society struggling to define standards of government conduct in the face of economic and social change. Ethical questions were given short shrift in Peter Lougheed's Progressive Conservative Party. His were governments of action wherein questions of conduct were ignored as impediments to Alberta's drive to economic diversification. Lougheed's ethical posture and his public record highlight an enduring democratic issue. Do leaders, as mere mortals, often manifest a balance of effectiveness skills (for example, energy, a belief in the correctness of their positions, and a clear agenda) and ethical skills (for example, thoughtfulness and genuine respect for dissenting views)? Harder still, if democratic leaders seldom have a balanced repertoire of the required qualities, on which side of the ledger do we want the shortage to occur?

Tory indifference to ethics has had serious consequences. A long-term neglect of serious ethical discourse, when combined with abiding concerns about too-close links between politicians, businessmen, and officials, has contributed to the view that the Alberta government is certainly unfair, probably corrupt, and, in the aftermath of the NovAtel report, managerially ineffective.

Since the mid-1970s, the opposition parties and Alberta's media have found the Tory approach to ethics deficient. The critics demanded a conflict of interest statute as an alternative to Lougheed's *laissez-faire* approach. Such a law was passed in 1991, but discontent is already evident. Disillusionment will grow as the reformers realize that a conflict of interest law, however tough, deals primarily with 'individual legislators alone with their bank accounts'.[52] That is, the statute defines the problem as the abuse of public office for personal financial gain. But with the exception of the cooling-off period for ministers, the act cannot easily control the cronyism that is often defined as the root of Alberta's ethical problem.

In her study of government ethics in the United States, Suzanne Garment argues that American government has 'a growing capacity and taste' for the generation of scandal.[53] So too has Alberta politics, although the elevation of scandal to centre stage is neither complete nor inevitable. The province's recent politics are dominated by concerns about the conduct of public officials. Particularly noteworthy is the media's growing interest in conflict of interest and its willingness to devote substantial resources to investigative journalism. Major stories have appeared about former premier Getty, Joe Dutton, a former Lougheed aide, and Steve West, the former solicitor general, who in December 1992 was appointed minister of municipal affairs. These exposés are linked by a concern with the lifestyles and personal affairs of politicians. The new office of the ethics commissioner can be pursued for opinions about the appropriateness of almost any action by an elected official. Ethical controversy now has a focal point in the machinery of government.

The modern mass media have institutional biases and a well-known capacity to shape the agenda. They are a major actor in Alberta's fledgeling ethics industry. My hunch is that today's muckrakers are disdainful and suspicious of modern Alberta politicians who expect, and, in most cases, enjoy upper-middle-class lives. Journalists dislike this trend and are critical of public policy, like generous expense allowances, that sustains it. More ominously, Alberta's journalists are not immune from the powerful 'infotainment' trend in North American journalism, which stresses the sensational, the personal, and often the bizarre at the expense of serious political analysis. Carl Bernstein, the prominent American journalist, argues that the modern media is shaping an 'idiot culture' and that the 'infotainment' ethos, as driven by competition, pervades the commanding heights of modern media.[54]

Modern Alberta is having severe problems developing an ethical balance. The province has moved from indifference under Lougheed to the present, when ethics are high on the agenda but no consensus is emerging about proper standards and how they can be achieved. Media-led muckraking is no substitute for intelligent ethical discourse. It allows conspicuous, but minor, issues like parliamentary expense allowances to be blown out of proportion and to be addressed without context. Moreover, an obsession with minor ethical transgressions can deflect public attention from serious problems. For example, the *Edmonton Journal* expended substantially greater resources on the issue of MLAs' expense allowances than it did on the province's 1992 budget, which was to have been balanced but instead resulted in a deficit of $1.6 billion. How much debate can we afford about how public officials do or should use aeroplan points accumulated in the conduct of public business? Finally, as G.R. Searle reminds us, corruption is the easiest charge to make and the hardest to refute.[55]

After two decades of Conservative dominance, many observers see a change of government as a panacea. For optimists, a new government would breath fresh air into a stale government and thereby heighten ethical sensitivities. But would a Liberal or New Democrat victory in a future provincial election much alter the ethics agenda? Either party, if elected, will be inexperienced and in today's demanding ethical climate will be prone to errors of judgement. The media and the opposition will pounce on the slightest indiscretion. And both opposition parties, especially the New Democrats, have relentlessly pursued the government for its ethical failures and have thereby generated high expectations for themselves. In the New Democrats' case, journalists will wonder what skeletons lurk in the closets of the self-righteous social democrats. The Liberals, if victorious, will be expected to eschew patronage and show that they are ethically superior to the Tories. In these obvious ways, Alberta's ethics debate has its own momentum.

Deeper questions arise. If one-party dominance, as measured by either the size of legislative majorities or time in office, underpins the Conservatives' insults to democracy, then more frequent changes in government may solve the problem. A regular changing of the guard would make difficult the creation of a self-perpetuating and self-serving circle of insiders as has grown up around the Conservative governments. And the regular rotation of political élites would also work against the view, frequently found in dominant parties, that public office is a personal possession whose ownership is merited by the virtues of the incumbents. But if, as in modern Alberta, the competing parties are ideologically alike, their competition can take the form of a 'purity duel', each claiming moral superiority over the other, with the result that standards of conduct spiral upward to become so high that no one can meet them. Another interesting scenario would be the election of a new dominant party like the provincial Liberals, whose electoral prospects are improving in the early 1990s. Almost by definition, a Liberal government would have the support, sooner or later, of Alberta's legal and business élites. After a period of humility, Liberal government might begin to resemble Conservative government and be characterized by close relations between politicians, senior officials, and corporate élites. The real problem might then be deeper and perhaps ultimately unsolvable: ensuring ethical government in a small but complex political system where the élite is small, intertwined, and by definition influential. Seen in this light, Albertans may have to find virtue in an unfortunate political necessity.

Notes

I would like to thank Stéphane Dion, Ken Kernaghan, John Langford, and Tom Pocklington for their helpful criticism. I am especially grateful to Sharon Sutherland for her extensive, insightful, and collegial critique.

1 Theodore J. Lowi, 'Foreword' in A. Markovits and M. Silverstein, eds, *The Politics of Scandal* (New York: Holmes and Meier, 1988): xii.

2 Critics of this paper have consistently raised an important concern. Is my emphasis on political leadership warranted? Are government's ethics really established by a person or small group? To this concern, I have several responses. First, I acknowledge that the conduct of other ministers, senior appointed officials, and MLAs is important to an understanding of government ethics. But the public debate in Alberta has stressed the role of the premier and I am following that debate. Second, every serious analysis of modern Alberta politics has stressed Peter Lougheed's dominance of his party, his government, and his province's political life. If the worry is that other actors held different ethical views that are obscured by my focus on the leaders, I can only argue that serious ethical dissent among Tories remains remarkably well hidden.

3 For an elaboration, see Suzanne Garment, *Scandal: The Culture of Mistrust in American Politics* (New York: Times Books, 1991).

4 Bruce L. Payne, 'Devices and Desires: Corruption and Ethical Seriousness', in Joel L. Fleishman *et al.*, eds, *Public Duties: The Moral Obligations of Government Officials* (Cambridge, Mass.: Harvard University Press, 1981): 187.

5 Lewis Thomas, 'Alberta 1905-1980: The Uneasy Society', in P. Dunae, ed., *Rancher's Legacy* (Edmonton: University of Alberta Press, 1986): 187.

6 Alberta, Legislative Assembly, *Debates*, 2 May 1973: 2739-40. Hereafter referred to as *Debates*, date, page.

7 *Edmonton Journal*, 4 May 1973: 7.

8 For details, see Dave Margoshes, 'Premier's free flights fly through flak', *Calgary Herald*, 28 Nov. 1978: A1, and 'Lougheed firm on flights', *Calgary Herald*, 29 Nov. 1978: A1.

9 *Edmonton Journal*, 2 Dec. 1978: A4.

10 Alberta, Mr Justice Brennan, *Report of a Public Inquiry* (Calgary, 1982). Hereafter referred to as the Brennan Report.

11 Brennan Report: 24.

12 Ibid.: 57.

13 Ibid.: 57.

14 Ibid.: 52.

15 *Debates*, 17 Nov. 1975: 1109.

16 *Edmonton Journal*, 10 July 1979: A4.

17 For details, see Larry Pratt, 'Grant Notley: Politics as a Calling', in Larry Pratt, ed., *Socialism and Democracy in Alberta* (Edmonton: NeWest Press, 1985): 26-9.

18 Jeffrey Simpson, *Spoils of Power* (Toronto: HarperCollins, 1988), especially 222-7.

19 *Debates*, 28 May 1979: 36.

20 For a fuller development, see Ron Chalmers, 'Insults to Democracy During the Lougheed Era', in Pratt, ed., *Socialism and Democracy in Alberta*,: 131-45.

21 For details, see *Debates*, 25 May 1979: 12.

22 For details, see *Debates*, 6 April 1982: 523-9.

23 *Debates*, 17 April 1985: 434-7.

24 W. Lippmann, 'A Theory about Corruption', in Heidenheimer, ed., *Political Corruption* (New York: Holt, Rinehart and Winston, 1970): 294-7.

25 For an overview of modern Alberta politics, see A. Tupper, 'Alberta Politics: The Collapse of Consensus', in H. Thorburn, ed., *Party Politics in Canada*, 6th ed. (Scarborough, Ont.: Prentice-Hall, 1991): 451-67.

26 C. Donville, 'Minister defends proposal for controversial Alberta-Pacific mill', *Financial Post*, 22 Jan. 1990: 4.

27 Alberta, Conflict of Interest Review Panel, *Report* (Edmonton, 1990).

28 See in particular M. Cernetig and P. Moon, 'Getty speculates in oil, gas', *Globe and Mail*, 24 Nov. 1990: A1; M. Cernetig and P. Moon, 'Getty's job "tough" on living standard', *Globe and Mail*, 26 Nov. 1990: A1 ; M. Cernetig and P. Moon, 'Getty denies wrongdoing', *Globe and Mail*, 27 Nov. 1990: A1; and M. Cernetig and P. Moon, 'Backers saved Getty over debt to bank', *Globe and Mail*, 28 Nov. 1990: A1.

29 *Globe and Mail*, 24 Nov. 1990: A1.

30 For a thoughtful assessment of the *Globe and Mail* stories, see M. Lisac, 'Coverage of Getty became media feud', *Edmonton Journal*, 4 Dec. 1990: A17.

31 *Edmonton Journal*, 27 Nov. 1990: A14.

32 S. Noel, 'Dividing the Spoils: The Old and New Rules of Patronage in Canadian Politics', in Thorburn, ed., *Party Politics in Canada*, 6th ed.: 94-111; J. Simpson, *Spoils of Power*; and R. Whitaker, 'Between patronage and bureaucracy: Democratic politics in transition', *Journal of Canadian Studies* 22 (1987): 55-71.

33 For an assessment of Premier Getty's use of patronage, see M. Lisac, 'Ministry of patronage Getty's portfolio', *Edmonton Journal*, 20 July 1991: A14.

34 For details see A. Boras and J. Adams, 'Investors cry foul', *Calgary Herald*, 14 March 1992: A1.

35 R. Helm, 'NDP leader blasts gov't patronage', *Edmonton Journal*, 21 March 1992: A5.
36 M. Lisac, 'Dutton a Tory with right connections', *Edmonton Journal*, 19 March 1992: A12.
37 Ibid.
38 Alberta, Auditor General of Alberta, *Report of the Auditor General on NovAtel Communications Ltd* (Edmonton: 1992): 20.
39 *Debates*, 20 June 1991: 1868-70.
40 M. Lisac, 'Old club brings in new rules', *Edmonton Journal*, 9 June 1991: A7.
41 D. Braid, 'New law merely an exercise in PR', *Calgary Herald*, 8 June 1991: A7.
42 For details, see the fascinating argument in S. Chibnall and P. Saunders, 'Worlds Apart: Notes on the Social Reality of Corruption', *British Journal of Sociology* 28 (1977).
43 The commissioner, having assumed office in early 1992, is already beset by requests for inquiries. He has been asked to review the Joe Dutton case, to examine MLAs' expense accounts, and to judge the controversies about the payment of ministers' living expenses through funds provided by their constituency associations. See A. Boras, 'Opposition wants new ethics boss to enforce law', *Edmonton Journal*, 15 March 1992: A5.
44 R. Helm, 'Ethics watchdog wants Rostad to let him off his leash', *Edmonton Journal*, 30 Oct. 1992: A8.
45 For useful introductions to this topic, see Dennis F. Thompson, *Political Ethics and Public Office* (Cambridge, Mass.: Harvard University Press; 1987), S. Garment, *Scandal*, especially ch. 7; A. Donahue, ed., *Ethics in Politics and Government* (New York: H.W. Wilson, 1989); and Thomas C. Reeves, *A Question of Character: A Life of John F. Kennedy* (New York: The Free Press, 1991).
46 B.L. Payne, 'Devices and Desires'.
47 *Edmonton Journal*, 17 Nov. 1983: A6. See also G. Oake, 'Is sex still seen as the ultimate sin?', *Edmonton Journal*, 18 Nov. 1983: B2; and D. Sellar, 'Harle's demise greased by double standard', *Calgary Herald*, 18 Nov. 1983: A5.
48 B. Laghi, 'West's jail time doesn't bother Getty', *Edmonton Journal*, 22 Feb. 1992: A7.
49 *Edmonton Journal*, 3 March 1992: A6.
50 For details, see *Debates*, 20 March 1992: 8-17.
51 I. Mulgrew, 'West's vow to quit drinking leaves experts wondering', *Edmonton Journal*, 21 March 1992: A6.
52 Thompson, *Political Ethics and Public Office*: 99.
53 S. Garment, *Scandal*: 1.
54 Carl Bernstein, 'The Idiot Culture: Reflections on post-Watergate journalism', *The New Republic*, 8 June 1992.
55 G.R. Searle, *Corruption in British Politics, 1895-1930* (Oxford: Clarendon Press, 1987): 8.

8

Kenneth Kernaghan

Rules are not enough

Ethics, politics, and public service in Ontario

In Ontario, as in all other parts of Canada, public concern about government ethics has increased significantly, and steadily, since the early 1970s. The Ontario government has responded to this concern with several measures designed to deter unethical conduct by public officials and to sensitize them to the ethical dimension of their behaviour. However, continuing reports of unethical conduct, combined with enduring and emerging ethical dilemmas, suggest that much remains to be done to enhance the ethical behaviour and ethical sensitivity of public officials.

We will examine four ethical areas in this essay: conflict of interest; relations between politicians and public servants, with particular reference to political neutrality, political rights, and patronage; privacy and confidentiality, including reference to whistle-blowing; and the management of a diverse workforce. This latter issue is examined by way of illustration of the very large proportion of ethical issues in the public service that revolve around human policies and practices. Particular attention is paid to the influence of Ontario's political and public service cultures on the evolution of government ethics. It is argued that impending changes in the culture of government service, resulting from the politicization of the public service and the service quality approach to management, will make more difficult the already daunting task of managing ethical behaviour. In addition, politicians and public servants are alerted to the important ethical implications of the systemic links between the constitutional conventions of ministerial responsibility, political neutrality, and public service anonymity.

The management of government ethics in Ontario has been handled largely through the development of written rules in the form of statutes, regulations, and guidelines. The major theme of this essay is that rules alone are not sufficient to cope with current and anticipated ethical problems. Certain problems, such as conflicts of interest or the leaking of government information, can be regulated to some extent by written rules, but even in these areas written rules are often difficult to apply to concrete cases. Many other ethical issues, such as deciding if or when lying is justified, or the appropriate measure of risk to the public, cannot be managed effectively by written rules. Other approaches, especially ethics education and ethics leadership, must complement the traditional reliance on rules. It is, moreover, sometimes necessary to rely on the ethical standards of the individual official and ultimately on his or her conscience. An Ontario deputy minister has concluded that 'a first principle of professional morality is that being accountable to others does not make you any less accountable to yourself. . . . the vitality of government is partly dependent on how well we understand and respect this principle of personal ethics.'[1]

We will begin with an examination of the current ethical landscape of Ontario government, with particular focus on recent ethics issues and on the political, legal, and administrative framework within which these issues arise. This is followed by an analysis of the major influences leading to the present state of the government ethics in Ontario. The third section contains a sketch of the future ethical landscape in the province, and the concluding section evaluates the current ethics regime and proposes several reforms.

Surveying the landscape

Constitutional considerations

The shape that ethical issues take in Ontario government is greatly influenced by the province's political, legal, and administrative institutions and traditions. Of central importance is the fact that the Ontario political system is based on the Westminster model of parliamentary-cabinet government with its accompanying constitutional conventions of ministerial responsibility, political neutrality, and public service anonymity. These conventions provide the framework for relations between politicians and public servants, and between government officials and the public.

The efficacy of individual ministerial responsibility requires the preservation of political neutrality and public service anonymity. It is argued that ministers cannot be expected to accept public responsibility for the errors of public servants if those public servants take the public stage by engaging in high-profile partisan politics or public comment on government policies, programs, and personalities. The convention of political neutrality requires that public servants avoid involvement in activities that bring into question the fact or appearance of their political impartiality. It is, therefore, central to discussions of the ethical and other implications of extending the political rights of public servants and of making patronage appointments to the public service. According to the anonymity convention, public servants should provide advice to Cabinet ministers in confidence and should not defend or speculate on government policies in public. This convention has obvious ramifications for issues of political rights and confidentiality.

Another central constitutional factor in the realm of government ethics is the Canadian Charter of Rights and Freedoms which came into full force in 1985.

The provisions of the Charter and judicial interpretation of these provisions have already had an extremely important influence in such areas as political rights and individual privacy where decisions affecting the federal sphere of government have significant implications for the provinces.

Ethics rules

Aside from broad constitutional factors, the ethical behaviour of public officials is affected by a plethora of rules in the forms of statutes, regulations, and guidelines. At a very general level, the Criminal Code, a federal statute, provides for the imprisonment of public officials at any level of Canadian government who commit such offences as accepting a bribe, committing a fraud or breach of trust, and selling or purporting to sell an appointment. Another federal statute, the Official Secrets Act, provides Draconian penalties for public officials who engage in the unauthorized release of confidential information.

There are also statutes that are applicable only to Ontario public officials. These include the Members' Conflict of Interest Act and the Election Finances Act covering elected officials; they include also the Public Service Act and its regulations that cover appointed officials and deal with confidentiality, conflict of interest, and political activity. Other statutes, such as the Freedom of Information and Protection of Privacy Act, affect the activities of both elected and appointed officials.

In addition to statutes and regulations, there are many guidelines devoted partly or solely to ethical conduct. In 1985, the Management Board Secretariat developed a Statement of Corporate Values that calls for ethical conduct both by and within the public service. The paragraph on excellence in service to the public notes that 'quality service . . . demands that the actions of the Ontario Public Service be consistent and based on ethical conduct and sound administrative practices.' And the paragraph on employees as a critical resource emphasizes the need for 'leadership that ensures fair treatment, personal growth and the development of each individual'. To enhance these standards of conduct, the Civil Service Commission drafted a Statement of Principles modelled on the Statement of Principles of the Institute of Public Administration of Canada and covering accountability, political neutrality, confidentiality, privacy, and conflict of interest. This draft Statement was widely circulated and used as a basis of discussion and analysis in ethics workshops, but was not formally adopted. In addition, individual ministries have developed specific ethical guidelines or mission statements containing references to desirable ethical behaviour. For example, the Mission Statement of the Ministry of the Solicitor General enjoins employees to develop fair policies, to consult widely, to promote social justice through fair and equitable treatment of all members of society, to eliminate systemic barriers to recruitment and advancement within the ministry, and to reduce risks to the public.

Finally, there are customs, informal practices, and traditions regarding ethical conduct that supplement, complement or, in some instances, run counter to, the formal rules. For example, section 14 of the Public Service Act provides a strict prohibition on public comment by public servants, but in practice this section has been given a much less restrictive interpretation than the literal one.

Problem areas

Conflict of interest

Conflict of interest is easily the most publicized area of unethical conduct in government and offences in this area, especially over the past decade, have done substantial damage to the careers of politicians and the electoral prospects of governing parties. It has become the primary ethical issue by which the public and, more specifically, the electorate, measures political integrity. The involvement of Cabinet ministers in conflict of interest scandals in 1972 led Premier William Davis to replace unwritten rules with formal conflict of interest guidelines that forbade ministers from purchasing real estate unless it was for personal use and required them to divest themselves of stocks or put them into a blind trust.

Little change was made in these guidelines until two ministers in the government of Premier David Peterson became involved in serious conflicts of interest in 1986. On the basis of a report that was critical of the 1972 guidelines,[2] the government replaced them in 1988 with conflict of interest legislation applying to both Cabinet ministers and members of the legislature.[3] The legislation also provided for the appointment of a conflict of interest commissioner to promote compliance with the legislation. Ontario was the first government in Canada to make such an appointment. The commissioner has described his primary duty as providing assistance to members of the Legislature in outlining their obligations under the conflict legislation; assisting in the identification of areas of possible conflict of interest and providing advice to prevent the situation from developing, or resolving it if it has occurred; and investigating complaints made in conformity with the act.[4]

Under the act, a conflict of interest arises 'when the member makes a decision or participates in making a decision in the execution of his or her office and at the same time knows that in the making of the decision there is the opportunity to further his or her private interest.' Members are prohibited from involvement in such activities as using insider information, exerting undue influence, or accepting fees, gifts, or personal benefits not arising from their normal protocol or social obligations.

Ministers are also prohibited from engaging in employment or in the practice of a profession, carrying on a business, or holding an office or directorship other than in a social or religious organization or a political party, unless these activities are required or permitted as part of their ministerial responsibilities. Ministers may use a trust to administer their financial interests or a business, but this trust must be approved by the conflict of interest commissioner. They must also disclose to the commissioner within sixty days of their election and annually thereafter their own assets, liabilities, financial interests, and income, those of their spouse and dependent children, and those of private companies controlled by any of them. The commissioner is required to prepare a public disclosure statement containing much of this information. Finally, the post-employment provisions of the act specify a 'cooling-off period' of one year during which former ministers cannot accept government contracts or benefits, or lobby for such contracts.

In 1990, Premier Bob Rae imposed additional rules on Cabinet ministers and their parliamentary assistants in the form of guidelines that were described by the conflict of interest commissioner as 'pretty Draconian'.[5] Ministers and their assistants are required to divest themselves of virtually all business interests and any other assets that might involve them in a conflict of interest. Not only are they forbidden to enter into contracts with the government, but their spouses and minor children are permitted to do so only when the contract is publicly tendered. The guidelines are interpreted and enforced by the premier, not by the commissioner.

With respect to appointed officials, the regulations under the Public Service Act were amended in 1973 to provide conflict of interest coverage for public servants. No definition of conflict of interest was provided, but five types of conflict of interest were spelled out and public servants were required to disclose actual or possible conflicts of interest to their deputy minister and, if necessary, to divest themselves of an outside interest, transfer the interest to a trust, move to another part of the organization, or resign. Similar requirements are contained in the current regulations and consideration is being given to including specific conflict of interest provisions in a proposed revision of the Public Service Act itself.

Both politicians and public servants are subject to the provisions of the Criminal Code mentioned above. The code is, however, an unwieldy instrument for handling many conflict of interest situations, especially those that fall into the grey area between criminal activity and mildly questionable behaviour, and which are better dealt with by administrative action than by the courts.

Conflict of interest problems also arise in the area of political party financing. Elected officials can make use of their public office to reward those who contribute financially to their personal campaigns or to the party as a whole. The 'greyness' of this area of political ethics is evident in the allegation in 1990 that several Liberal members of a legislative committee examining the auto insurance industry were in a conflict of interest because they had received campaign contributions from the insurance industry. The then premier, David Peterson, rejected the notion that 'fair-minded' people would perceive this situation as a conflict of interest.[6]

Much more damaging conflict of interest problems arose in 1989. These revolved around Patricia Starr, a Liberal fundraiser and chairperson of the Toronto section of the National Council of Jewish Women who had been appointed chairperson of the Ontario Place amusement park. It was alleged that she had made illegal political contributions, most of them to provincial Liberals.[7] It was also revealed that the Council had received questionable tax breaks, apparently for low-income housing that it was building in partnership with a large development company, whose president was also the president of the Ontario wing of the federal Liberal Party. During the investigation of the Starr case, one of the premier's chief assistants resigned after it was alleged that he had accepted a gift from a firm doing business with the government. The premier used a cabinet shuffle to remove most of those ministers associated with Patricia Starr's questionable activities, but not before it became evident to the public that the Election Finances Act did not sufficiently deter unethical conduct in respect of campaign contributions.

Politicians and public servants
The ethics of relations between politicians and public servants are influenced by the constitutional conventions explained above and, in such areas as partisan political activity and public comment, by written rules. Considerable uncertainty remains, however, as to how these conventions and rules should be interpreted. Moreover, because the rules in some areas are either vague or non-existent, reliance must be placed on the personal ethical standards of public officials.

For example, in the normal course of their duties, public servants are expected to be politically sensitive but not politically partisan. During the 1990 provincial election, some ministers were accused of using public servants for partisan purposes and some public servants were perceived as being unduly accommodating to the ministers' requests. An official of the Ontario Public Service Employees Union (OPSEU) noted how difficult it is to determine whether a public servant who prepares material that is helpful to a minister during an election campaign is engaging in partisan political activity as defined in the Public Service Act. He argued that while the act prohibits public servants from taking part in political activities, it does not provide protection for those who are requested to do so by their political masters.[8] The act does state that public servants 'shall not during working hours engage in any activity for or on behalf of a political party'. This is not, however, very precise guidance for public servants who want to act ethically while safeguarding their careers by maintaining harmonious relations with their hierarchical superiors. The underlying ethical principles here are that it is improper for political superiors to request public servants to provide partisan assistance, and that public servants have a duty to resist such requests.

Ethical issues are often intertwined with considerations of political power and political rights. For example, during the 1990 provincial election, OPSEU took out newspaper advertisements in opposition to the Liberal government. In addition, the union continued its vigorous quest for an expansion of the political rights of its members. The 1990 election of the New Democratic Party, with its close political ties to the public unions and its long-time support for the expansion of political rights, has greatly enhanced the prospects for a liberalization of the current political rights regime. In its first Throne Speech, the new government promised legislation to extend the rights of public servants to engage in partisan political activity and public comment. This promise was followed by a discussion paper outlining a three-tier model for defining political rights.[9]

Opposition to a major extension of political rights for public servants is based largely on concern for the preservation of the constitutional conventions of political neutrality, ministerial responsibility, and public service anonymity, and the public service values of efficiency and effectiveness.[10] Part of the concern is that the involvement of large numbers of public servants in high-profile partisan politics, combined with other moves in the direction of a more politicized public service that are explained later in this essay, will lead to a resurgence of patronage in the form of politically motivated appointments and promotions of public servants.

The ethical dimension of relations between politicians and public servants often comes to the force with a change in the governing party. For example, reports of deteriorating relations between certain Cabinet ministers and senior public servants began to circulate within a few months of the NDP election victory in 1990. Senior public servants spoke anonymously to the press about the alleged incompetence of certain ministers and their political advisers, both of whom, it was claimed, refused to listen to frank advice offered in the public interest. Public servants were in turn accused of obstructing government policies, sometimes on ideological grounds. Within eighteen months of the election, seventeen of twenty-seven deputy ministers had left the government, for a variety of reasons, and several of them had been replaced by NDP partisans.

Confidentiality and privacy
The increasingly central role of information in contemporary society has impor-tant ethical implications for both politicians and public servants. In the manage-ment of information, governments are required to balance the public's right to know not only with the need to keep certain government information confiden-tial, but also with the need to protect the privacy of individual citizens. The Official Secrets Act is of limited usefulness in managing the ethics of government information in that its intention appears to be the prevention of foreign espion-age; it is unlikely to be used against public officials who disclose other types of information without authorization. In Ontario, the major mechanism for manag-ing the government's collection and use of information is the 1988 Freedom of Information and Protection of Privacy Act. The philosophy underpinning the act is that the public has a right of access to information held by government institutions; exemptions to this access should be limited and specific; decisions to deny access should be reviewed by an independent body; and individuals have a right to have information about themselves protected and have access to that information.

All public servants are also required to take an oath of secrecy that includes the requirement that they will not, except as legally required, disclose information that they acquire by virtue of their public office. This oath has not prevented public servants from leaking government information to the media and opposition parties, a practice that has become increasingly frequent over the past two decades. In 1991, the NDP government was seeking imaginative ways of tracking down public servants who leaked highly sensitive cabinet documents to opposition parties, ostensibly for partisan purposes.[11]

Within the framework of written rules designed to ensure ethical information practices, politicians and public servants exercise considerable discretionary authority in deciding what measures of confidentiality and privacy are appropriate. The task is not an easy one. According to an Ontario deputy minister, the complexities of knowing what you can and cannot do, what you should or should not release, can be mind-boggling. One of the reasons for this confusion is that people want to know at what point the individual's right to privacy is superseded by the public's right to know, and nobody seems to have the answers.[12]

It is increasingly acknowledged that the meaning of the oath of secrecy is too vague to provide sufficient guidance.[13] A literal interpretation of the oath suggests that disclosing information acquired by virtue of one's public employment is prohibited. However, in a 1982 whistle-blowing case, the Crown Employees Grievance Settlement Board ruled that invoking the oath in its literal form was inconsistent with the principle of open government.[14] Recognition that the ethics of whistle-blowing has become an issue of considerable public debate in Canada,[15] and that the Ontario government has not made adequate provision for managing the issue, led the NDP government to promise legislative protection for public servants who disclose confidential information about serious government wrongdoing.[16] This protection would extend to public servants who blow the whistle on such matters as illegal activity and gross abuse of public funds, not to those who leak information about policies to which they are opposed or in order to embarrass the government.

The whistle-blowing issue demonstrates that public servants must on occasion resolve clashes between their personal ethical standards and the ethical duties and obligations imposed by the organizations they serve. For example, a public servant with knowledge of wrongdoing within government may have to choose between loyalty to the government of the day and personal conviction that the public has the right to know about the wrongdoing.

Public and media concern about the ethical management of the confidentiality issue has been matched by heightened anxiety about ethical behaviour in the privacy field. Opposition legislators and the news media are focusing increased attention on real and alleged breaches of individual privacy. An opposition member's suggestion that the premier should resign for revealing the salary of the former head of a provincial agency was largely wishful thinking. However, a minister resigned after inadvertently revealing the name of a drug addict who had received treatment in the United States. Still another minister took a lie detector test *to prove that she was lying* when she said publicly that she had seen information on the billing practices of an Ontario doctor whom she named; her aim was to avoid censure and possible resignation for using confidential information for partisan purposes. During a legislative inquiry into this case, it was revealed that a journalist had knowledge about an internal government document containing confidential information on the doctor's billing practices that had been circulated among several public servants.

The Ethics of Diversity

The Ontario government, especially since the mid-1970s, has been strongly committed to ensuring that the public service reflects the diversity of the province's population. The management philosophy underlying efforts to achieve this objective is employment equity. Ontario was the first province to adopt an affirmative action program for women in the public service and considerable progress towards employment equity for women was made by the mid-1980s. Then in 1987 the government announced an employment equity program covering five designated groups: women, francophones, disabled persons, aboriginals, and racial minorities, and in 1988 it passed pay equity legislation.

The government has learned that simply recruiting members of the designated groups is insufficient and that a diverse workforce requires the removal of organizational barriers to their full participation and advancement. Despite various initiatives to overcome such barriers, including programs to train employees to manage cultural diversity, a task force report on employment systems in one ministry revealed that its working climate did not encourage upward mobility for designated group employees. Moreover, there was 'an alarming number of incidences of sexual and racial harassment'.[17] It seems reasonable to conclude that similar problems exist in other ministries.

The challenge in this area is not simply that of unethical behaviour in the form of discrimination and harassment. The management of a culturally diverse workforce requires a high level of sensitivity to different peoples, styles, and values and the ability to resolve ethical dilemmas arising from these differences. For example, an Ontario deputy minister has explained that recruiting members of ethnic minorities can really muddle our morals. How, for example, do you conduct a fair job interview when, in certain cultures, making direct eye contact is considered bad form? In other cultures it is unheard of to talk positively about yourself. Our notions of right and wrong go right out the window when confronted with other ways of doing things. We are forced to admit just how ethnocentric our ways of judging others really are.[18] It is essential for government to achieve a high ethical performance in the management of cultural diversity so that it can promote or require employment equity programs in the private sector with clean hands.

Analysing the status quo

The current ethical landscape in Ontario government has been shaped by influences of varying degrees of specificity. These influences include broad societal concern about ethics in general, developments in the political system in Canada and other countries that have affected ethical behaviour in all government jurisdictions, political characteristics unique to the Ontario scene, and contributions of particular political parties and their leaders.

Societal influences

The public's sustained anxiety about government ethics over the past two decades is not simply a response to continuing reports of unethical behaviour involving public officials; rather it is part of increased society-wide concern about ethical issues in general. Ethical problems in government and the widespread negative image of public officials have contributed substantially to this broad concern, but much public attention has been directed also to ethics in business, medicine, journalism, sports, and many other areas of Canadian society. In Ontario, the Toronto-based print media have been especially effective in stimulating and maintaining the public's interest in ethical issues.

The public and the media have pressured government not only to ensure that public officials act ethically but also to resolve ethical dilemmas in various policy fields (e.g., AIDS) and to regulate ethical conduct in business and other non-governmental organizations. Business organizations in particular have responded to public and governmental concern about their ethical performance by such means as adopting codes of ethics, providing ethics workshops for their employees, and emphasizing the importance of ethical leadership. The Ontario government's efforts to preserve and enhance the ethical behaviour of public officials have benefited from concepts and practices developed for private sector organizations.

Broad political influences

A second set of influences on the government's ethical climate are developments in the political system that are common to all government jurisdictions, but to which different governments respond differently. An Ontario deputy minister has noted the emergence of new ethical issues and new insights on old issues.

> Twenty years ago we didn't see as clearly the indirect methods by which politicians and public servants can become beholden to, or influenced by, developers or others seeking government benefits. . . . As well, the issues have become much more complex because, for example, there is no longer a dominant system of values, new technology has revolutionized fields such as the health care system, and information is much more readily available.[19]

Widespread media coverage of unethical behaviour involving public officials in other countries, especially in the United States and Britain, has increased concern in this country about government ethics. Similarly, extensive publicity about unethical behaviour, especially conflicts of interest, involving officials in Ottawa has stimulated and reinforced concern in Ontario, which not only houses the federal capital but whose residents have strong political identification with the national government.

While conflict of interest scandals are nothing new in Ontario politics, they have been viewed in recent years with increasing gravity, especially since the election of the Peterson government in 1985—a date that coincided with the beginning of a series of well-publicized conflict of interest incidents featuring ministers in the federal government. Over the next several years also, the news media focused a great deal of attention on conflicts of interest involving politicians and, to a lesser extent, government employees in various Ontario municipalities. There were frequent demands from opposition parties that the government conduct a formal inquiry into municipal conflict of interest problems, especially those arising from relations between elected officials and developers.

The political and personal embarrassment arising from disclosures and allegations of conflict of interest has prompted the Ontario government's political opponents to focus on this problem area, to exaggerate the gravity of some offences, to make irresponsible allegations, and to lump as many questionable activities as possible under the general rubric of conflict of interest. The heightened public concern about conflicts of interest can be attributed in substantial part to the general tendency, especially over the past decade, to inflate the meaning of what constitutes a conflict. As a result, there is considerable confusion as to precisely what activities should be characterized as a conflict of interest. Ian Greene has identified four types of conflict in which Canadian cabinet ministers have been involved, namely, private profit from public office; violation of the appearance of impartiality, either through being in a real conflict of interest situation through breach of the conflict code or through failure to avoid the appearance of conflict of interest; giving favours to friends or associates; and conflicts of interest involving party patronage.[20] And for public servants, eight variations of conflict have been identified, namely, self-dealing, accepting benefits, influence-peddling, using government property, using confidential information, outside employment, post-employment, and personal conduct.[21] In addition, *apparent* and *potential* conflicts are often treated as seriously as real conflicts—a development not lost on opposition legislators. Moreover, as in the Members' Conflict of Interest Act, restrictions on the activities of legislators are applied to their spouses and dependent children as well.

Increasingly also, the meaning of conflict of interest is not limited to the use of public office for private *financial* gain; it can also include benefits to friends or relatives—and even to political parties or candidates. For example, ministers can grant preferential treatment to business firms that have been especially helpful in party fundraising, and public servants can leak information to assist the fortunes of a particular political party.

The activities of certain ministers of the NDP government have led to a further expansion in the scope of application of conflict of interest. In 1991, the premier admitted that two ministers broke the conflict of interest guidelines by trying to influence the College of Physicians and Surgeons, a quasi-judicial body, to suspend a doctor who had been convicted of sexual assault. While an argument could be made that these ministers, as well as the 'lie-detector' minister mentioned earlier, were pursuing the public interest, the fact remains that they were using their public office to seek objectives not directly within the sphere of their ministerial authority. Still other ministers were embarrassed by, or forced to resign for, involvement in conflicts of interest of a more conventional nature.

The ferocity and persistence of opposition attacks on these ministers for real or alleged conflicts can be explained in part by the perceived self-righteousness of the premier's criticism of the ethical performance of government ministers when he was in opposition. In response to the premier's refusal to dismiss one of the ministers under attack, an opposition member claimed that when the premier was in opposition he had time and time again 'stood in his self-appointed judge's chair . . . and demanded blood'[22] from government ministers. Not only in Ontario, but in other Canadian governments, politicians have often found that the practical realities of governing make it difficult to adhere to the ethical standards they have demanded of others.

Political and public service cultures

The dominant political culture in Ontario is a conservative one, characterized by such values as élitism, ascription, hierarchy, continuity, stability, and social order.[23] Historically, both the Conservative and Liberal parties have adopted and protected these values. There is, however, a significant reform element in the political culture that has been expressed most strongly by the CCF and NDP. The influence of this reform element, combined with the fact that even the Conservative and Liberal parties have been somewhat progressive, suggests that the dominant political culture might best be described as a 'progressive' conservative one. In terms of attitudes towards the political system, Ontarians are a 'participant political culture' in that they view themselves as politically effective and have a high level of trust in government. There is, at the same time, a large number of 'critics', that is, Ontarians who are high on efficacy but low on trust; this may be the result of the continuing influence of the CCF/NDP and the one-party dominance which, until recently, has characterized the Ontario political system.

Pierre-François Gingras contends that there are two political cultures in Ontario—one of 'affluence, centrality and satisfaction with a progressive conservatism', and one of 'deprivation, remoteness and alienation'.[24] These latter characteristics are associated with the province's large immigrant population, especially in Toronto, and with Northern Ontario with its many ethnic communities, its concentration of Franco-Ontarians, and its support for the CCF and the NDP. Neither of these populations has been completely integrated into the dominant culture. The increasingly multicultural nature of Ontario society and the growing political power of ethnic communities explains in large part government support for employment equity and concern about individual and organizational ethics in the management of an increasingly diverse workforce.

Long periods of one-party dominance in the province, by one or the other 'conservative' party, has had an important impact on business-government relations and on the ethical milieu in which these relations have been conducted. From the time of Confederation, there have been very close relations between Ontario governments and the province's business community. Elite accommodation in Ontario 'is a natural relationship between the dominant business representatives of the financial and industrial interests in the economic heartland of Canada and the dominant political spokesmen represented there.'[25] The financial backing of business interests for the governing party, whether the Conservatives or the Liberals, has helped to keep the party in office once it has been elected.

During the long period of Conservative Party rule (1943-85), close links between government and business were accompanied by numerous conflict of interest allegations and by the use of political patronage to reward the government's business friends with appointments to the many semi-independent agencies of government[26] and with government contracts. The electorate's concern about integrity in government was not, however, a major factor in the defeat of the Conservative government by the Liberals in 1985. With respect to the use of patronage, it is notable that 'the provincial culture was no less shot through with patronage than others, but a certain subtlety and discretion often accompanied its use.'[27] Like his predecessor, the new Liberal premier, David Peterson, was very adept at the patronage game. He used the system to reward friends quietly and to broaden the party's political base by appointing to government agencies a large number of women and representatives of the ethnic and francophone communities. Moreover, partly in response to the public's outrage at the patronage practices of Prime Minister Mulroney, Premier Peterson promised to reform the Ontario patronage system.[28] While his successor, Premier Bob Rae, promised to put an end to the system, the end does not appear to be near.

Premier Peterson was also adept at managing conflict of interest problems during the early years of his government. As explained earlier, he responded quickly and vigorously to conflict allegations against two of his ministers. However, the Patricia Starr affair, which began in 1989, caused considerable political damage. It involved not only conflict of interest but political patronage and breaches of the Election Finances Act as well; it also drew attention to the close ties between the Liberal government and the business community. The low level of public trust in governments generally and the continuing revelations of unethical behaviour in Canadian political life doubtless led some voters to believe that the Starr affair was part of a larger measure of political corruption in the province. Government integrity was an important theme in the 1990 election and the new premier began by toughening the conflict of interest rules for cabinet ministers. We have seen that this was not sufficient to ward off ministerial conflicts of interest and resignations.

Ontario's public service culture reflects the main features of its political culture. The predominantly conservative political culture, combined with the cautious, managerial style of most Ontario premiers, has resulted in close adherence to the classical model of public administrations with its emphasis on hierarchy, merit, impartiality, and continuity. An important aspect of Ontario's political and public service cultures is a long-standing commitment to a politically neutral public service appointed on the basis of merit, in the sense of 'best qualified'. As a result, patronage appointments, especially to the regular public service as opposed to agencies, boards, and commissions, have been much less frequent than in several provincial jurisdictions. This can be explained in part by the factor of one-party dominance, which has meant that there have been fewer instances in which a new governing party was pressured to reward its political friends with government jobs by turfing out its political enemies. The traditional emphasis on an impartial, professional career public service helps to explain also Ontario's reluctance to extend the political rights of public servants. As explained later in this essay, some changes in the governing party in recent years, especially the election of an NDP government, are tending to move the public service in the direction of politicization.

It is notable that the progressive element of Ontario's political culture has helped to stimulate significant public service reforms that have served as a model for other provincial governments. In the sphere of government ethics, Ontario was the first province to introduce conflict of interest guidelines for public servants, and its workshops on public service ethics have served as a model for other provinces.

Parties and their leaders

We have seen that the seriousness with which elected officials view alleged unethical activities depends significantly on whether they are in or out of power. This is especially the case in the conflict of interest sphere, where there is considerable debate over what constitutes a real conflict and what political or personal price should be paid by those involved. The pattern in Ontario has been for opposition parties to proclaim their capacity for higher levels of ethical performance than the governing party, to develop 'new and improved' rules when they come to power, and then to see ministers and their political staff become involved in serious ethical problems. It has become painfully obvious to recent governments that written rules cannot provide for every contingency and that in the final analysis considerable reliance must be placed on personal ethical standards.

Ethical leadership, especially by premiers and ministers, can also have an extremely beneficial effect on the ethical conduct of politicians and public servants. In assessing the ethical performance of political leaders, however, it is essential to keep in mind the distinctive and pressure-filled ethical milieu in which they must operate.

Premier Peterson was castigated by opposition legislators and punished by the electorate for conflicts of interest involving his ministers and his political staff, but there was no suggestion that he personally used his public office for private gain. Moreover, a number of measures taken by his government were aimed specifically at enhancing the ethical performance of both politicians and public servants. Shortly after his government came to power and before conflict of interest allegations began, Liberal members of the legislature, including cabinet ministers, were briefed on the nature of conflicts of interest and the need to avoid them. On the day after his government was sworn in, the premier met all deputy ministers to inform them that government business should be conducted according to the values of openness with the public, fairness and equity, integrity and honesty, caring for people, and trust between his government and the public service. The Peterson government was also more active than most governments in Canada in supporting measures to sensitize public officials to the ethical dimension of public service. These measures included the development of ethics rules for both politicians and public servants, the creation of the office of conflict of interest commissioner, and the mounting of ethics workshops, first for senior executives and then for managers and supervisors. In addition, the Peterson government, in August 1990, appointed a consultation committee to conduct a review of the conflict of interest issue in municipal government.

Decisions by the New Democratic Party government under Premier Rae are also likely to have a lasting effect on the ethical milieu and performance of public officials. As explained earlier, the premier prescribed strict conflict of interest guidelines for cabinet ministers and parliamentary assistants. Notable also were the Throne Speech announcements that the government would expand the permissible political rights of public servants and provide legislative protection for public servants who blow the whistle on government wrongdoing. Not only in Ontario but across the country, the NDP and the public service unions have been among the foremost proponents of the expansion of political rights for public servants. While considerations of political power as well as ethics are involved in this issue, a persuasive argument can be made for permitting as many public servants as possible to exercise the fullest possible measure of political rights. In addition, the circumstances under which public servants are justified in blowing the whistle is an ethical issue of considerable current debate. The Rae government is the first in Canada to declare its intention to protect whistle-blowers from reprisal. Moreover, the government responded to the report[29] of the Municipal Conflict of Interest Consultation Committee, appointed by its predecessor, by publishing a white paper entitled *Open Local Government*.[30] The white paper proposed, among other things, to amend the Municipal Conflict of Interest Act to provide more effective regulation of conflicts of interest involving politicians.[31] The Committee also suggested that a model code for local government employees should be developed. In response, the Association of Municipal Clerks and Treasurers of Ontario has developed a model code which it is encouraging municipalities to adopt.

Prospects and portents

Analysis and action in the sphere of government ethics must take account not only of the current ethical landscape but also of the likely contours of this landscape several years down the road. Recent developments and emerging trends suggest that over the next decade there may be dramatic changes in the ethos, and therefore in the ethical climate, of the Ontario public service. These changes will have especially important ramifications for relations between public servants and politicians. Even the constitutional pillars of ministerial responsibility, political neutrality, and public service anonymity are being eroded by the shifting sands of political and administrative change.

A consensus has emerged among public officials that the importance of the ethical dimension in government has increased steadily over the past two decades and is likely, at the very least, to maintain its importance in the foreseeable future. Moreover, it is likely that the problem areas discussed in this essay will continue to be high on the ethics agenda a decade from now. There is increasing recognition that certain ethical problems (e.g., conflict of interest) can be much more easily managed by resort to written rules than are other problems (e.g., lying, lack of integrity in the competition process), and that ethics leadership and ethics education are, therefore, important complementary means of enhancing ethical behaviour.

There is continuing debate over what constitutes ethical or unethical conduct in various problem areas, and what penalties should be paid when there is agreement that unethical conduct has occurred. Even in the conflict of interest sphere, where written rules have significantly narrowed the area of previous disagreement, expansion of the meaning and application of this offence has complicated the task of managing ethics. Similarly, if the political rights of public servants are expanded, the broad ethical debate over the right to exercise these rights fully would be resolved, but new ethical issues would arise. For example, just because it becomes legal for welfare case-workers to engage in door-to-door canvassing after working hours does not mean that it is ethical for them to seek permission to put up lawn signs at the homes of clients they visited during working hours. Moreover, the ethical mettle of ministers and public servant managers will be tested when they are making human resource decisions affecting employees who have campaigned, in a high-profile way, for the 'wrong' party.

The extent to which a greater consensus on government ethics emerges will depend significantly on the extent to which the reforms discussed in the next section of this essay are adopted. The prospects for reforms are good because of the foundation of ethics rules and ethics education that has already been laid, and because of the knowledge, especially in the political realm, of the painful consequences of even perceived unethical conduct.

On the other hand, reforms designed to enhance ethical behaviour in the Ontario government may be undermined by broad, long-term developments whose likely consequences have been largely ignored. Specifically, there are two developments that will have significant ramifications for the culture of the Ontario public service, especially in respect of relations between politicians and public servants. The first development is the politicization of the public service;

the second is the adoption of the service quality approach to management (SQM). Implementation of these two systemically related developments seems to be proceeding as if they can reasonably be considered in splendid isolation from one another.

As noted earlier, the NDP government proposes to extend the political rights of public servants in respect of both partisan political activity and public comment. As a result, a much larger number of public servants would be permitted to engage in high-profile partisan political activities and in public criticism (or praise) of government policies, programs, and personalities. A related development is the government's decision to provide legislative protection against reprisals for public servants who blow the whistle on government wrongdoing. A strong argument can be made that these interrelated developments will tend to erode the fact and the appearance of political neutrality and undermine the related conventions of ministerial responsibility and public service anonymity.[32] Moreover, these conventions are already being threatened by other developments. For example, the NDP government has made several partisan political appointments at the highest levels of the public service, and the anonymity of public servants is continuing to be diminished by their appearances before legislative committees and at public meetings, their negotiations with interest groups, and increasing media attention to their activities. Taken together, these developments will have a significant politicizing effect on the public service.

At the same time as the forces for politicization are gathering speed, the NDP government has committed itself to the government-wide implementation of the SQM approach, with its emphasis on improving service to the public, empowering public servants, and operating more efficiently. An essential feature of this approach is the delegation of real decision-making power down the administrative hierarchy and out to public servants on the front lines. Empowered public servants will be expected to provide better service by being in close contact with their clients and by being more innovative and taking some risks. They will also have more discretionary authority to affect the rights and livelihood of those they serve.

It follows that public confidence in the political impartiality of these public servants will be more important than in the past. Yet these same public servants are included among those whose rights to engage in high-profile partisan politics and public comment the government proposes to expand. Another concern is that innovative, risk-taking public servants are likely to make more mistakes and thereby embarrass their political superiors. Thus, it will be more important than ever that ministers be willing to accept public responsibility for the errors of departmental subordinates. Ministers are less likely to fulfil this responsibility, even in the interest of improved service to the public, if at the same time public servants are publicly criticizing or campaigning against them.

Still another consideration is that the successful implementation of SQM requires a high level of trust between ministers and public servants and between public service managers and other employees. This, in turn, requires harmonious relations between ministers and senior managers on the one hand and public service unions on the other. Yet the strongest proponents of more political rights for public servants are the public service unions whose motivation is not only enhanced individual rights but also enhanced political power. One concern about a more politicized working environment is that it will be a less efficient one because of increased tension between managers and other employees and among the employees themselves. This would be at odds with the efforts of SQM to bring about greater productivity. Certainly, the empowered-workteam approach to decision making, which is characteristic of SQM, will not work as well if team members are highly visible partisans of different political parties.

If both the politicization and the SQM movements are allowed to proceed without account being taken of their interrelationships and long-term consequences, the culture of the public service will be greatly affected. It will be characterized by a high level of politicization and a low level of empowerment. The level of trust among politicians, public servants, and the public required for successful implementation of SQM will not be achieved. Moreover, the productivity and morale of the public service will suffer. This will not be a milieu conducive to high levels of ethical performance. It is essential, therefore, to consider measures that are likely to enhance political and public service ethics.

Evaluation and reform

Not only in Ontario, but in all democratic governments, public servants play a critical role in safeguarding the public against unethical behaviour by politicians as well as by other civil servants. Thus, the integrity of government depends significantly on trust and respect between politicians and public servants. Many elected officials, including cabinet ministers, do not understand the delicate nature and the high ethical content of these relationships. In particular, there is insufficient sensitivity to the systemic connections among the constitutional conventions discussed above. A frequently expressed regret among senior public servants is that politicians, especially new cabinet ministers and their political staff, are not sufficiently attuned to the behaviour required by these conventions and to the ethical and value issues facing public servants. It would, therefore, be beneficial to provide ethics workshops for politicians, or joint workshops for politicians and public servants, to examine these issues. This would provide a valuable opportunity also to emphasize the important influence of ethical leadership by ministers and senior public servants on the ethical performance of public servants at all levels of the hierarchy.

Since 1987, more than half of the province's most senior public servants have participated in ethics workshops and an effort is being made to provide the same opportunity, either centrally or through individual ministries, to all managers. Given the increasing importance of ethical issues in government, the inclination of public servants to choose workshops dealing with managerial and technical matters rather than ethics, and their misperceptions about the purpose and nature of ethics education, it is desirable to make ethics workshops a required rather than an optional component of education programs. While workshops can heighten ethical sensitivity and performance, resources may not be available to provide workshops for public servants below the supervisory level. Hence, it is essential that managers provide strong ethical leadership and that ethics education be complemented by ethics rules of appropriate comprehensiveness, specificity, and accessibility.

As noted earlier, Ontario has a considerable number and variety of ethics rules in the form of conventions, statutes, regulations, and guidelines, especially for public servants. The rules for public servants are scattered in various places because they cover a broad range of problem areas and many of them were ad hoc responses to particular problems. The rules are, however, unnecessarily dispersed; it is a difficult task for public officials—or anyone else—to get an overall picture of the rules and their interrelationships and to find them easily when they are needed. Ontario would be well advised to review its rules in the various problem areas, amend those that need to be brought up to date, formulate new rules where there are significant gaps, and provide as coherent and comprehensive a statement of them as possible (or references to their location) in a single publication.

This code of ethics or code of conduct could contain general ethical principles covering at least the areas of conflict of interest, political rights, confidentiality, privacy, and equal opportunity. Each of the principles could be followed by a commentary that elaborates on their meaning, provides examples of unethical behaviour, and refers to statutes, regulations, and guidelines found elsewhere that bear on the interpretation and application of the principles. For example, the commentary could explain the several variations of conflict of interest and make reference to coverage of this matter in the Criminal Code, the Public Service Act, Management Board guidelines, and the Manual of Administration. In addition, this service-wide code could be supplemented by each ministry with information and advice relevant to the ministry's particular needs.

Rules are clearly not a cure-all for unethical behaviour. As explained above, some ethical problems cannot be easily addressed by written rules. Moreover, by breaking or circumventing the rules, a small number of public officials will add credence to the adage that you can't legislate morality. Nonetheless, the prospect of disciplinary action, including dismissal, for ethical infractions can be an effective deterrent to unethical behaviour. Moreover, given the cost of extending ethics education down the hierarchy and the possible absence of ethical leadership, rules may be virtually the only means of managing the ethical conduct of public servants at the middle and lower levels of the public service. The fact remains of course that voluntary commitment to high ethical standards is preferable to compliance to written rules motivated by fear of sanctions.

As suggested earlier, both the success of SQM and the public's trust in public servants are likely to be heightened by assurance that public servants' decisions are not based on partisan considerations. Thus, reform of the political rights regime in Ontario must take account of the goals of public trust in government and public service efficiency and effectiveness. A dominant theme of the rules on political rights should be the principle that public servants have ethical duties that go beyond the formal requirements of the law.

Ethics commissioners[33] and counsellors can enhance ethical conduct by enforcing ethics rules and providing ethics education. Ontario already has a conflict of interest commissioner and a chief election officer to manage ethical rules affecting politicians, but the law enforcement function performed by these officers has obscured the function of ethics education. Ontario's chief election officer has argued that 'whereas the law enforcement function is directed to the administration of means by which to deal with serious ethical problems, ethics education is directed to eradicating the problems themselves.'[34] He recommends that government ethics agencies promote ethics education among the public, the media, schools, and universities. Moreover, ethics education for political parties and interest groups would help ensure that they 'are sensitive to the principles and practices of government ethics so that actions leading to potentially unethical behaviour would be identified, circumscribed and avoided long before actual unethical behaviour resulted'.[35] Similarly, an ethics commissioner or counsellor for the public service as a whole or for individual ministries could not only manage ethics rules but also promote ethics education and provide advice on ethical issues and dilemmas in such areas as conflict of interest, political rights, whistle-blowing, and human resource practices. Still another model worthy of serious consideration is that of a government-wide ethics counsellor whose office would perform administrative, advisory, investigatory, and educational functions for both politicians *and* public servants.[36] One virtue of government-wide or public service-wide ethics offices is that they can encourage consistency in the treatment of similar ethical issues from one ministry to another.

In recognition of the enduring debate as to whether public morality is different from private morality, ethics education should include an examination of the special ethical demands on public officer holders. It is important to consider whether it is appropriate for an individual to apply different ethical standards when acting as a politician or public servant than when acting as a private citizen. A strong argument can be made that holding public office imposes obligations that may clash with generally accepted ethical rules. For example, in certain circumstances public officials may be excused for lying in the interest of national security.

We have seen that public officials are entwined in an intricate web of interests and obligations that affect their ethical standards and behaviour. Politicians and public servants face many of the same ethical issues, but each group operates in a distinctive ethical milieu. Moreover, the ethical obligations of Cabinet ministers, with their substantial power in the policy process, differ from those of backbench legislators whose power and, therefore, whose opportunities for unethical conduct are more limited.

Politicians are subject to influences that are of little or no concern for public servants in that politicians face strong and direct *political* pressures, including the need to be re-elected. For politicians, the demands of partisan politics and of their representative role create ethical complications that do not trouble public servants. Consider, for example, the ethical issues associated with election campaigns and political party financing. Moreover, politicians are obliged to consider the interests not only of the province and a broad range of pressure groups, but also of constituents, party colleagues in the legislature, and the party organization outside the legislature.

In the conflict of interest sphere, the line between the politicians' representation of their constituents' interest and their pursuit of self-interest is often indistinct. For example, a farmer representing the interests of a farming area may unavoidably serve, or appear to serve, his or her own interests at the same time. This problem is formally recognized by Ontario's 1988 Members' Conflict of Interest Act which 'does not prohibit the activities in which members normally engage on behalf of their constituents'.[37] The public is likely to be less forgiving if a ministry of agriculture employee who owns or operates a farm makes decisions, even if they are ostensibly in the public interest, that favour his or her personal interests.

It is important to keep in mind that public servants vastly outnumber elected politicians and the number of discretionary decisions made by public servants greatly exceeds those made by these politicians. Public servants exercise enormous power in making, implementing, and evaluating policies and in managing programs and people. Moreover, unlike politicians, whose ethical performance is usually the subject of public debate, the ethical behaviour of public servants is normally handled within the public service itself, away from the glare of publicity.

In conclusion, it is worth re-emphasizing that ethics rules are not enough. The critical importance of the personal ethical standards that public officials bring to their decisions argues for widespread ethics education and exemplary ethics leadership. The political and bureaucratic cultures in Ontario have gradually become more sensitive to the significance of ethical behaviour as a result of government efforts over the past two decades to prevent and punish ethical misconduct. While much of the stimulus for these efforts has come from widespread public concern about government ethics in Canada and elsewhere, Ontario has had its fair share of unethical behaviour among public officials. To its credit, the province has adopted several mechanisms to deter unethical conduct and to make public officials, especially public servants, more conscious of the ethical conflicts and dilemmas in government. By accepting the reforms and warnings discussed above, Ontario would move a long way towards ensuring that sensitivity to the ethical dimension of government is sufficiently integrated into the province's political and public service cultures.

Notes

1 George Thomson, 'Personal Morality in a Professional Context', in Kenneth Kernaghan, ed., *Do Unto Others: Ethics in Government and Business* (Toronto: Institute of Public Administration of Canada, 1991): 29.

2 The report, requested by the premier, was prepared by John Black Aird, the former lieutenant-governor of Ontario.

3 Ontario, Statutes, Members' Conflict of Interest Act, 1988, ch. 17.

4 The Hon. Gregory T. Evans, *Commission on Conflict of Interest Annual Report 1988-1989* (Toronto: Publications Ontario, 1990): 2.

5 *Globe and Mail*, 13 Dec. 1990: A6.

6 *Globe and Mail*, 18 Jan. 1990.

7 See Georgette Gagnon and Dan Rath, *Not Without Cause: David Peterson's Fall From Grace* (Toronto: HarperCollins, 1991): 61-73.

8 *Globe and Mail*, 5 Sept. 1990: A8.

9 Ontario, Management Board of Cabinet, *The Extension of Political Activity Rights for Ontario Crown Employees: A Discussion Paper on Issues, Options and Proposals for Reform*, May 1991.

10 For an examination of the arguments on each side of this question, see Kenneth Kernaghan, 'The Political Rights of Canada's Federal Public Servants', in Michael Cassidy, ed., *Democratic Rights and Electoral Reform*, vol. 10 of the *Report of the Royal Commission on Electoral Reform and Party Financing* (Toronto: Dundurn Press, 1992).

11 *Globe and Mail*, 23 Sept. 1991.

12 Elaine Todres, 'The Ethical Dimension in Public Service', in Kernaghan, ed., *Do Unto Others*: 14.

13 See, for example, Ontario Law Reform Commission, *Report on Political Activity, Public Comment and Disclosure by Crown Employees* (Toronto: Ministry of the Attorney General, 1986): 88-93.

14 *Re Ontario Public Service Employees Union (MacAlpine) and the Crown in Right of Ontario (Ministry of Natural Resources)*, unreported, 18 Nov. 1982: 65.

15 Kenneth Kernaghan, 'Whistle-Blowing in Canadian Governments: Ethical, Political and Managerial Considerations', *Optimum* 22, 1 (1991/2): 34-43.

16 See Ontario, Management Board of Cabinet, *Whistleblowing: A Discussion Paper on the Protection of Public Employees Who Disclose Serious Wrongdoing*, Sept. 1991.

17 Ontario, Management Board of Cabinet, *Breaking Down the Barriers: Report of the Human Resources Secretariat Employment Systems Review Taskforce*, May 1991: 2.

18 Todres (above, n.12): 16.

19 George Thomson, 'Personal Morality in a Professional Context', in Kernaghan, ed., *Do Unto Others*: 23.

20 Ian Greene, 'Conflict of Interest and the Canadian Constitution: An Analysis of Conflict of Interest Rules for Canadian Cabinet Ministers', *Canadian Journal of Political Science* 23 (June 1990): 253-4.

21 Kenneth Kernaghan and John Langford, *The Responsible Public Servant* (Halifax: Institute for Research on Public Policy and Toronto: Institute of Public Administration of Canada, 1990): 142-53.

22 *Globe and Mail*, 13 Dec. 1991: A8.

23 Rand Dyck, *Provincial Politics in Canada*, 2nd ed. (Scarborough, Ont.: Prentice-Hall, 1991): 269.

24 François-Pierre Gingras, 'Ontario', in David J. Bellamy, Jon H. Pammett, and Donald C. Rowat, eds, *The Provincial Political System: Comparative Essays* (Toronto: Methuen, 1976): 31-45.

25 Norman Penner, 'Ontario: The Dominant Province', in Martin Robin, ed., *Canadian Provincial Politics*, 2nd ed. (Scarborough, Ont.: Prentice-Hall, 1978): 209.

26 By 1985, about a thousand of the 4,750 order-in-council appointments were considered the premier's personal prerogative. Jeffrey Simpson, *Spoils of Power: The Politics of Patronage* (Toronto: HarperCollins, 1988): 219.

27 Ibid.: 220.

28 Ibid.: 219.

29 Ontario, Municipal Conflict of Interest Review, *Report of the Municipal Conflict of Interest Consultation Committee to the Minister of Municipal Affairs*, July 1991.

30 Ontario, Ministry of Municipal Affairs, *Open Local Government* (Toronto: Ministry of Municipal Affairs, 1991).

31 For elaboration on these developments, see David Siegel's essay in this volume.

32 Kernaghan (above, n.15): 39.

33 See Ian Greene, 'Government Ethics Commissioners: The Way of the Future?', in Kernaghan, ed., *Do Unto Others*: 165-70.

34 Warren R. Bailie and David Johnson, 'Governmental Ethics and Ethics Agencies', in Kernaghan, ed., *Do Unto Others*: 162.

35 Ibid.: 163.

36 See the proposed model contained in Canada, *Ethical Conduct in the Public Sector, Report of the Task Force on Conflict of Interest* (Ottawa: Supply and Services, 1984): 13.

37 Ontario, *Statutes* (1988), ch. 17, sec. 5.

9

Cities: 'The dilemmas on our doorsteps'

More than half the Canadian population (56.1 per cent in 1986) lives in twenty-four census metropolitan areas. Our largest cities are more populous than the smaller provinces. The economic significance of large Canadian cities is reflected by the fact that, measured by purchases of goods and services from small businesses, Edmonton was ranked Canada's nineteenth largest corporation in 1984; in 1992, municipally-owned Edmonton Power was the fifth most profitable corporation in the country.

Large Canadian cities are important because most of us live in them and they are usually the provincial capitals. Moreover, their behaviour commands the attention of their provincial 'superiors' and their ethical activities set the standards for municipalities, large and small. Large cities are the focus of the metropolitan media and hence establish the popular benchmarks for the range of permissible governmental conduct.

The systematic study of, and debate about, political corruption in North America began in large American cities in the late nineteenth century. Ironically, given these intellectual and political roots, we know little about government ethics in large Canadian cities. The subject is little studied probably because city government is still thought to be trivial in its pursuits and in the damage engendered by its conflicts of interest. For instance, local politicians still attract little attention when they themselves go directly about drawing the boundaries of the constituencies they are to represent. Moreover, municipal activity seldom justifies national media attention, local stories are rarely put in context with events in other cities, and there is little likelihood that we may soon share a national urban political culture with the common ethical standards this might set.

The pursuit of high ethics and 'good' government remains the heart of the objectives of city government reformers. The early study of urban government tried to devise structures that would protect citizens from various evils of urban life, including the nasty activities of their governors. John Stuart Mill and Alexis de Tocqueville saw municipal government as the cornerstone of democracy, but another influential writer, James Bryce, presented a very different interpretation. Deeply worried by the 'boss politics' of America's burgeoning northeastern cities, he concluded in 1888:

> The deficiencies of the National government tell but little for evil on the welfare of the people. The faults of the State governments are insignificant compared with the extravagance, corruption and mismanagement which mark the administration of most of the great cities. . . . [1]

Bryce's pessimistic assessment of American cities led to a comprehensive set of institutional reforms that were enthusiastically adapted to Canadian cities, even though we seldom thought of them as hotbeds of corruption. This benign view of ethical conduct in Canadian cities is probably attributable to a lingering acceptance of romantic ideas about big-city politics. As Harold Kaplan argues, competing ideas about the essence of urban government forged in the nineteenth century reflect the common, continuing notion that city government is, and should be, non-partisan and non-ideological. 'Municipal government would be a refuge from political conflict and rancour, a haven for unadorned common sense.' [2] My view is that important ethical issues abound in city politics, despite their non-ideological, technocratic, and non-partisan veneer.

This chapter covers a lot of ground. It employs material from several cities, with particular attention to the 1980s and early 1990s. Several perennial ethical dilemmas are probed through examination of three main issues: the consequences of unregulated municipal campaign finance, the patent manipulation of the land development process by those with an immediate interest in the outcome, and, finally, the consequences of the more traditional exploitation of public position for direct personal gain.

We will learn that city elections are a costly process and that those who give often expect to receive tangibly. We will examine several instances where donors very much expected a quid pro quo in the days following the vote. Our questions are about how far both civic and provincial authorities ought to go in regulating the contribution process to ensure that holding local public office is more about serving an objective public trust. Seldom is the supposed selflessness of non-partisan councillors more clearly called into question than on occasions when electoral boundaries must be considered. Our evidence clearly indicates not only that fairness withers under the onslaught of re-election considerations but also that there are important consequences for whose agenda wins priority status at city hall. There is more to this issue than just jigging the rules of the game.

Our second area of concern is the perennial question of lobbying. In our cases we will consider officials' response to developer behaviour in the practical realm of the approvals process. We will specifically explore the nature of 'insider trading' in information. What are the practical lessons to be learned by citizens? What are the important ethical questions at stake for those with standing in the game? Finally, we will look at those traditionalists who simply abuse their office-holding tenure. The relatively extreme case of Edmonton's mayor William

Hawrelak will outline the fundamental ethical problem. But Hawrelak's persistent wrongdoing raises a more modern question, again illustrated by example, concerning the extent to which a person's private behaviour may, or should, disqualify them from eligibility for office-holding. And, ultimately, who should make what rules?[3]

Seen together, these discrete issues highlight the broader point that Canadian city politics is mostly about land development and who should benefit from the enrichment that follows the enhancement of property. The apparently symbiotic relationships among councillors, those of us with an interest in land, and public office-holding lies at the heart of most ethical conflict in city politics. It would seem that boosterism and civic altruism, for so long so conceptually compatible in the after-dinner speeches to Canada's big-city chambers of commerce, are pretty well mutually exclusive in the real world at city hall. Let us now look at some basic issues.

Elections

Canadian city elections are expensive and their financing is a constant source of concern. In the 1990s a challenger for the mayor's chair should anticipate a minimum budget of a quarter of a million dollars to make a credible impression.[4]

Throughout his work, James Lorimer describes the close relations between the property industry and local elections. These relationships have deep implications for who may be elected and what they will do once in office. First, developers may provide financial support in times of hardship, such as elections, and in the employment of close relatives. Even perceived labour representatives on council may be believed to have invoked the cloud of greater employment among the construction trades, as they did during debate for city concessions to Edmonton's Eaton Centre development in the mid-1980s, to mist over employment prospects for not-too-distant relations. At the same moment there is an understanding among the booster media, some municipal politicians, and the missionaries for urban growth that development and the concomitant public works are more generally desirable and 'progressive'. Finally, and naturally, the basic medium of exchange, as it was in the old boss systems, has been 'friendship', a rise in social status particularly for new migrants and a sense of belonging due to one's financial link, no matter how nebulous, to those in authority.

Urban fundraising is a major source of ethical concern. At an early stage of Laurence Decore's victorious 1983 Edmonton mayoralty campaign, his senior policy adviser asked that he be cautious in his solicitation of developers' funds; the answer was, 'There are basically no other sources!' Six weeks before the election, this led to headline problems when the city's largest developer denied assertions that it funded its own slate of hopefuls. The story read, 'The Journal received information Monday suggesting Triple Five gave a $5,000 contribution to the Decore campaign in August. It was claimed that Decore returned the money last week after a request was made for a meeting between Decore and Triple Five officials.'⁵ Corporation officials also denied giving money to Decore's incumbent opponent, but apparently this was not the case: " 'We did get a contribution from them [Triple Five] . . . about a week ago," said Gary Davidge, Purves' campaign manager.'

The matter of local councillors' dollar leftovers after campaigns seldom comes to light, but it raises interesting questions. In Calgary, columnist Don Martin found that, 'In municipal politics there are no rules to twist, bend or break. Ethical discretion is the only obstruction to council members taking outside financial help for personal gain.'⁶ Martin notes that Mayor Al Duerr, who annually holds fundraisers for up to 400 guests, 'could legally take the $10,000 now sitting in a blind trust for his reelection and buy a private golf club membership or pay down his mortgage'. Councillor Sue Higgins frankly stated: 'There are no receipts issued because it's not tax deductible. That makes it tough to get donations, but you don't have to account for the money.' The question should be asked, Are politicians only accountable to the highest bidder? And, Martin concludes: 'The temptation to pocket money generated for political purposes is compounded for popular incumbents. As sure bets for re-election, they attract the larger donations, but require less money to top the polls.'⁷

Even the far-reaching campaign finance legislation enacted in Ontario in December 1987 contained no tax credits or deductions that permitted municipal campaign supporters to recover a part of their donations. The province ignored the sticky problem of controlling amounts raised over and above its proposed spending limit of about $28,000 (for instance, Toronto mayor Arthur Eggleton legitimately used his surplus 'to pay for his wife's attendance at official functions'), overlooking in the process the creation of an independent authority to scrutinize financing irregularities, as recommended by its advisory committee on the issues. In Toronto in 1985, the amounts spent by the ten councillors who voluntarily disclosed them ranged from $12,500 to $45,909: *The Globe and Mail* estimated that some councillors had raised, undisclosed, two or three times the average expenditure of $18,000, and the majority (13 of 23) received a total of $300,000 in largely undisclosed amounts (in the two years preceding the election) from the development industry.⁸

To codify behaviour with respect to campaign funding procedures Ontario's new Liberal government enacted legislation in 1987 that demanded full disclosure, and put ceilings on revenues and expenditures. A partial reason for this action is the federal-provincial-municipal partisan linkages, which also reveal how problematic the enforcement of even strict local rules not founded in strong common assent can be. Liberal and Conservative local politicians have had access for campaign purposes to the electoral war chests of the development industry while local social democrats have not. To undertake the higher cost of 1980s city campaigns, Ontario's New Democrats counterstruck by funnelling municipal donations through the provincial coffers of sympathetic MPPs, candidates, and constituencies, thereby enabling them to issue provincial tax receipts to the individual donors who are their dollar bulwark. This sparked Queen's Park, in 1986, to overcome its traditional foot-dragging,[9] to recognize that local candidates no longer conformed to the model by exclusively financing their own campaigns (therein tacitly recognizing a major-league cities category), and to prohibit the diversion of provincial campaign funds into municipal elections. The New Democrats found sanctuary in the federal church—the federal election machinery, in this way being able to issue receipts for up to a third of their municipal donations. (The federal elections expenses act did not prevent ridings from spending their sums as they saw fit except during federal election campaigns; moreover, the ridings found themselves able to skim about 20 per cent for their own direct purposes.)

In the absence of provincial initiative elsewhere in Canada, municipalities are still on their own. For example, Edmonton councillors wrestled with the ethics of election expenditures after public allegations in the early 1970s that some councillors were the undue beneficiaries of a small number of very large developer donations. In 1973, council resolved, without an enforcement provision, that its members should disclose property holdings within city limits to the city clerk. In 1975, Mr Justice William Morrow held forty-four days of hearings, heard fifty-four witnesses, and concluded only that 'one alderman had collected more than $13,000 in commissions for acquiring land for a land developer, but did not abstain from voting when the developer's matters came before council or the Development Appeal Board, of which he was a member.'[10] Although that particular councillor chose not to seek re-election, thereby testing 'community standards', in the absence of provincial enabling legislation council could agree neither on spending limits nor disclosure. In its revised municipal elections by-law governing the campaign of 1989, there was no mention of campaign financing. In January 1992, council amended its 1973 voluntary property disclosure by-law to permit 'public review of campaign contributions and expenses of all candidates for civic office' by requiring a statement indicating all contributions of $300 or more, and the rejection of any anonymous donations exceeding $300, and an itemized list of all campaign expenses, the penalty to be a fine between $500 and $1,000.[11] This by-law governed the conduct of all candidates, *successful or not*, in the October 1992 civic election.

Thus, one province on its own, and one city by itself, legislated specific standards of behaviour in election finance. But very few comprehensive sets of rules exist to regulate other activities within the municipal arena. Major-league civic campaigns are increasingly expensive, but contributions are not normally tax-deductible or publicly disclosed.

The dilemma for political gladiators is that to be successful you must 'dance with the gang that brung ya'. Obviously, major donors are unlikely to support candidates who are not broadly sympathetic to their overall disposition; serious problems, as noted below, have arisen from quid pro quo expectations of immediate payoffs. In our cities New Democrat and other left councillors have, and not exclusively for altruistic reasons, most aggressively hawked campaign finance reforms even while playing the games with provincial and federal tax rebates. In Toronto, for instance, NDP councillor Jack Layton made no bones about seeing receipts issued for his municipal contributions: ' "If we want the affluent to run City Hall, then don't allow tax rebates," he said. "But if we want politicians not beholden to developers, then we had better provide a way for the average person to contribute to political campaigns." '[12]

The 1990s will be the age of campaign financial disclosure in Canada's major cities. Unlike the situation with the other two levels of government, the fundamental ethical problem has been, and will be, rooted in the fact that municipally contributions are very much an individual's concern. The individual solicits the dough (let us not subscribe to the fiction of 'arm's-length' intermediaries) and the individual votes on very specific matters directly affecting personal gain. One's ethics in the matters of fundraising and voting are never hidden within the murky pool of party in Canadian big-city politics. It is precisely this conjunction of giving to personal campaigns with the potential of very specific individual favours that is the issue. An individual's personal fairness in the difficult weighing of the equation of money, the power of office-holding, and electoral politics cannot really be legislated, either, although disclosure, expenditure ceilings, and tax deductibility will be. The shrewder councils will endeavour, initially, to make their own rules. This raises the obvious question: How impartial are these lawmakers likely to be?

One illustrative test of the partiality of big-city councillors arose during the 1960s and 70s over the question of striking electoral boundaries. For federal and provincial governments, constituency boundaries are now generally by set autonomous commissions: But even in the major cities of Canada, and even where local parties have been manifest, the prevailing belief is that council decisions are neither ideological nor partisan and that councillors should try to accomplish an 'objective public interest'. In this world of purportedly unadorned common sense there has been no compelling need to remove electoral considerations from political meddling since few people perceive that this issue is very important.

It seems evident that to argue that an issue is 'common-sense', or 'value-free', or 'technical' is a shrewd first step towards imposing one's own values. As E.E. Schattschneider argued: 'All forms of political organization [represent] the mobilization of bias. Some issues are organized into politics while others are organized out.'[13] For city politicians, elections at large generally favour the interests and political resources of business, certain of the professions, and upper-class civic reformers; smaller, block, wards benefit local community leaders, some single-issue pressure groups, neighbourhood ratepayers' associations, and political activists with a left-progressive bent. Heterogeneous 'strip' wards are modest compromises with the overall business advantages of at-large elections.

City of Toronto councillors wrestled with the problem in 1969. James Lorimer, in his account of these activities, documents the curiosity of sitting aldermen advocating the advantage of personal preservation as community interest in the form of strip wards at the expense of neighbourhood representation and its block-type ward apologists.[14] Patent gerrymandering was crudely engineered in the guise of, and in an appeal to, community well-being.

This Toronto hornet's nest revealed that there are major stakes in cities' electoral reforms. At the heart of the 1971 Unicity reform of Winnipeg was a system of fifty small, block-shaped, wards which NDP provincial ministers (all former municipal councillors) anticipated would correct the business/farm gerrymander of 1920, in the aftermath of the Winnipeg General Strike, to three, large, strip wards.[15] In 1991, the provincial Conservative government of former city councillor Gary Filmon proposed a system of fifteen pie-shaped, strip wards in which suburban, presumably decently middle-class, voters would swamp inner-city leftists.[16] These were in place for the October 1992 elections. Edmonton's councillors approved four elongated strip wards the north-south length of the municipality for a city the population-size of Toronto in 1971; quasi-at-large elections but at a quarter of the cost! In 1973, the Saskatchewan provincial New Democrats introduced wards to Regina and Saskatoon which were shrilly opposed by the respective cities' boards of trade. In 1987, under Premier Grant Devine, the provincial Conservatives returned to elections at large for both cities.

Vancouver's case, from the 1960s to the present, is predictable in this light. It was the only community in the province to possess a provincially issued charter, and issues such as local electoral boundaries have quickly bounced into the provincial legislature's lap. In the 1930s labour was defused with the imposition of a general vote. Although a plebiscite in 1973 supported at-large elections (59 per cent), subsequent pressures by left-progressive local activists led to support for a ward system in plebiscites in 1978 (51.7 per cent) and 1982 (56.9 per cent). But the conservative bent of the provincial administration, and its minister of municipal affairs, William Vander Zalm, abetted the subtle lobbying of its municipal allies within the Civic Nonpartisan Association. Hence, Vancouver remains the single major Canadian city still conducting civic contests city-wide.[17]

Such manipulation of electoral boundaries, always justified as a realization of community interest, invites the question, 'When is self-interest not?' Councillors act as individuals and are unlikely to engineer a loss of personal incumbency; at the same time there always exists one face of the civic culture to which there may be an appeal for legitimation. Gerrymandering may be distasteful to some, but does a genuine act for the betterment of the community 'as a whole', say, always mask a more crass intent? There are no sure-fire answers.

The ethical issue here is not complex: should those with a direct interest in the outcome make the decision? The practical problem with boundaries, as with dollars, is *who* ought to decide in this arena of strong, conflicting traditions and personalities. In Metro Toronto, with direct election, and in Ontario with election finance, it was the province that flinched. To the extent that municipal councillors, systemically, no longer have either the moral authority or political legitimacy to act, the provinces *will* act. Or, to put it differently, only when city governors appreciate the serious questions about their own legitimacy will they feel compelled to act by hiving off their powers to devise the formal rules of elections. Should cities choose not to act, the provinces will feel it necessary to do so, further eroding the legitimacy of city councils in the process. Will the provinces then feel pressure to regulate more closely the core policy making at city hall?

Making decisions

Another worrisome side of business influence appears in its direct impact on the workings of city councils. This has appeared in the form of pro-development politicians openly promoting the 'growth means progress' line. Alan Artibise, describing Winnipeg's emergence, was speaking generally of the early twentieth-century Canadian city when he wrote that other important considerations were often subordinated to rapid and sustained urban growth: 'Winnipeg was established by businessmen, for business purposes, and businessmen were its first and natural leaders. . . . Indeed, the common outlook of Winnipeg's businessmen that the expansion of the economic enterprise should be the prime concern of the local government is a dominant theme throughout the period.'[18] Business people quite naturally bring to political life those attributes that made them successes: 'Businessmen are accustomed to giving contracts to friends and relatives. Manufacturers woo purchasing agents with gifts. "Spiffs"—cash paid to salesmen and store managers for pushing a brand of merchandise—are common practice.'[19] Is it unethical to pursue your class interest within city politics?

No, but municipal politicians may get so carried away with boosterism during official performance of duty that they equate their own personal aggrandizement as one significant measure of community well-being. As Ari Hoogenboom has written: 'What is meant by graft? . . . Honest graft, that estimable Tammany Hall politician said, was the profit that flowed from advance information on future government action. . . '.[20] As detailed with Edmonton's fabled Mayor Hawrelak later in this chapter, for some municipal councillors Harry Truman's dictum that 'the buck stops here' takes on tangible meaning for personal property. Some have made an impressive escape from personal poverty. For instance, evidence of personal corruption in Mayor Jean Drapeau's 'clean government' administration came in the fallout from the 1976 Olympics: 'The most serious incident involved the chairman of the executive committee [whose] country house had been built for him without payment by one of the major Olympic contractors.'[21]

There exist many tangible rewards. Helpful councillors may find themselves the recipients of sage land investment advice. For instance, in early 1981 Edmonton mayor Cecil Purves came under pressure to resign for alleged conflict of interest, having voted in support of that city's major annexation (part of which encompassed lands he owned). Although council brought him to court, and he was exonerated, his public statement of defence includes this: 'On September 28,

1979—seven months after the city had made public the proposed annexation boundary—*I was invited by longstanding friends to purchase* a one quarter interest in a 39.84 acre parcel of land outside the current city boundary but within the proposed annexation area.'[22] The identity of the friends was not revealed. Second, certain professionals on council (e.g., engineers, architects, real estate agents, and insurers) may find new business opportunities appearing at their doorsteps. For example, the architectural component of Edmonton's new city hall was let untendered to well-known former city alderman Gene Dub (although he had won the design competition for a more grandiose version in 1986) once a more realistic budget was set. Third, there is life after politics and the carrot of future employment may indeed be powerfully inducive for those interested in public relations or experienced in development procedures. Former mayor Ivor Dent of Edmonton (1968-74), a well-known New Democrat, now sells commercial real estate. Bureaucratic professionals may sell their expertise: James Lorimer observes that, 'Metro Toronto's first chief planner, Eli Comay, moved out into the consultant business. Toronto's first development department head, Walter Manthorpe, moved over to become vice-president of one of Toronto's major developers, Meridian, after he left city hall.'[23] William Allen, the chairman of Metro Toronto, became, first, the president of Kinross Mortgage Company and later president of Dominion Realty.[24]

In several columns, Toronto journalists Jock Ferguson and Dawn King describe the legendary card games within the York Region (north of Toronto) engineering community: 'Around the table on a given night you might find town engineers, municipal councillors, and some of the people who need them most: Rudolph Bratty, a lawyer, director of several major Canadian corporations and multi-millionaire developer; Alfred De Gasperis, his equally successful development partner and president of Con-Drain, the largest sewer and water-main contractor in Southern Ontario; Stanley Leibel, Mr Bratty's partner in Canada Homes; and Carlo Baldessarra, Mr De Gasperis' partner in Greenpark Homes.'[25]

The players and the venues varied (the Markham municipal offices, law office boardrooms, participant-owned restaurants) as did recollections about stakes, winnings, and locations. The point is that supplicants for, and suppliers of, fields of dreams could privately chat things up after a round of golf, often organized by town engineers, and over a few drinks. Perhaps innocent enough but, nonetheless, in the realm of land-use development even a giant lacking sanitary connectors remains a dwarf. After interviewing some 200 politicians, municipal staff members, competing developers, industry consultants, and other participants in land-use planning, the authors conclude that the poker players were somehow able to take the major risks out of linking their land to sewer capacity allocations. Ferguson and King quote one former associate: 'I used to think they were very smart to guess where the pipes were going. But I realized that where they buy land is where the pipes will go.'[26]

Anyone familiar with the development process, from concept to design, through amendments to approvals, has probably found it an irksome, legally burdened process. Changing rules and capricious decision making are hardly unknown. But in York Region, the poker players 'moved swiftly and surely through every stage of the development process' to the point where 60 per cent of additional sewage allotments were to their properties. Even land owned by others, who became frustrated by development refusals, would suddenly receive swift approvals once purchased by Messrs Bratty and De Gasperis. Ferguson and King conclude: 'A senior partner with a highly respected consulting engineering firm said he had great difficulty getting information from [regional engineer] Mr Hodgson about sewer capacity while he was doing engineering studies for the municipalities of Vaughan and Markham. He said he faced the same roadblock when working for a developer who was denied sewer capacity in both Newmarket and Markham.'[27] Perhaps Mr Bratty's concession that 'he and his partners have a successful record because they are better, smarter and luckier, and not necessarily in that order' is fairly accurate. Or did they just play their cards right?

As we have observed, most contributors to civic political campaigns expect to garner some certainty with respect to future government action that extends beyond ensuring a climate favourable to business. The etiquette of the game generally dictates that these understandings are undertaken and executed in private, and often not even in specifics. Where the wheels fall off the trolley is when the results of complex negotiations end up on a council agenda as a line item to be put to the vote. This may lead to situations as in Edmonton where in 1986, during the final votes on detailed amendments to a complex concessions package for the Eaton Centre development, the developer from the public gallery was so boisterously gesticulating yeas and nays to his advocates on council that Mayor Purves inadvertently tried to summon 'alderman' Ghermezian to order.[28] In a similar case in Toronto in 1987, developers' lawyer Patrick Devine stood up, reached over, and tapped Alderman Betty Disero on the shoulder 'to vote in favour of a 13-story luxury condominium project he was representing'.[29] Ferguson and King describe similar behaviour by a Toronto lobbyist who sat in the public gallery during difficult proceedings. He found it prudent to nod to aldermen when it was time for them to vote. They report that 'a frustrated Ward 6 Councillor Jack Layton said Mayor Arthur Eggleton should "ask Mr. Blott to come and have a seat here (at the council table) so he can at least direct things from down here rather than from a seat in the council chamber."'[30]

Canada's low voter participation in municipal elections has masked the very close attention paid the policy process by persons who are focused on real property. As we have seen, there is a closely symbiotic relationship between those who own land and their agents and those with the power to regulate its servicing and use. The individuals most intensely involved in major city politics may find themselves leading one of many possible triple lives of lawyer, development lobbyist, and fundraiser; small businessman, councillor, and civic booster; or city planner, home-maker, and careerist. Any one of these packages has in it the possibility for serious conflict of interest.

Public expectations for the 1990s will likely demand more than the disclosure of personal and family property holdings 'within or immediately adjacent to City boundaries in which the councillor or the councillor's family have a direct or indirect interest; and all contracts involving the City in which the councillor, or a member of the councillor's family residing in the councillor's household, is a party. . . '.[31] It has been personal abuse in the extreme that has at least focused public attention upon the need for systemic constraints on those exercising the powers of public office, an area to which we now direct our attention.

Public office, public trust

We learn about ourselves and our communities through studying the transgressions of others and our reactions to them. As the behaviour of public officials pushes limits of tolerance, we begin to realize the boundaries of community standards. Two cases here present different sides of a similar coin, men whose private behaviour and the public judgement thereof set forth a measure of calibre for public character in the 1990s. Both are considered for what they did as lawbreakers, one as an old-style combination 'ward-heeler' and gains politician, the other a subject of family violence, and for what they tell us about contemporary expectations of public officials.

People in business must exercise caution in public office, but especially is this so at city hall, where the normal quick profit or private phone call may directly violate public mores, leading them to run afoul of public expectations. William Hawrelak, nicknamed 'Wild Bill', had certainly one of the more turbulent terms among Edmonton's three dozen mayors; his periods in office raise questions about the obligations set for elected municipal officals.[32] Hawrelak's career was that of an 'ethnic' politician. It possibly illustrates that while second generations may violate dominant group norms in the process of assimilating, it is not unusual for the third to exploit them to the point where a later successor could say of his 'charter group' opponent that, 'Any elected official who deals in land is a fool.'[33]

William Hawrelak was first elected councillor in 1949 and in 1951 became the youngest mayor (and first of Ukrainian descent) of a major Canadian city. Throughout his career Hawrelak showed an inability to differentiate between public and private business affairs. Of all Canada's more prominent municipal actors his unscrupulous behaviour while in office is the most clearly detailed judicially. By the standard of virtually any day or place, he was corrupt.

To summarize, Hawrelak exploited the knowledge gained in his office of land developments throughout the city, his personal suasion over professional staff, and the secrecy of his dealings, to profit himself, his two brothers-in-law, and sundry friends and business associates. For example, in the late 1950s Hawrelak purchased land for motel development for his brother-in-law opposite an existing motel strip whose hoteliers had understood from planning documents that further development was legally prevented. Hawrelak personally intervened for the necessary rezoning. While mayor he worked on retainer (understood to have been $20,000 yearly) for Loblaws after 1957, ostensibly in a public relations capacity, but in reality flipping land deals and at the same time ensuring that Dominion Stores, a Loblaws competitor, had favoured intersection sites. The 1959 inquiry into his behaviour as mayor came to this very simple conclusion: 'The Calgary Trail, Loblaws transaction, Boulevard Heights, the Namao property are all instances in which the Mayor was serving two masters at the same time.'[34] As to how Hawrelak ran his affairs, at one crucial point in 1956 he visited Toronto to attend the Grey Cup, to meet with the agent for Dominion Stores, and to leave not only the requested legal description of one of his brother-in-law's properties (in which he himself held a half interest) but also the proposed plans for the subdivision. The subsequent correspondence to consummate the deal coursed through the mayor's home and not his civic office.[35]

He acquired land from the city at deflated prices for further motel construction adjacent to the downtown airport. In short, Mr Justice Porter found 'that there was gross misconduct on the part of the Mayor and a complete abandonment of responsibility on the part of the town planner. . .'.[36] The *Report*, concluding that in all his dealings with and for Dominion Stores he had persistently misled council, was delivered on 9 December 1959; Hawrelak resigned at noon during a special meeting of council. The city sued for its lost land profits and, in May 1962, council agreed to a settlement of $100,000 and costs. Hawrelak had claimed in public that he was unaware of his brother-in-law's interest in one particularly lucrative land swap. Mr Justice Porter was not convinced: 'The Mayor's statement that he was unaware of Shandro's interest in acquiring the property I find difficult to understand.'[37]

Hawrelak overcame the stigma of his past by winning an especially ferocious campaign in 1963 by 8,000 votes. Less than a year later a tenacious aldermanic watchdog, who had been one of the diddled motel owners, charged that the mayor held an indirect financial interest in a controversial land swap with Chrysler, the car maker.[38] In this deal Chrysler was permitted to exchange certain lands with the city for a site it preferred for commercial development; the lands the city received would meet Planning Act provisions for parkland which in turn would permit it to proceed with preferred residential development on adjacent property owned by Sun-Alta Builders, a company in which Hawrelak held 40 per cent of the shares. The 'technical' problem was that the City Act prohibited voting (as Hawrelak had done) on any matter in which the participant had greater than 25 per cent ownership of the stock of the respective corporate actor. The mayor was brought to court by 'a politically interested citizen': in 1965, Chief Justice McLaurin disqualified Hawrelak, who stoutly maintained that it was all a technicality.[39] The city initiated legal action to recover $133,000 in excess profits and damages; Hawrelak appealed the Alberta Court's judgement against him to the Supreme Court of Canada, ultimately receiving vindication in 1975 (3-2) after campaigning, and winning, the mayoralty race in 1974. Immediately upon assuming the chain of office, Hawrelak promised the citizens of Edmonton that he would never again unwittingly err. His chief of staff would personally advise him on the 'ethics' of any dealing: the latter was a fellow Ukrainian-Canadian, a longtime friend, and a disbarred lawyer. Since it is inconceivable that Hawrelak himself did not know the formal rules, had he never learned his lesson, or did he just not grant it significance? What are the lessons?

Who plays by whose rules, and the nature of the refereeing, can colour our assessment of ethical behaviour in city politics. On the use of patronage and various forms of graft in the United States, V.O. Key once observed that it 'serves to solidify a "political class" lacking the tie of tradition or those resources necessary to sustain a benevolent oligarchy. Whether this is "right" or "just" is a matter for professors of ethics. The phenomenon is true.'[40] Robert Merton also wrote that the 'boss' system was a serviceable means of social adjustment: 'By this centralized organization of political power, the boss and his apparatus can satisfy the needs of diverse subgroups in the larger community which are not adequately satisfied by legally devised and culturally approved social structures.'[41]

In Canada, in Edmonton, Hawrelak's politics were certainly boss-style, providing access to traditional levers of power to a new untraditional community, who in turn would overlook his transgression of what were held to be 'anglo' standards. That his actions to advance his constituents' self-worth were often only symbolic it is true, and that he crassly exploited his office for personal enhancement is also fair judgement. It 'worked'—for them and for him—nonetheless.

But the problem is, what of the electorate if we are to devise and enforce 'community' standards? The man was, after all, re-elected after twice being stigmatized from office. The rules set by British precedent, as evident in land-use planning, might be fine for those who subscribed to 'fair play' on the British model, and had well sustained the development practices of the small British town of Edmonton. Unfortunately, in 1947, the nearby discovery of oil at Leduc changed both the scale and the very nature of the community as new employment and entrepreneurial opportunities became a magnet for the rural underemployed of Edmonton's hinterland. Those who moved in were successful survivors, the products of the land and the application of their wits. Almost at once the question would become, who municipally personified those standards?

The problem presented by Hawrelak as a personification is that in a rapidly evolving community there were *two* countervailing sets of community standards at play at the same time. Marcia Sypnowich is perplexed by the setting in place of formal ethical standards for a complex society: 'This is an especially complex issue in a multicultural society where moral standards vary among religions, communities and cultures.'[42] Yet she is merely concerned with matters related to size, age of settlement, and geographic (as in regional) location. What happens when the fundamental differences lie *within* one community's boundaries? Is it really enough for her to conclude that 'Ethical behaviour is promoted by an electorate that holds the municipal council accountable for what it does'?[43] Hawrelak was last held 'accountable' by his electorate in 1974, and won, in the process doubling the vote of his nearest challenger and trouncing an incumbent mayor in the bargain!

The reformers of the mid-nineteenth century set conflicting standards for town hall but shared a common distinguishing mission. Edmonton held a somewhat similar distinctive objective a generation ago, a common purpose in unbridled economic growth and spatial expansion. The question was how best to get there. Hawrelak's re-election campaign theme in 1963 emphasized dynamic leadership, not trust: 'You've seen the council on television—no leadership; no direction.' And the theme in 1974 was progress: 'Let's Get Edmonton Rolling Again.' The style was personality, not participation: in quashing a proposed city council question period he said, 'I don't like that idea at all. It's not the way to run a city efficiently.'[44] The shortcomings of personal greed were, after all, penny ante compared to the public goods acquired by the city through his terms in office; the marketing of municipality overrode private malfeasance. This was trickle-down politics! Except in that segment of the city most dearly subscribing to the middle-class ethos, Hawrelak won consistently. He won the older, established, heavily populated sectors of the city, not the newer suburban areas. In offending the latter it is evident that Hawrelak's was a personal style that went beyond cutting corners to get the job done. But his brashness evidently met his constitutents' needs and manifestly overcame 'public' approbation. Nonetheless, by the time of his last term it seems clear that the public morality of the community was beginning to congeal to a shared standard much different than that from which he had once benefited. This evolution would mean trouble for another councillor whose personal life became controversial.

Edmonton councillor Ken Kozak became nationally famous because he was convicted of a summary offence related to family violence. Kozak sought to divert public attention from this, and an array of unconventional behaviour, by claiming that his electors could best render judgement of him. He did not test his ward incumbency directly though, running instead for the mayoralty in 1992, when he garnered less than 4 per cent of the vote.

In the spring of 1990 Alderman Kozak pleaded guilty to assaulting his estranged wife, was given a suspended sentence, and was put on probation for twelve months. Although the conviction brought calls for his resignation, he refused to quit and, since the offence was punishable by less than five years in jail, he was allowed to remain in office. After recognizing the futility of moral suasion, council decided to request the minister of municipal affairs to amend the Municipal Government Act to disqualify any councillor convicted under the Criminal Code, but permitting such an individual to stand in a subsequent by-election or election if the conviction involved only the less serious summary offences. As the mayor wrote, 'We feel that these amendments . . . address the public's "community standards" demands of civic elected officials without placing unduly onerous or impossible requirements on such officials.'[45]

Provincial officials could find no general legislation in any other province respecting either MLAs or councillors that dealt specifically with family violence issues. The problem, generally, came to be defined by the recognition that the Criminal Code does not specifically define 'family violence' offences in isolation from common or aggravated assault, except that the victim of the offence is a family member of the accused person. Six potential alternative courses of action, ranging from 'no change' to 'petition to recall an elected official convicted of any offence under the Criminal Code', were publicly presented for debate.

Edmonton's city council considered the package. Kozak opposed the option recommended by the city's law department, which called for the removal of councillors convicted of all criminal offences, although permitting those with summary offences the right to run subsequently. Interestingly, Kozak was supported by social democratic councillor Brian Mason, who had found himself on the brink of arrest for public mischief while exercising picket line solidarity on another issue. Speaking of his own 'legitimacy of social disobedience', Mason noted that 'There could be times when people of conscience would find it better to go to jail to stand up for what they believe in.'[46] Edmonton's council accepted (9-3) the most inclusive alternative, with the proviso that for non-indictable offences disqualified council members would be eligible to run in a subsequent by-election or election.

The Kozak case raised the issue of whether the council, the courts or, ultimately, the electorate—by petition or through by-election—should determine community standards. No Canadian jurisdiction has a recall provision at present and the urban citizens' movement of the 1970s is by now sufficiently inert that little legitimacy would attach to any such proposal. So it will be up to the courts to decide, acting most likely upon citizen-initiated complaints under the auspices of more general legislation. On a second matter, ought city councillors now be subject to a general standard applied to all federal, provincial, and municipal elected officials respecting their personal activities? I believe the answer shortly will, and should, come to be 'Yes'.

Third, direct political action in the world of industrial or race relations, and income or gender inequities, will increase in Canada. In the absence of imaginative provincial initiatives, local councillors will increasingly need to respond with codified standards for behaviour sensitive to their assessments of local community expectations and evaluations, at least as a first step towards a more generally enforceable statement. And finally, to introduce the concept of 'family violence' would be to inject a vital new principle in evaluating the private behaviour of public representatives: unlike pecuniary conflicts it is unlikely any alderman would commit an offence related to family violence in the conduct of their official duties. The question then becomes, should these standards be established *across the board*? To introduce 'family violence' as a provision for disqualification of councillors would introduce a new principle, one that is not presently in the Criminal Code and one that does not now pertain to provincial legislators themselves. Such a change will clearly mean that definable community standards for the personal lives of legislators *can* be applied during their office tenure.

Conclusion

My cases cover a lot of turf, from an appeal to the broadest sense of 'community' to endorse advantageous electoral arrangements and perennial questions about campaign finance, through conflict of interest, to questions that result from activities in private life that do not directly affect the legal responsibilities of public office-holding, but which may violate community standards. As to the last, and not frivolously, are we at the point where a smoker cannot hold office? The range of transgressions is a natural consequence of the mixed missions of Canadian local government forged over a century ago, and which still remain powerful in our civic culture of today. But the issues are still largely like those that confront the other levels of politics.

William Mishler has observed that 'Gladiatorial activities are distinguished from other forms of electoral participation in that they tend to be full-time occupations requiring political professionals.'[47] Most people who seek local public office are 'good people' prepared to sacrifice their personal lives and private pursuits for the betterment of the public good. Most elected officials devote long hours to their municipal tasks, especially in the cities. For even the citizen amateur as civic politician the remuneration is usually minimal with modest pensions as compared with senior governments. The general problem is that the city system is much less regulated than other politics in Canada.

Councillors commonly run into difficulty with those issues directly at the heart of municipal governance. For most city councils, complex policies for the environment and garbage, conditional grants and debentures, service delivery and taxation equity boil down to James Lorimer's comment a generation ago, 'In fact, the real business of city government *is* property.'[48] He accurately notes that virtually everything that municipal government undertakes is somehow related to real estate. This can become, very quickly, a high-stakes game. In any such game both the official rules and regulations, and the expectations of what constitutes appropriate behaviour, although largely unwritten, were once pretty well understood and accepted by the principal players. When the rules are broken, or when they are changed or not understood, or when they are challenged by an outsider, the players are punished. Developers learn very quickly, or they don't survive, that the basic law of local government is that it is easier to beg forgiveness than to ask permission. Contemporary councillors have little such leeway.

The dominant ethos still underpinning civic governance in Canada closely parallels the bourgeois, anglo-saxon, protestant pattern of ideals of American cities three decades ago, which emphasized that persons should seek office to protect, efficiently and rationally, the common good of the 'community as a whole' and that 'politics should be based on public rather than private motives and, accordingly, should stress the virtues of honesty, impartiality, and efficiency', the traits that one essentially equates with public servants and not politicians.[49] Ari Hoogenboom correctly catches the roots of the problem in encoding adaptive ethical change when he says that 'the civil service reform movement fits into a pattern of those out of power versus those in power. Reformers invariably wished to curtail the appointing power after they thought it had been abused, and to them abuse occurred when men of their own social station or politicial faction were not appointed to office.'[50] In local politics, where the immutable law is, in a perverse construction of parliamentary supremacy, very simply that no decision is ever final at city hall, we must be wary of 'us versus them' prescriptions.

Personal experience leads to the conclusion that no absolute checklist of correct political standards overrides common sense, no matter how relative that concept must be. Experience leads also to the conclusion that no matter how comprehensive and well-conceived they may be, codified reforms may be manipulated, subverted, or ignored. This is especially true where élites are closely intertwined, money has an immediate impact, and the definition of conflict of interest is still rather elastic. Occasional freelance corruption may be apprehended. It is the systemic and pervasive influence of those whose livelihoods are on the line—realtors, construction companies, speculators—that makes the legislation of morality at best elusive and, at worst, ineffective pending deep changes in our urban democratic behaviour.

So in devising an ethical code for municipal political behaviour in the 1990s, the reality may be that, given the various constraints, choice is usually but not always possible.[51] To believe otherwise is to be stuck with the story of Buridan's ass, named after medieval philosopher Jean Buridan. Stuck exactly between two indistinguishable piles of hay, lacking a reason to go to either rather than the other, the ass starves to death. But suppose it were a municipal councillor. Why cannot it make an arbitrary choice to the right or to the left? Does provincial statute not specify its choice? What do 'community standards' mean and by whose ethnic traditions? Will critical donors seek out another mule? Whose tastes may be offended?

In the 1990s, the development of codes of conduct for councillors will be difficult. In our new decade one must begin to reconcile old precedents with three developments. One, the demands imposed upon the state by the evolving technology of the age of the fax machine and cellular telephone. Two, the impact of the cultural traditions and historic honour codes of new migrant communities. Three, the new agendas of issue-oriented citizen activists in which policy and personality are not as clearly distinguishable as in traditional left-right platform politics. New codes for the 1990s will neither solve nor prevent intense and frequent controversy. Rules will apply, but how much can really be subject to the new edicts?

Notes

1 As quoted by Wallace S. Sayre and Nelson W. Polsby, 'American Political Science and the Study of Urbanization', in P.M. Hauser and L.F. Schnore, eds, *The Study of Urbanization* (New York: Wiley, 1965): 117.

2 Harold Kaplan, *Reform, Planning and City Politics: Montreal, Winnipeg, Toronto* (Toronto: University of Toronto Press, 1982): 64.

3 On this point, see Marcia Sypnowich, 'Promoting Ethical Behaviour for Municipal Councils', *Canadian Public Administration* 34, 1 (Spring 1991): 146-52.

4 For details of a campaign's strategy, style, and expenses see James Lightbody, 'The First Hurrah: Edmonton Elects a Mayor, 1983', *Urban History Review* 13: 1 (June 1984): 335-41. See also Stephen Clarkson, *City Lib: Parties and Reform* (Toronto: Hakkert, 1972).

5 *Edmonton Journal*, 27 Sept. 1983.

6 'City Council has no law for gifts', *Calgary Herald*, 21 June 1991.

7 Ibid.

8 *Globe and Mail*, 11 Dec. 1987.

9 In her essay (above, n.3), Marcia Sypnowich hints at the rationalization that underpinned historic reluctance to act: 'The government had to try to accommodate a disparate municipal system in which six hundred of eight hundred lower-tier municipalities have populations of fewer than five thousand and in which Metropolitan Toronto has a population of two million—more populous than eight of Canada's provinces.'

10 *Edmonton Journal*, 16 March 1977.

11 By-law 9938, 'A By-law to Require Disclosure by Candidates and Council Members', 14 Jan. 1992.

12 *Globe and Mail*, 15 Dec. 1987.

13 E.E. Schattschneider, *The Semi-Sovereign People* (New York: Holt, Rinehart and Winston, 1960): 71.

14 James Lorimer, *The Real World of City Politics* (Toronto: James, Lewis and Samuel, 1970): 37-52; James Lorimer, *A Citizen's Guide to City Politics* (Toronto: James, Lewis and Samuel, 1972): 112-20.

15 James Lightbody, 'The Reform of an Electoral System: The Case of Winnipeg, 1971', *Canadian Journal of Political Science* 11, 2 (June 1978): 307-32.

16 *Globe and Mail*, 11 April 1991.

17 Donald J.H. Higgins, *Local and Urban Politics in Canada* (Toronto: Gage, 1986): 325-31; Lorimer, *A Citizen's Guide*: 110-11.

18 Alan F.J. Artibise, *Winnipeg: A Social and Political History, 1896-1914* (Montreal: McGill-Queen's University Press, 1975): 23, 25.

19 Alan Philips, 'Graft in Civic Office', in Kenneth M. Gibbons and Donald C. Rowat, eds, *Political Corruption in Canada* (Toronto: McClelland and Stewart, 1975): 102.

20 Ari Hoogenboom, 'Spoilism and Reformers: Civil Service Reforms and Public Morality', in A. Heidenheimer, ed., *Political Corruption: Readings in Comparative Analysis* (New York: Holt, Rinehart and Winston, 1970): 277.

21 Andrew Sancton, 'Montreal', in Warren Magnussen and Andrew Sancton, eds, *City Politics in Canada* (Toronto: University of Toronto Press, 1983): 74.

22 'Statement by Mayor Purves'—7 Oct. 1981. Emphasis added.

23 Lorimer, *A Citizen's Guide*: 140.

24 Lorimer, *A Citizen's Guide*: 107.

25 Jock Ferguson and Dawn King, *Globe and Mail*, 28 Oct. 1988. See also the series written by Jock Ferguson and Paul Taylor, 'Developers back Toronto politicians', beginning 11 Dec. 1988, and Andrew McIntosh, 'Belleville mayor's real estate activities raise concerns', *Globe and Mail*, 7 April 1988.

26 *Globe and Mail*, 28 Oct. 1988.

27 Ibid.

28 Personal notes.

29 *Globe and Mail*, 14 Dec. 1987.

30 Jock Ferguson and Paul Taylor, 'Lawyer grows wealthy on development lobbying', *Globe and Mail*, 17 Dec. 1987.

31 This wording is taken from City of Edmonton By-law 9938 (14 Jan. 1992): 8.

32 For an overview of his career see James Lightbody, 'Hawrelak', in Allan Levine, ed., *Your Worship: The Lives of Eight of Canada's Most Unforgettable Mayors* (Toronto: Lorimer, 1989): 30-50.

33 *Edmonton Journal*, 13 Oct. 1983. In 1983, Laurence Decore (an alderman during Hawrelak's final term in office) became Edmonton's thirty-sixth mayor, returned by the largest plurality in the city's history. A prominent member of the Ukrainian-Canadian community, throughout the campaign he emphasized how greatly he was indebted to Hawrelak for much of his political education: 'Hawrelak taught me the method of dealing with people at city hall. That's what I learned from him and I'm proud of it.' *Edmonton Sun*, 13 Oct. 1983.

34 *The Report of the Honourable Mr Justice M.M. Porter* (Edmonton, Office of the Attorney General, 1959): 88.

35 Ibid.: 25ff.

36 Ibid.: 37.

37 Ibid.: 10.

38 The land swap, widely used in Canadian urban development, builds profitability whenever a promoter is either able through 'insider' knowledge to exchange his property for a similar amount of more valuable civic land which is, say, more proximate to his project, or when he, a relative, or associate is able to pick up a property at assessed value and then receives market value or more (after development) for it. See Philips (above, n.19): 88.

39 The findings of the inquiry by Chief Justice McLaurin are reprinted in detail in the *Edmonton Journal*, 11 March 1965.

40 V.O. Key, Jr, 'Techniques of Political Graft', in Gibbons and Rowat, *Political Corruption*: 52.

41 Robert Merton, *Social Theory and Social Structure* (Glencoe: The Free Press, 1957): 72.

42 Sypnowich (above, n.3): 146.

43 Ibid.: 147.

44 *Edmonton Journal*, 31 Jan. 1975.

45 Mayor Jan Reimer to the Hon. Raymond Speaker, Minister of Municipal Affairs, 30 April 1991 (Ref. No. 2861).

46 *Edmonton Sun*, 13 Sept. 1991.

47 William Mishler, *Political Participation in Canada* (Toronto: McGraw-Hill, 1979): 47.

48 Lorimer, *A Citizen's Guide*: 4.

49 See Edward C. Banfield and James Q. Wilson, *City Politics* (New York: Random House, 1963): 41, 123.

50 Hoogenboom (above, n.20): 283.

51 The practical difficulty often lies in the very devising of the statutory declaration of good intentions, as happened with the unseating of four aldermen in Thunder Bay in 1972: 'Probably only one of all these deserved this fate. The others, whose motives were beyond reproach, were caught in the meshes of the conflicts of interest provisions of The Municipal Act, a statutory trap for the honest but unwary local politician.' Ian MacF. Rogers, 'Municipal Conflict of Interest: The New Ontario Law', in Gibbons and Rowat, *Political Corruption*: 251.

David Siegel   **10**

Small-town Canada

Many observers of local government see small towns as ideal local government structures. They see them as being close to the people and therefore susceptible to effective democratic control. In an ideal world, small local governments embody civic virtue.

The reality is sometimes very different. Small-town politics can be mean-spirited and venal, a saga of family disputes handed down from generation to generation and personal intrigues that would make a soap opera seem tame.[1] Small-town councils can be run like a private old boys' club with the 'old boys' making decisions over some beer at the Legion Hall and then ratifying them at a public council meeting.

> Local government, in its various forms, may be the closest and most accessible to the people but that does not therefore make it the most democratic. Some local government administrations have proved to be as autocratic and/or corrupt as those found anywhere.[2]

In sum, small town politics can embody the best democratic traditions. They can also bring out the worst in people.

This chapter is about ethical dilemmas in small towns. These are frequently not the same problems seen in larger communities writ small. Many ethical problems are unique to smaller jurisdictions.

The first section discusses some of the characteristics of small towns that make them qualitatively different from larger jurisdictions.[3] The second section then focuses on some of the ethical dilemmas particular to smaller towns, while the third section probes some new developments and trends.

No precise definition of a 'small town' is advanced. The type of place under discussion should be clear enough from the characteristics discussed in the next section. At the risk of generalizing, it is possible to distinguish between two broad types of small towns. One type is the small, isolated community which will remain a small town for the foreseeable future. A second type is the small town that is in the process of changing its size and character as it comes under the influence of an expanding central urban area.[4] It is changing from a small town into a dormitory suburb. This describes what has happened to many former sleepy villages on the outskirts of Montreal, Toronto, Vancouver, and other expanding cities.

The ethical problems of the latter type of community are similar to those of the larger jurisdictions of which they are becoming a part, although the pressures generated by rapid development present particular problems. This chapter will focus mainly on those small towns that are likely to remain small towns for the foreseeable future, although there is some discussion of the problem of rapid development.

A word needs to be said about the empirical basis of this chapter. Some of the information and examples here have been generated from a review of the limited literature on small towns, but a great deal derives from my own experience in teaching courses to, and sharing stories with, small-town government officials. Some practices are discussed without benefit of formal reference because they have come from my personal experience or confidential discussions. The advantage of this approach is the distinctive flavour provided by the commentary from those directly involved in the events.

This method of data gathering is also the product of necessity. Small-town politics are not the subject of intense academic scrutiny.[5] Other methods of documenting activities are also sparse. Many small towns do not have their own newspapers. Their political life is the subject of sporadic reports in the weekly newspapers of nearby towns.

Small municipalities are different

The politics and administration of small municipalities differ qualitatively from their counterparts in federal or provincial governments or even larger municipalities for several reasons. These differences are instrumental in determining the kinds of ethical problems that occur in smaller municipalities and the ways in which they are played out. This section reviews the key differences.

Small towns are, well, small. One effect of this is that municipal politicians become involved in a more 'hands-on' way in the details of decision-making. Legislatures at the federal and provincial levels pass laws that establish broad, general policies. These policies are then implemented by public servants at several removes from the law-makers. By contrast, municipal councils, especially those in small jurisdictions, are much more likely to make very specific implementation decisions. Small-town politics and administration are very much hands-on processes compared to other jurisdictions. For example, a provincial legislature will appropriate a large sum of money at the beginning of the year for road construction. The details of how and where the money is spent will be made in the bureaucracy with occasional consultation with the minister. Generally, decisions will be taken by administrators acting on technical principles. Provincial legislators know or care very little about the details of these individual decisions.

The situation is very different at the municipal level. Municipal councils ordinarily have a hands-on approach in making detailed decisions on specific projects. They decide to upgrade the intersection on Third Street instead of the one on Fourth Street and they can frequently spend a great deal of time discussing the upgrade's precise form.

The hands-on nature of decision-making means that small-town politicians are more likely to find themselves in situations where they are called upon to make decisions that transparently affect themselves, their families, or their friends (or enemies).

Small towns have only a limited number of potential suppliers of particular products and services, and one of these suppliers could easily be a councillor. Small towns are also more likely to generate situations where councillors or municipal civil servants must deal with relatives, long-time friends (or enemies), and members of the same hockey league.

This situation personalizes decisions in small towns. When federal and provincial law-makers consider legislation, they usually have a general idea of which broad groups in society will benefit from the legislation, although even this is sometimes unclear. When a municipal council is making decisions, it is frequently very clear which individuals and groups will benefit from a decision.

Small-town politicians also remain very much a part of their community in ways that federal and provincial politicians, who conduct their business in far-away capital cities, do not. Members of Parliament and most provincial legislators are full-time politicians. By contrast, most municipal elected offices are part-time positions which pay part-time wages. The levels of remuneration are such that municipal politicians must continue in their full-time employment or profession, usually in the same municipality in which they serve on council. Municipal politicians simply cannot forgo their full-time occupations for a part-time job paying as little as $1,000 a year.

Open party politics is seldom found in small towns. No opposition party exists to apply pressure, to increase the visibility of government action and to keep the council honest. De facto coalition groupings can develop,[6] but even these are usually absent in small towns.

> The other outstanding difference between legislative behaviour at the two senior levels of government and the local one is the high incidence of unanimity or near unanimity and the low incidence of lengthy debate on motions at council or school board meetings. This is especially so in those small municipalities that have relatively homogeneous populations and where all or most of the local politicians can be seen to represent much the same constituency.[7]

David Rayside describes this situation in the town of Alexandria, Ontario. 'Occasionally, a deviant will be elected, or deviant voices raised, but transgressions of the informal rules will almost always be met with disapproval.'[8]

Small town councils are sometimes criticized as functioning like 'old boys' clubs.'[9] One hears stories of councils that meet informally before meetings, discuss the issues, and decide. After the decisions are made, a public meeting is then held where the private decisions are ratified.

Sometimes this pattern develops informally. If most councillors have businesses downtown, they might all belong to the same service club or have lunch at the same restaurant. During lunch, they are likely to discuss items of importance to the town and arrive at a consensus on how best to deal with them.

> Dundas [Ontario] is a quiet community near Hamilton whose affairs have long been dominated by the commercial interests of its main street. Until recently, many political decisions were made at the Lions Club, to which most council members belonged.[10]

This form of interaction engenders an attitude of 'you have to go along to get along'. In the long run, it is better to be a team player and not be too critical of any decision. Thus, you might have to suffer a short-term loss, but it is in your long-run interest (and the long-run interest of your constituents) to be a team player.

The lack of a formal opposition is exacerbated by limited media coverage. Small-town newspapers usually hire only young and inexperienced reporters who seldom know a lot about local government and who may overlook serious problems. Even when the reporter is competent, he or she may cover several beats and several towns and thus be spread too thinly to undertake serious political analysis. When a reporter is critical, he or she can frequently be reined in by upper management. As Rayside argues:

> The room for press manoeuvre in criticizing established institutions or dominant ideas is even narrower in small communities, where the need to avoid controversy that 'makes the town look bad' imposes severe limits on what a reporter or editor can write.[11]

Cause and effect are hard to sort out, but the low media interest in local politics is usually accompanied by low citizen interest. In small towns, contacts that individuals have with the town hall are episodic. Most issues concern such matters as the establishment of a children's playground or the realignment of an intersection. The usual pattern is that a few citizens meet with councillors and/or staff about specific matters and then return to their passive roles. Broad policy issues seldom galvanize entire communities. Gerald L. Gold describes a typical council meeting in Saint-Pascal, Quebec: 'Other than the *échevins* the Conseil room is empty and silent unless an important civic issue musters a group of interested spectators.'[12]

In this environment, the council takes on the flavour of an old boys' club. It consists almost entirely of white, middle-class males, which (except for the gender distribution) makes it fairly representative of most small towns. With no serious opposition or even careful observers, a homogeneous group of councillors can sometimes forget that the municipal council is not their private club.

Councils can be self-perpetuating bodies. When a member of the club chooses not to run again, the remaining members often select a replacement candidate. Like God at creation, the new member is made in their own image and likeness. And normally, the newly-anointed person is easily elected. Acclamations are common, and if there is a serious threat, a few telephone calls will ensure that the proper person is elected. Again, Gold's description of Saint-Pascal is typical:

> Saint-Pascal's local elections are rarely contested. . . . Thus elections to the school board, to the various committees of the Caisse Populaire and often to the Conseil are won by acclamation. Occasionally an *échevin* is contested, but the mayor's candidate has always won. No mayor has ever been defeated at the polls.[13]

An important principle is that municipal civil servants work for council as a whole, not for its head or individual councillors. However, when council takes on the club atmosphere, this principle can be easily forgotten. For example, councillors commonly approach staff members for assistance in dealing with small problems. When this happens in limited ways that do not violate council policy no problems arise. However, sometimes councillors forget their roles and demand that employees do things at odds with council policy.

The old boys' club atmosphere can also cause councillors to identify themselves personally with the interests of the overall municipality. This attitude leads them to see challenges as personal attacks. Members of council become accustomed to functioning without serious challenges.

In large, diverse municipalities, it is understood that such matters as community planning will evoke diverse views. Some councillors welcome conflict because it sometimes leads to creative solutions. Others accept it only grudgingly, but in large heterogeneous areas, councillors recognize that conflict is a consequence when large numbers of people live in close quarters.

Members of small-town councils may deal poorly with dissent. Policy issues can be personalized so that dissent is seen as a personal affront to the councillors and a sign of disloyalty to the town. This latter issue takes on importance because the economic viability of small towns may be more fragile than that of economically diverse larger cities.

Small towns are frequently characterized by the lack of a diverse commercial or industrial base. They are often supported by one employer. Many isolated northern communities are totally dependent on a mining or lumbering company. Other small towns, tourist towns for example, have several employers that are all related to one industry.

In both cases, there is a sense that the town's success is tied to the success of the single company or industry. This gives that company or industry an inordinate amount of influence over councillors.

In effect, these managers and owners exert influence on local government without ever participating in it, simply by virtue of the unspoken threat of shifting investment or reducing employment.[14]

Many councillors or their kin will depend on the continued success of the one industry for their own livelihood. They can be directly dependent if they are an employee of, or a supplier to, the major industry. Or they can be indirectly dependent when they are small-business operators and most of their customers are employees of the dominant industry. Jack Masson points out that 'many of Alberta's growth communities are one-industry towns in which it is difficult to recruit councillors who are not somehow connected with the dominant industry.'[15]

Even if a councillor has no direct relationship with the major industry, middle-class councillors naturally identify with the local economic élite. 'There tends to be an affinity between the interests of the corporate sector and the business or professional background and perspectives of a large proportion of local elected officials.'[16] Or, as Rayside found: 'The merchant's and entrepreneur's background and their place in the economy predisposes them to believe that the interests of Alexandria and of its local industries coincide.'[17]

Small towns usually do not have highly developed administrative rules to govern council procedures, purchasing practices, and personnel matters. In the informal environment of small towns, formal rules seem unimportant. Town staff members are usually sufficiently overworked they have no time for 'frills' like standard operating procedures.

A basic rule for a council is a 'procedure by-law' which governs its operation by specifying when council meets, how it conducts its business, and who may appear before it. Its purpose is to structure the relationship between council and citizens and to control council's discretion in dealing with cases.[18]

Councils can also adopt by-laws dealing with administrative processes such as purchasing and personnel administration. The purchasing by-law will specify when tenders must be called and what procedures must be followed to ensure fairness in awarding contracts. The procedures dealing with personnel should establish a merit system of hiring and promotion, and provide safeguards against unwarranted firings.

The absence of such formal rules allows for broad discretion and the possibility of political penetration into obviously administrative terrain. Most rules of procedure establish and enshrine the line of demarcation between political involvement and administrative activities. For example, when the purchasing by-law specifies the procedures administrators must follow in the purchasing process, councillors are thus blocked from easily intervening in cases. It even makes it awkward for the full council, which could legally change its by-law, to intervene except in extraordinary circumstances.

The absence of a formal merit system has similar consequences. The federal and provincial governments and large cities have merit systems enforced by a semi-autonomous commission or personnel department.[19] In many smaller municipalities, hiring is done by the old boys' club, which leads to favouritism and nepotism. While most councils avoid excesses, the lack of a formal hiring process leads to an emphasis on a candidate's connections and viewpoints.

The absence of a merit system also limits the protection that municipal employees have against arbitrary demotion or dismissal. They have the same right to bring an action for unjust dismissal as any other employee, and in some provinces, senior municipal employees have a right to a hearing in front of the full council before they can be dismissed. These remedies fall short of the protection from firing or demotion for inappropriate reasons afforded employees of other governments.

The combination of informal hiring procedures and minimal protection from arbitrary dismissal makes public servants subservient to their political masters. This subservience may make it difficult for public servants to resist inappropriate demands made by politicians. Civil servants may be dismissed because of the venal personal attitudes of a councillor.

Close-knit communities or nasty cliques?

One frequently hears two extreme characterizations of life in a small town. At one pole is the strong sense of community associated with a small group of like-minded people, all concerned about their town. Everyone gets along well and works together for the common good. This overview aptly describes many small towns.

One would expect high levels of ethical behaviour in such a situation. People who respect one another would likely respond to peer pressure to do the right thing, and since everyone in a small town tends to know everyone else's business, there is less opportunity to hide inappropriate behaviour.

The opposite pole is a town riven by strife and cliquishness, such as the small Newfoundland towns studied by Matthews where politics were dominated by ancient family feuds.[20] The small size of the community makes it impossible for rivals to ignore one another.

This kind of community is frequently characterized by 'winner-take-all' politics. Whoever dominates the civic government uses every means available to thwart the enemy. High ethical principles are obviously not front and centre.

The polar extremes are small-town life as the idyllic existence of a group of neighbours working together peacefully for the common good, contrasted with a group of enemies forced to share the same small geographic area with one another. Most small towns fall between the polar extremes, but the location of a particular town on the continuum will have a significant influence on its ethics.

Ethical problems in small towns

This section examines the particular ethical problems that can occur in small towns. It is not meant as a picture of life in a typical small town. All these problems would never occur in a single town. But it is worth noting that the characteristics of small-town life identified above could lead to ethical problems that are not unique to small towns, but can be a bit different in their development and in the way they play out because they take place in small towns.

Conflict of interest

The position of part-time politician and the detailed nature of decision making present ethical dilemmas. In larger jurisdictions where politicians are paid a full salary for their political work, the standard way of avoiding conflict of interest is to require that they cease to engage in a business or profession that might lead to a conflict situation. Such a prohibition is not possible where elected public office is a part-time job with part-time remuneration. In some cases, a councillor might operate a business providing a good or service the town needs. Preventing the town from dealing with a business owned by a councillor might cause serious problems if there are only a limited number of suppliers in the town. Forcing a councillor to give up her or his business interests would significantly limit the number of people who would be interested in serving on council.

Prince Rupert, British Columbia, has three travel agencies, one of which is partly owned by a longstanding mayor.[21] The city does business with all three agencies. The mayor makes it clear that he has never directed the town to do business with his agency. Should the city only do business with the two remaining agencies? Is it appropriate to prevent the mayor's agency from doing business with the city just because he is a part-time mayor?

The usual procedure in such cases is for councillors with a pecuniary interest in a matter before council to declare openly the nature of the interest and refrain from participating in the debate and voting. This works well in cases such as the one described above, where the interest is a purely personal one. However, this approach can run into difficulty when the councillor's interest is shared by many of her or his constituents. A councillor may then be unable to represent the valid concerns of her or his constituents.

In the Township of Tarbutt and Tarbutt Additional (near Sault Ste Marie, Ontario), a property-owner wanted to rezone some shoreline property so it could be used as a commercial dock. Many nearby property-owners opposed the rezoning and asked their councillor to make their case before council. The problem was that the councillor also owned property in the area that would be affected by the rezoning. He decided to participate in the discussion and was subsequently found in contravention of the legislation. The councillor stated his case in these terms.

> It's very hard to speak on that council in such a small township when you might have an interest nearby. The only thing I did wrong was that I had about 150 shoreline people who wanted me to speak in their interests who were opposed to the development.
>
> All I was doing was my job, representing the people. My own feelings on Sutton Island was it didn't matter to me personally.[22]

Legitimate disagreement can easily arise about whether a situation is a conflict of interest.[23] But how can we foresee every situation? How do we make meaningful the elusive idea of 'conflict of interest'?

In Stoney Creek, Ontario (just outside Hamilton), a councillor voted in favour of allowing a deviation from established planning policy to permit retail and professional use on the ground floor of an apartment building.[24] Does the fact that the councillor owned part of a similar building about a kilometre away (although in a different kind of neighbourhood) constitute a conflict of interest? A citizen filed a suit alleging that it did and argued that changing the policy in the one case paves the way for altering the policy in other cases.[25] Who is right and on what grounds?

Some conflicts arise from oversight. For example, in Howick Township in southwestern Ontario, a councillor, who also operated a small construction business, gave quotations over the telephone to several contractors for the hourly rental of equipment. Some of these contractors relied on these quotations to prepare bids they subsequently submitted on a new township office building. Apparently not realizing that he had been identified as a sub-contractor on several bids, the councillor voted to award the contract to the lowest bidder, who happened to be one of the contractors who was using his quotation.[26] The courts subsequently ruled that this was a conflict of interest even though the action was inadvertent and the amount the councillor stood to earn was about $300.

Transfer of town resources to personal use

The idea that councils operate as an old boys' club can cause members to forget that they cannot convert town resources to their personal use. Councillors may ask civil servants to commit an inordinate amount of resources to a project in their ward. In extreme cases, they might even ask staff to use town resources for their personal benefit. 'Mr Road Superintendent, as long as your crew is putting gravel on the shoulder in front of my house, could they just throw a few shovels of it in my driveway?' At some point in this process, a councillor has crossed the line and acted unethically. The councillor is also asking the staff person to be complicit in the unethical behaviour as well.

The transfer of public resources to private use is probably a common ethical transgression. The fact that it is seldom brought to public attention reveals the ease with which it can be covered up.

The unfair exercise of discretion

The private club atmosphere may cause councillors to exercise their discretion unfairly. Almost unconsciously, personal considerations may influence their behaviour. That this can be done for apparently benevolent purposes does not make it any less unethical. For example, most provinces have legislation that requires municipalities to commence proceedings to take over property when tax arrears reach a certain point. The legislation might provide discretion about how to proceed, but action is demanded. However, what happens if the property is owned by a councillor or by someone friendly with a group of councillors? What happens if the arrears results simply because a citizen has been hurt by an economic downturn? The benevolent action to take in this case is to extend the time period for a person who is temporarily down on her or his luck. But such a response violates the legislation and is unfair to the residents who pay their taxes on time. In the old boys' club atmosphere, members can forget their broader obligations.

Another problem arises when dissidents challenge the old boys, who in turn see dissent as a personal attack and respond with attacks of their own. This attitude militates against the sensible discussion of issues.

A side effect of extreme opposition to dissent is that councillors may develop a proprietary attitude to information that ought to be available to the general public. Since councillors see discussions of issues as 'we-they' confrontations, they often view the release of pertinent information as providing ammunition to the enemy. They sometimes even refuse to provide basic information.

Muddling of the public interest and special interests

Many small towns are single-company or single-industry towns. In these situations, the prospects of the town can be closely identified with the prospects of the industry. This can lead councillors to focus on the interests of a special group and to identify the interests of that group with the broader public interest. What is good for General Motors, to paraphrase a famous line, is good for the town!

Occasionally allegations of bribery arise, but bribery is seldom necessary. Councillors are easily convinced that business interests and the public interest are synonymous. The lack of an aware media and an attentive citizen body makes it likely that undue business influence is widely discussed.

The ethical problem is that councillors can put the interests of a single powerful group ahead of those of the town. They might look the other way rather than enforce pollution control regulations or building standards by-laws. They might provide improved streets to one area of the town rather than more needy areas. They might make planning decisions that help the major industry, but hurt other large areas of the town. In some provinces, councils can provide grants or reductions in property tax to major industries, thereby increasing the tax burden on other members of the community.

Violation of professional standards and political neutrality

Municipal employees in small towns usually do not have the protection of merit systems like those found in the 'senior' governments. The absence of this protection has an impact on the relationship between councillors and staff. Some small towns still see municipal employment as a gift to be given to councillors, family members, and supporters.

This attitude has several consequences. The ideal relationship between politicians and experts is one where the experts are secure enough in their positions that they can provide independent advice to their political masters. This is very important for politicians, who should not surround themselves with sycophants. When staff people constantly fear for their jobs, they will be inclined to act like the 'eager beavers' described in John Langford's chapter on British Columbia. They will be too eager to please their masters.

In the absence of a merit system, staff are more likely to be compliant and turn a blind eye to ethical transgressions. In the situation mentioned earlier, where the councillor asked the road superintendent to put a bit of gravel on his own property, clearly the superintendent should refuse. Will employees be independent when their jobs are at risk? Councillors can engage in some kinds of unethical activity without the assistance of staff, but in many cases staff must at least acquiesce in the activity.

The lack of security of tenure also has an effect on the political neutrality of the staff. Municipal employees ought to remain outside the political fray so that they can serve all councillors loyally. If an employee becomes too closely associated with a councillor or a group of councillors, then other councillors may doubt the civil servant's loyalty.

In federal and provincial governments, laws protect public servants from being drawn directly into the political process, but no such protection exists for municipal employees. It is not unusual to hear of politicians making veiled threats about what they will do to employees who do not assist them in their campaigns. Employees can be unfairly pressured to become involved in partisan politics.

The challenge of rapid development
Particular ethical problems beset small towns that experience rapid growth. This commonly happens on the fringes of major cities, when towns that were once sleepy hamlets suddenly become attractive to people working in the nearby city. At this point, these towns become attractive to major developers who are looking for large tracts of land that are still relatively cheap.

Rapid development means that the councillors and staff who are accustomed to working in a particular environment will suddenly be working in a very different one. Councillors who have been making decisions about the amount of gravel to put on a concession road will suddenly be asked to approve major subdivisions.

Rapid change also affects staff. The planner who is very competent at handling requests for zoning changes will suddenly be asked to examine a plan for a complex subdivision. The road superintendent who is capable of maintaining concession roads will be asked to plan and build a much more complex road system. Competent people may find that their jobs have changed radically.

Developers do not experience similar problems. They are skilled at their work because they have done it many times. In some cases, competent but relatively inexperienced staff people will be outgunned by experienced developers who will apply pressure to the town to get the best possible deal. The town will be pushed to do things under threat of having the developer move to an adjacent municipality.

The developers will have a lot of money at stake. Occasionally that money will be used for bribes, but more likely it will be used legally to provide campaign funds to those candidates for council who favour rapid development. Symbiotic relationships develop in which councillors who operate small businesses realize that if they make certain decisions the entire community will prosper and their businesses along with it.

In this environment, opportunities for unethical conduct abound. For example, a developer could sell a house in the new subdivision to a councillor or staff person. In developments where each home is custom-built the actual price of the home may be difficult to determine. In Markham, Ontario (just north of Toronto), the mayor and some senior officials made an agreement in 1984 to purchase homes in a new development at 1984 prices even though the homes would not be built until 1986. The apparent saving in one case amounted to $50,000.[27] These actions assumed particular significance when building inspectors, who formerly worked for the town, alleged that infractions by the developer were being overlooked by their superiors.[28]

Other ways can be found to curry the favour of key decision makers. Repeated invitations to view major sporting events from developers' private boxes are an excellent way to allow councillors to develop an appreciation for developers' proposals. Invitations to lavish parties may be extended.

Many of these activities are not unethical. There is nothing inappropriate about going to a party or an occasional baseball game. However, citizens who see their elected representatives as frequent guests in the private boxes of developers may wonder about the relationship between the developer and the councillor and the latter's autonomy.

Another ethical concern arises when a town employee has an opportunity to work for a development company. Such companies can often pay more than the town. This movement from the town to the developer raises several concerns. If the staff person and developer are negotiating the change of employment at the same time that a developer's proposal is before the staff person, will the proposal be objectively assessed? Second, is the development company buying preferential treatment at the town hall by having someone on staff who knows the relevant policy makers?

Some municipalities have developed post-employment rules for councillors and staff. But considerable controversy remains. Does an employer have the right to dictate rules about future employment? What penalties or restrictions can a municipality impose on someone who is no longer in its employ?

Emerging trends

In the 1990s, Canadians are concerned about ethics in government. But many politicians in small towns are oblivious to the concern. They want to play by the old rules and to operate local government as an old boys' club. They are incensed when citizens' groups challenge the established order. But change is in the wind, some of it coming from within councils and some of it externally imposed.

Greater provincial involvement in ethical matters
In response to public demand and the reluctance of municipalities to regulate themselves, provincial governments are imposing stricter ethical regimes on local governments. Alberta is embarking on a comprehensive revision of municipal legislation that will involve some limited changes in matters dealing with ethics.[29] Ontario is considering significant changes under the heading of 'open government' which we will examine here.[30]

The most prominent change in Ontario is a tightening of the Municipal Conflict of Interest Act. This change is coupled with other legislation dealing with the process for the disposal of municipal property and limitations on closed council meetings. Another major initiative is an overhaul of the provincial Planning Act, prompted in part by alleged irregularities in the planning process in municipalities just north of Toronto.

The major changes in Ontario's conflict of interest legislation relate to disclosure and enforcement. One idea asserts that councillors must disclose certain financial information at the beginning of their term of office. This would probably not be the full disclosure required in other levels of government, but would involve disclosure of assets and liabilities most likely to result in a conflict.[31] The idea is very controversial. Critics raise the conventional argument that the requirement would discourage good candidates from running for municipal office.[32]

A second point of contention is the enforcement mechanism. In Ontario, citizens must now take a civil action against a councillor. This could involve significant cost to the citizen, who usually does not stand to benefit from the action. Obviously, this is a significant deterrent to proper enforcement of the Act.[33]

This method of proceeding can also be unfair to councillors who must spend large sums to defend themselves against possibly frivolous charges. A councillor who incurred a $200,000 legal bill to defend himself against a conflict of interest charge remarked that 'A wealthy person can bankrupt an official through the court system.'[34]

The Ontario government has proposed an independent commission to investigate allegations of conflict of interest.[35] The commission would work informally to resolve problems. In many cases, complainants are not interested in winning a big court decision; they just want a particular behaviour to cease. The idea is that the commission could encourage errant councillors to change their ways. In more serious situations, if a citizen made a prima-facie case of conflict before the commission, the commission would then fund the legal action.

Municipalities complain about the imposition of provincial rules. Small municipalities also complain about having to follow the complex rules drafted with larger cities in mind. However, if citizens demand higher standards, and if individual municipalities do not establish their own rules, provincial governments will impose tough ethical rules on municipalities. It is unfortunate that sweeping provincial legislation may impose unexpected hardships on certain jurisdictions. But unless municipalities regulate themselves, the provincial governments will intervene.

Changing composition of municipal councils
Evidence is difficult to obtain, but there is a shift in the composition of councils. Where change is occurring, municipal politics are becoming more complex and councils are becoming more heterogeneous. The old boys' club is being broken up.

The heterogeneity occurs almost automatically in municipalities experiencing rapid development. Some of the 'new people' were politically active in their former neighbourhoods and want to continue that activity in new surroundings. Others, who were not politically involved before, might find themselves involved because of concerns about their new community's future.

Even in more stable municipalities, changes are occurring as new blood is injected into the council from women and local interest groups. Women are being elected to councils in growing numbers. Citizens' groups are sometimes challenging the old boys' club by sending their own representatives to council.[36]

Women are probably more involved in local politics than at other levels for several reasons.[37] They are less likely to have the business connections necessary to raise the money needed to campaign in federal or provincial elections.[38] Local elections are more likely to be won by hard work and demonstrated competence than large sums of money. Moreover, those political parties that dominate federal and provincial politics allegedly discriminate against women who want to run in attractive ridings.[39] Women's concerns for their family obligations might also cause them to shy away from the demanding time and travel commitments of federal or provincial politics.[40]

Women are usually too busy juggling work, family, and personal obligations to want to join an old boys' club. Their interest in politics is more likely to be motivated by policy problems. There are numerous stories of women who have become involved in local politics because they were concerned about pollution in a nearby creek, or the quality of recreational facilities available to their children. As one woman put it in a recent study:

> Three years ago the injustices which exist in our society were forcibly brought home when I realized that a decision to construct a high school in the city was not taken, as stated, based upon enrolment but the fulfilment of a political promise.[41]

Another source of new blood is local coalitions such as taxpayers' revolt groups.[42] A second type of group frequently forms around a particular issue, such as the location of a landfill site. These groups can become quite powerful in their area. They sometimes decide to extend their influence by putting some of their members forward for office. Where there are ward elections, even relatively small groups can focus their attention on a limited geographic area.

These 'new' councillors—women and representatives of citizens' groups—frequently bring to council a clear agenda.[43] This makes them different from the old boys who are on council for social reasons and whose only agenda is the status quo. The idea that the municipality should actually do something new or different can be quite unsettling to the old boys' club.

New blood usually causes conflicts. In areas experiencing rapid development, there is the inevitable fight over whether the town should accept development or retain the old ways. In the long run, the pro-development forces almost invariably win, but usually only after wounds are inflicted.

Another kind of tension can arise between the old boys who see council as their private preserve and newer members of the community who are frequently more affluent and better-educated. The new people usually want to build a strong community with a high level of public services while the old guard wants basic services and low taxes.[44]

Increasing professionalization of municipal staff

Municipal employment was formerly based largely on patronage and residence. It certainly helped to be related to a councillor and it was essential to be a resident of the community. Suitable employees from outside were not sought out if there was an able-bodied person on the welfare rolls or a councillor with an unemployed niece.

A consequence was that many employees were not well trained. They had little education in ethics or local government, and hence held widely different views about proper conduct. As Frank Cassidy and Marilyn Gore put it:

> There are significant ambiguities on the part of municipal administrators concerning matters that involve moral dilemmas and the standards which should apply to them. On this basis, it may be concluded that the problem is not just one of obtaining ethical administrative behaviour in government, it is also one of arriving at a consensus, at least among municipal administrators, about what such behaviour looks like.[45]

This is changing. Municipal employees are becoming more professional and much better trained.[46] They are more likely to be graduates of college or university programs or holders of professional certification or members of a professional association. This means that municipal public servants may now understand ethics better. They may have taken a formal ethics course in their academic training. Their professional association may have a code of ethics that has been the subject of discussion at association meetings. This not only influences the staff members' own behaviour, but it also provides them with greater expertise in steering their political masters away from unethical conduct. Professionalism may also make managers more independent of politicians. This might cause politicians disposed to cut ethical corners to think twice if they know that municipal civil servants will not conceal their misconduct.

Conclusion

Ethics will always be a problem in government. Unethical practices breed on the kind of secrecy found in many small towns. However, the times are changing; a number of trends are combining to produce a higher standard of ethical conduct.

The first trend is simply a greater understanding of, and sensitivity to, ethical concerns. A second is the greater interest of provincial governments in municipal ethics. It would be better if municipalities regulated themselves, but this is not happening. In the absence of this self-regulation, provincial governments will clean up the problems. Finally, municipal councils are changing from old boys' clubs to heterogeneous bodies representing diverse interests.

Notes

1 Canada has had more than its share of fiction writers with an ability to discuss the good and evil in small towns. Some of the best-known are Roch Carrier, Robertson Davies, Anne Hébert, Margaret Laurence, Stephen Leacock, Alice Munro, Andreas Schroeder, and W.D. Valgardson.

2 James C. Simeon, 'Polemical Incantations on Local Government Education', *Municipal World* (August 1989): 200.

3 The fact that different size can result in qualitative differences in addition to quantitative ones has been explored fairly well in some areas, but not so well with regard to local government. See Graham White, 'Big Is Different from Little: On Taking Size Seriously in the Analysis of Canadian Governmental Institutions', *Canadian Public Administration* 33 (1990): 526-50.

4 This phenomenon is well described in Christopher R. Bryant and Philip M. Coppack, 'The City's Countryside', in Trudi Bunting and Pierre Filion, eds, *Canadian Cities in Transition* (Toronto: Oxford University Press, 1991): 209-38.

5 An excellent recent exception is David Rayside, *A Small Town in Modern Times* (Montreal and Kingston: McGill-Queen's University Press, 1991). He summarizes (pp. 303-4) the sparse literature. Much of this has been written by anthropologists or sociologists and so touches only peripherally on the political aspects of towns.

6 Scott McAlpine and Stan Drabek, 'Decision-making Coalitions on Non-partisan Councils: A Small City/Large City Comparison', *Canadian Journal of Political Science* 24 (1991): 803-29.

7 Donald J.H. Higgins, *Local and Urban Politics in Canada* (Toronto: Gage, 1986): 374.

8 Rayside, *A Small Town in Modern Times*: 250.

9 The use of the word 'boy' is not inadvertent sexism. In fact, most of these councils are composed overwhelmingly of males.

10 Kevin Marron, 'Conflict-of-interest charges shatter small-town tranquility', *Globe and Mail*, 3 March 1988: A18.

11 Rayside, *A Small Town in Modern Times*: 250.

12 Gerald L. Gold, *Saint-Pascal: 'Changing Leadership and Social Organization in a Quebec Town* (Toronto: Holt, Rinehart & Winston, 1975): 183.

13 Ibid.: 184.

14 Ibid.: 240 (footnote in original text omitted here).

15 Jack Masson, *Alberta's Local Governments and Their Politics* (Edmonton: Pica Pica Press, 1985): 152.

16 Higgins, *Local and Urban Politics*: 291.

17 Rayside, *A Small Town in Modern Times*: 249.

18 Ibid.: 268.

19 Other chapters in this book indicate that even these organizations do not work as well as they should in preserving the merit system.

20 Ralph Matthews, *'There's No Better Place Than Here': Social Change in Three Newfoundland Communities* (Toronto: Peter Martin Associates Limited, 1976): 51, 65.

21 Gordon Clark, 'Mayor's travel biz ties to city studied', *The Province* (Vancouver), 19 July 1992: A4.

22 Jackie Hoffman, 'Two councillors voluntarily suspended', *The Sault Star*, 3 Feb. 1990. Similar cases are not unusual: Malcolm McNeil, 'Decision next week on Lisko conflict charge', *The Times* (Oshawa), 31 Aug. 1982; Sterling Taylor, 'Vaughan councillor risks conflict charge', *Toronto Star*, 15 Sept. 1987.

23 Joe Warmington, 'Separate board after "defined" conflict terms through committee', *The Sault Star*, 26 April 1991; Denis St Pierre, 'More bite urged in municipal conflict regulations', *The Sudbury Star*, 27 April 1991; John Tollefsrud, 'Keep rules simple, conflict-of-interest committee told', *The Nugget* (North Bay, Ont.), 2 May 1991.

24 Kevin Marron, 'Stoney Creek councillor denies allegation of zoning conflict', *Globe and Mail*, 20 Sept. 1988: A18.

25 Kevin Marron, 'Councillor not penalized for error', *Globe and Mail*, 10 Nov. 1988.

26 'Conflict of interest case is adjourned', and 'D'Arcey Affidavit', *The Listowel Banner*, 13 June 1990; *Municipal World* (October 1991): 17.

27 Maureen Murray, 'Markham mayor denies allegations of improper deals', *Toronto Star*, 30 Oct. 1988; Jock Ferguson and Dawn King, 'Municipal officials make sweet housing deals', *Globe and Mail*, 29 Oct. 1988.

28 Jock Ferguson and Dawn King, 'Former Markham building inspectors tell of frustrations', *Globe and Mail*, 29 Oct. 1988; Lila Sarick, 'Markham mayor denies special deal', *Globe and Mail*, 1 Nov. 1988.

29 Alberta, Municipal Statutes Review Committee, *Municipal Government in Alberta: A Municipal Government Act for the 21st Century* (March 1991).

30 Ontario, Ministry of Municipal Affairs, *Open Local Government* (n.d.)

31 Ontario, Municipal Conflict of Interest Consultation Committee to the Minister of Municipal Affairs, *Municipal Conflict of Interest Review* (July 1991): 46-50.

32 Chris Vander Doelen, 'Conflict law a low blow, Hurst charges', *The Windsor Star*, 26 March 1991; Robert Sibley, 'Tighter conflict rules will drive away municipal candidates, says ex-alderman', *The Ottawa Citizen*, 10 April 1991; 'Proposed conflict guidelines excessive, area reeves say', *The Windsor Star*, 5 April 1991.

33 Stanley M. Makuch, *Canadian Municipal and Planning Law* (Toronto: Carswell, 1983): 316; Martha Jette, 'Conflict of interest act serves rich: alderman', *West Hamil-*

ton News, 29 May 1991; 'Local aldermen seek conflict policy change', *Examiner* (Peterborough, Ont.), 10 Dec. 1987; Geoffrey York, 'Greene wins conflict-of-interest appeal', *Globe and Mail*, 17 April 1985.

34 Phil Tyson, 'Conflict case cost too high—Rexe', *Examiner* (Peterborough, Ont.), 24 April 1991. For other cases, see Zuhair Kashmeri, 'Mayor of Mississauga thwarts bid to oust her but is told to pay costs', *Globe and Mail*, 23 July 1982; Don Brillinger, 'Municipal politicians who breached conflict laws must pay costs of ratepayers who challenged them', *Lawyers Weekly*, 7 June 1991.

35 Ontario, Municipal Conflict of Interest Review Consultation Committee, *Review*: 59-67.

36 Masson, *Alberta's Local Governments*: 83.

37 Janine Brodie, *Women and Politics in Canada* (Toronto: McGraw-Hill Ryerson, 1985): 51, 81-4; Sylvia B. Bashevkin, *Toeing the Lines: Women and Party Politics in English Canada* (Toronto: University of Toronto Press, 1985): 71.

38 Brodie, *Women and Politics*: 103.

39 Brodie, *Women and Politics*: 107-12; Bashevkin, *Toeing the Lines*: ch. 3.

40 Brodie, *Women and Politics*: 81 and 116.

41 Ibid.: 35. See also p. 52. Hal Quinn, 'A First in Victoria: Premier Rita Johnston Sets her Own Course', *Maclean's*, 15 April 1991: 14.

42 C.R. Tindal and S. Nobes Tindal, *Local Government in Canada*, 3rd ed. (Toronto: McGraw-Hill Ryerson, 1990): 172-3 and 242.

43 Higgins, *Local and Urban Politics*: 262-3.

44 Masson, *Alberta's Local Governments*: 137 (footnote from the original text omitted).

45 Frank Cassidy and Marilyn Gore, 'Ethics in Local Government: The Views of Municipal Administrators', *Optimum* 22 (1991/92): 52.

46 George B. Cuff, 'How Council Perceives the Manager', *Municipal World* (Feb. 1989): 45-7.